I0128307

Charles William Mansel Moullin

Sprains

Selections and Comments

Charles William Mansel Moullin

Sprains
Selections and Comments

ISBN/EAN: 9783744692892

Printed in Europe, USA, Canada, Australia, Japan

Cover: Foto ©Thomas Meinert / pixelio.de

More available books at **www.hansebooks.com**

THEIR

CONSEQUENCES AND TREATMENT

BY

C. W. MANSELL MOULLIN,

M.A., M.D. Oxon., F.R.C.S. Eng.

Assistant Surgeon and Senior Demonstrator of Anatomy at the London Hospital; formerly
Radcliffe Traveling Fellow and Fellow of Pembroke College, Oxford.

REPRINTED FROM WOOD'S MEDICAL AND SURGICAL MONOGRAPHS.

NEW YORK
WILLIAM WOOD & COMPANY
1891

CONTENTS.

INTRODUCTION.

PAGE

General Considerations, ... 5

CHAPTER I.

The Anatomy of Joints, ... 9

CHAPTER II.

Cause and Prevention of Sprains, ... 18

CHAPTER III.

Diagnosis, ... 30

CHAPTER IV.

Nature of the Injury, ... 40

CHAPTER V.

Inflammation and the Process of Repair, . . . 60

CHAPTER VI.

Imperfect Recovery, . . . 71

CHAPTER VII.

Treatment. Cold. Heat. Pressure, . . 82

CHAPTER VIII.

Treatment. Rest, ... 97

CHAPTER IX.

Forcible Manipulation, ... 105

CHAPTER X.

Massage, ... 120

CHAPTER XI.

Sprains of Tendons, ... 133

CHAPTER XII.

PAGE

Sprains of the Back and Neck, ... 152

CHAPTER XIII.

Internal Derangement of the Knee, . . 172

CHAPTER XIV.

Contraction of the Fingers, ... 179

CHAPTER XV.

Muscular Contraction, ... 187

CHAPTER XVI.

Muscular Wasting, ... 201

SPRAINS

AND THEIR CONSEQUENCES.

INTRODUCTION.

It has been my endeavor in the following pages to confine myself as closely as possible to the commoner forms of sprains, and to those after consequences which may be regarded as directly and immediately dependent on them. Of those which follow more remotely there is no end, and the briefest description would lead me far beyond the limits at my disposal. It has been said, and not untruly, that in all probability half the crippled limbs and stiffened joints that are met with every day, date their starting point from the occurrence of some apparently trivial accident of this description.

The question of treatment has been dealt with at some length; and if I have seemed to advocate the adoption of more active measures than those generally employed, especially in the case of long standing inability, it is only that I am firmly convinced of their efficacy and safety when properly carried out.

Few injuries are treated with so little consideration as sprains. It is impossible to overlook wounds, owing to the bleeding and pain that accompany them. Fractures, it is understood, require rest and care; but sprains, in which the tissues are torn to such a degree that the damage is far more serious than in many fractures, merely because they are so common, are considered of little or no consequence.

It counts for nothing that the part injured is one of the most complicated structures in the body, and particularly liable to inflammation from the constant use to which it is subjected. The construction of a bone is comparatively simple, and its function is merely the passive duty of support. A joint, on the other hand, is exceedingly complex, and must not only be as strong for support as the bones between which it lies, but must, in addition, be capable of executing rapid and often extensive movements. Two, three, or even more bones may enter into its construction; each of them where it forms part of the joint is faced with cartilage; around them is a protecting capsule of fibrous tissue, lined with a delicate secreting membrane; ligaments of different kinds hold the bones together; muscles of various size and strength move them one on the other; there is a very large supply of blood-vessels and nerves; and even the tissues round are so adjusted to the surfaces that with every change in position they fill up the constantly-varying spaces round and between the bones. Yet a fracture is regarded as very serious; a sprained joint as quite a trivial matter.

In the one the injury is simple and definite in its character; one broken bone does not differ very materially in this respect from another; in the other there is no limit to the variety of hurt sustained, or to the complications that follow. The ligaments may be torn across, or wrenched off the bone; the muscles may be lacerated; the tendons displaced bodily from their grooves; the discs of cartilage which are present in some joints between the bones, forced out from their position; the joint cavity filled with blood, and so much more extravasated into the tissues that the discoloration may reach from the ankle to the knee; in short, the tissues may be torn and bruised as extensively as in a dislocation. In many cases the injury is to all intents and purposes the same; the sole difference is that the bones which were wrenched apart at the time of the accident resume their normal relation to each other in the one, while in the other they either remain fixed, or slip a little further aside. Vidal de Cassis appreciated this when he spoke of sprains as temporary dislocations.

There is no end to the variety of the injuries that are classed together under this name. It is almost an impossibility for two sprains to be exactly alike. Joints differ from each other as widely as they can, both in structure and action; different kinds of tissue enter into their formation, and serve as many separate purposes; the violence that causes the accident is different in every case, both in its force and direction; and the position of the limb at the moment can rarely be the same. Some joints are much more liable to injury than others, those especially in the lower limb; and the ankle more than the hip or knee. In some the stress falls on the ligaments; in others, as in the shoulder, on the muscles; very often both suffer together, though in varying proportion; or without the joint itself being injured, the muscles and tendons may be strained, and give rise to stiffness or weakness that lasts for years.

Other considerations also step in and help to make the variety greater. No two persons ever resemble each other exactly; even if this were possible in the earliest years of life, age, habits, occupation, mental temperament, bodily constitution, and many other things, induce such modifications that the slightest difference must at length become immense. Repair is not carried on with the same degree of energy in all; in some complications occur much more easily than they do in others; inflammation breaks out more readily, or other troubles make their appearance; so that, even if by some strange chance the injuries were identically the same in any two cases, it is impossible for them to continue so for any length of time. In this respect peculiarities of constitution are of great significance; in the majority of instances the ultimate result, whether the joint recovers within a reasonable period, or remains cold, stiff, and untrustworthy for years, depends much more on them, and on the method of treatment adopted, than on the mere fact of a ligament having been torn or only stretched.

This, however, is not the only reason why sprains do not merit the neglect with which they are so often treated. Imperfect recovery in the case of a broken bone is quite exceptional. Failure of union does sometimes, but very rarely, occur. It is more common for the position of the broken ends to be faulty, so that there is some deformity, or loss of power; but even when this does happen the after-trouble or inconvenience is only of a temporary character, and at the end of a few weeks or months, at the most, the limb is as strong and firm as ever. Such a thing as yielding, weakness, or continued pain at the seat of fracture is almost unknown, unless there is some exceptional condition of things present. It is not so with sprains. An amount of the thickening round the seat of injury, so slight as altogether to escape notice in the case of a fracture, is quite enough to disable a joint.

It is true that a large number of sprained joints get well of themselves, or under ordinary domestic treatment, a few, it must be admitted, in spite of it; but even in the young and healthy, it is not unusual to find the action of the joint seriously impaired. There may be merely a general sense of weakness and insecurity, a feeling that it is not to be trusted as it was before; or the least attempt at movement may be attended with intolerable suffering. There may be no very visible or definite alteration, or every tissue of which the joint is composed may be more or less disorganized. The skin may be exquisitely tender; the subcutaneous tissues swollen and distended, so that the natural outline cannot even be recognized; the muscles may waste away; the tendons become glued to their sheaths, and the interior of the joint be damaged to such an extent that, even if everything else were restored, it would be impossible for the bone to work evenly or smoothly on the other.

Results of this kind, happily, may nearly always be prevented. It is true that in some people the power of repair is much more feeble than it is in others; and, no doubt, under some conditions, such as advancing age, joints are especially prone to stiffness and other troubles; but taking them as a whole, few kinds of accidents are more amenable to treatment than sprains, if only two conditions are observed: one, that it is commenced sufficiently early; the other, that it is carried out thoroughly and efficiently, not in a perfunctory manner.

Afterwards, if the time immediately after the accident has been allowed to pass by, and the joint is stiff, and recovery imperfect, a great deal may still be done; but as a rule, the longer the delay the more remote the prospect of perfect restoration. The sudden and startling cures that are so often heard of are really few and far between. It must always be remembered that in surgery, as in most other things, successes are trumpeted abroad, and always quoted as an encouragement, while failures are either never heard of, or quite unconsciously are forgotten. Much more often recovery is slow and tedious, requiring care and much patience, with days in which improvement is well marked, interspersed among a much larger number on which either no change at all is apparent, or possibly even the pain and stiffness seem actually worse.

CHAPTER I.

THE ANATOMY OF JOINTS.

THERE is no need in a work of this kind to enter into a detailed account of the structure of joints, or to describe minutely the different varieties. I shall only mention a few particulars to which it seems advisable to call attention, as the clinical symptoms that follow injuries do not always correspond with the structures as described in ordinary anatomical treatises.

A joint is the connecting link between two of the rigid parts of the skeleton. Both in the trunk and in the limbs the main support runs down the centre like an axis, and for the sake of mobility is divided into rigid and flexible segments. The latter are known as joints.

Yielding Joints.—Some are very simple. There is merely a tough layer, made up partly of fibrous tissue, and partly of cartilage, uniting the two bones, and allowing a limited amount of bending to take place between them in all directions. Bone and fibro-cartilage are developed from the same material; in one part lime salts are deposited, so that it becomes hard and dense; in another fibres make their appearance, and it is converted into ligamentous tissue, capable of bending with ease from side to side, but admirably adapted to resist longitudinal strain. The two are quite continuous, and shade off imperceptibly into each other. So slight, indeed, is the difference, that it not unfrequently happens, as a result of disease, or even of old age, that the whole becomes converted into bone, and the joint disappears as such.

Others are a little more complicated; but the changes that make their appearance during normal growth, or at certain special periods, show plainly that the difference between them and the more complex ones is only one of degree, and not one of kind. The ends of the bones, if carefully examined, are a little expanded, so as to form a wider surface for the attachment of the uniting disc; while the sides are cut away to lessen the weight and to economize material. At the same time the softer intermediate part becomes modified. Owing to the varied character of the strains that fall on its sides and centre, they become different in texture and in power of resistance. The centre, where, whatever the direction in which one bone is bent on the other, there must always be pressure with but little tendency to separation, remains cellular, or becomes so soft and yielding that in some cases it is almost fluid. At the circumference, where in every strain there is compression on the concave side and tension on the convex, the connecting medium gradually becomes more and more fibrous, until by degrees the originally uniform layer of fibro-cartilage is resolved into a central cavity surrounded by a fibrous capsule and separated from the surfaces of the bones by a layer of cartilage which undergoes no alteration.

Such are the joints in the backbone between the bodies of the vertebræ, though in them, at least in man, the change rarely progresses so far. The union is exceedingly strong; the amount of movement allowed at each very limited, though it may take place in any direction; and the aggregate result of a number close together is very considerable.

They are very rarely sprained; their strength, their position close together, so that any stress falling on one is distributed over a large number, and the limited range of movement, prove their safeguard. If the violence is so extreme that something must give way, they either tear across or separate from the bone on one side. Then the injury is to all intents and purposes a fracture, and like fractures is repaired by the deposition of bony material, so that the joint is lost.

Movable Joints.—It is only a step from joints such as these to those in which there is a well-defined central space, enclosed in a fibrous capsule, and lined with a delicate secreting membrane. The development of the various parts is carried further and further, until they differ from each other widely in appearance; but the degree of relationship between them is as near as ever it was; and they are as much connected together, and as closely bound up with each other, as they were before the change. The difference is only one of degree, not one of kind. They become varied in outward appearance and physical properties, because of the different services they have to perform; but they never lose their mutual sympathy or connection. It is impossible for one part of a joint to be injured, or to suffer in any way, without influencing the rest. Joints are not built up, like machinery, of different and separate parts, any one of which can be injured and replaced without interfering with the others; they are living organs, which cannot be healthy if the smallest part fails in its duty.

The Bones.—In the limbs and the more movable joints the modifications are especially great. First, the bones, which are the chief supporting structures, become more highly specialized. Instead of retaining the same uniform character the ends are altered in one direction, the middle in another. The shaft becomes hollowed out and assumes a cylindrical form, the shape well known to mechanicians as the one best calculated to withstand vertical pressure and lateral strain with the minimum expenditure of material. Here and there the compact walls are strengthened by outlying ridges, so that the cross section in some is almost prismatic. The ends, on the other hand, become wide and expanded, to increase the extent of surface that enters into the formation of the joint; often they are still further enlarged by processes jutting out to afford greater strength and security for the ligaments that hold them together, and more advantageous leverage for the muscles that move them. At the same time the internal structure loses its uniform arrangement. Where the range of movement is limited and equal in all directions, the interlacing network of bony spicules, of which the sponge-like interior is formed, shows no well-defined differences either in density or arrangement. The outer layer is merely a little more compact and smooth on the surface than the rest. In the more highly developed joints, no matter in what direction the bones are sawn, the dense tissue that forms the outer layer, and the open-work interlacing bars inside, are always so arranged in arches and curves as to diffuse as far as possible over the whole the pressure that falls on any one spot, and to secure the greatest amount of strength and elasticity with the least weight and the smallest expenditure of material.

Then the surfaces in contact with the opposite bone become varied in direction and outline in order to correspond to the movements. The more active and vigorous these are, the more changed and uneven they become. In the simplest joint they are flat, and face each other directly, only allowing a

certain amount of gliding between them.   In others—the
shoulder and hip, for example—the extremity of one bone is
hollowed out into a cup into which the other fits, more or less
accurately, according to the degree of support required.   In
the lower limb, where the need of this is much greater than
in the upper, the rounded extremity of the bone forms more
than half a sphere, and is so tightly embraced by the sides of
the cup, that, even when everything that holds the bones together has been divided, it requires very considerable strength
to pull the two apart.   In the shoulder, on the other hand, the
cavity is shallow, the head of the bone large in comparison,
and the range of movement increased thereby at the expense
of the security.   In a third class, the ends are so modified with
regard to each other, that movement can only take place in
one plane as on a hinge.   In the elbow, for example, the bone
is rounded from before backwards, and fits into a corresponding depression on the other, rotating in it on an axis that
runs from side to side.   In the ankle there are stout projecting processes, one on either side, so that movement is strictly
limited to one direction, and lateral bending is impossible.

When more complicated movements are required, the modifications become greater still.   In one instance a ligamentous
ring attached at one side is thrown round the neck of a bone,
so that it can turn securely in it on its own axis.   In another,
discs of fibro-cartilage are interposed between the bony surfaces to deepen the sockets and lessen the impact of shocks;
or, as in the case of the wrist and foot, a number of small
bones are so adjusted to each other that the pressure falling
on any one of them is diffused and distributed over all the rest.

The Fibrous Tissue.—These changes are not confined to
the bones; in the more movable joints the ligaments become
modified quite as much.   As already mentioned, in the simplest the fibrous tissue that joins the bones together passes
directly from the surface of one to a corresponding point on
the other.   Where the range of motion is a little more extensive, the part round the circumference becomes more fibrous,
the interior softer and more cellular.   In those which admit a
wide extent of movement the change is carried further still.
The soft central space becomes a well-defined cavity; and the
fibrous tissue round forms a firm ligamentous capsule, enclos-
ing it, and tying the two bones together.

The Capsule.—Simultaneously with this the point to which the capsule is attached undergoes an alteration. Freedom of movement is easily gained by increasing the length of the fibres; but at the same time stability and security are lost, unless, as in the case of the shoulder, the surrounding muscles replace the ligaments in checking and controlling the action. Accordingly, in all cases in which the range of movement exceeds a very small angle, the fibres no longer pass from surface to surface, or even from margin to margin, but are shifted further back on to the sides of the bones, so that the ends of these are enclosed by the capsule and lie inside the joint. By this arrangement one bone is enabled to glide on the other when any stress falls on it, and freedom of movement is gained without the sacrifice of strength. There are few joints in the body admitting of much angular movement in which one joint does not glide to some extent on the other.

The Ligaments.—The strength of the fibrous capsule becomes modified at the same time. Where the amount of movement is but little, and is equal in all directions, there is a uniform and even layer, extending all round the joint from one bone to the other. When the structure of the bones allows bending in one plane only, as in true hinge-joints, the side portions springing from the ends of the axis of motion are more highly developed than the rest. Each is attached to a point on the more fixed bone, and radiates from this in a fan-like way on to the other, so that the two are firmly braced together in all positions of the limb. At the back and front it is thin and loose, merely serving to protect the cavity of the joint. By steps such as this the capsule of a joint gradually becomes split up into four divisions, which appear to be so isolated and distinct from each other that they are often called anterior, posterior, and lateral ligaments. They are not, however, separate structures in any sense of the term. They are only subordinate parts of the same that have become differentiated from each other by the difference in the character of the work they are called on to perform.

In a ball and socket joint, which, so far as this is concerned, may be regarded as a kind of universal hinge, the capsule is modified in the same manner. In the hip, where unyielding support in front is required, that part is so strong that, even in dislocation, it very rarely gives way; behind, where there is but little strain, it is comparatively thin and weak. In the shoulder, everything else is subordinated to accurate and rapid action in all directions. The capsule consequently is, with the exception of one part, so loose and long that it only becomes tense when the angle of movement is extreme; the muscles here take the place of the ligaments almost entirely, and not only execute but also control and restrain the movements of the arm with a precision that would be impossible if it were dependent on passive and unyielding fibrous tissue.

The Synovial Membrane.—The cavity of a joint always contains a certain amount of an exceedingly viscid fluid, known as synovia. The quantity is very variable even in the same joint, but in general there is merely sufficient to moisten the surfaces that are in contact with each other, so as to avoid friction as far as possible. It is secreted by a delicate structure known as the synovial membrane. This lines the interior of the fibrous capsule, and is prolonged into all the outlying pouches in connection with it, but does not extend, at least in the adult, over the layer of cartilage that covers the ends of the bones. Before birth an exceedingly delicate film of cells, without any fibres, may be found in this situation; but they are soon worn off, and do not reappear. Where this membrane is folded on itself, as, for example, at the attachment of the capsule to the bone, it is often thrown into folds, which, under some circumstances, are capable of assuming a very considerable size. The inner surface is smooth and polished; the other is continuous with the fibrous tissue of the ligaments, where they serve to enclose the joint; but between them, and in the intervals found here and there extending under muscles, it possesses a delicate wall of its own, formed of connective tissue, and connected to the structures round by a few loose and scattered fibres.

This synovial membrane is in general regarded as a separate and distinct structure, found in those joints only in which there is considerable freedom of movement. In others, it is stated that an imperfect cavity is sometimes developed, but that it is never lined by a true synovial sac. This view is incorrect; neither the method of development nor the changes that take place in disease lend it any support. In reality, the synovial membrane is nothing more than the lining of the cavity, which is developed as the amount of movement increases; and under similar conditions, structures indistinguishable from synovial sacs may be developed in any part of the body.

In the centre of a joint the cells which fill up the space between the bones break down, become liquid, and dissolve away; round the circumference they persist. The outermost, as already mentioned, are converted into fibrous tissues, and form the ligaments, or the capsule, as the case may be; the inner ones, those that immediately line the cavity, form the synovial membrane. The cartilage on the ends of the bones is not covered with it, or it is at most covered with a single layer of cells, because of the relation it bears to the cavity, and because there is no fibrous tissue developed on its surface. In the intervals between the ligaments, where there is nothing to protect the cavity of the joint, it is a little stronger than elsewhere, and may be called a membrane; but it is not an isolated or distinct structure here any more than it is elsewhere. It is continuous on either side with the neighboring ligaments; where it comes into contact with the cartilage it shades off into it, so that it is impossible to say where one commences and the other ends; and its outer surface is part of the loose and delicate connective tissue that fills in all the irregularities round joints, extends under the muscles and tendons, and forms a layer under the skin.

Mutual Sympathy of all the Parts.—Joints are commonly regarded as composed of many different structures, all of them separate and distinct from each other, with different and independent functions. There are ligaments to hold the bones together; a synovial membrane to render the movements smooth; cartilages over the ends of the bones to lessen the impact of any shock; and round them, filling up all the interspaces, a quantity of loose and delicate connective tissue, containing the blood-vessels and nerves which supply the joint.

This view may serve for the purposes of ordinary descriptive anatomy; but it gives an altogether wrong impression of the nature of the injury sustained when a joint is sprained, and of the causes of the complications and after-troubles that follow with such frequency. The bones that form a joint, no matter how many there may be, or how great may be the varieties of their shape, are surrounded and held together by connective tissue, which is structurally continuous with them. It bridges

over the interval between them, fills up all the interstices left
by the muscles and tendons, and forms an investment for these
and every other structure near.   One part, where there is
much tension, becomes dense and unyielding, so that it is
known as ligament; in another the cells undergo a process of
liquefaction, and a cavity is formed; the limiting wall of this
is differentiated into a synovial sac, and a membrane more or
less distinct is developed from it.   The different structures
lose all external resemblance to each other.   What they do
not lose is their relationship from their common descent.
Throughout the whole of life the closest sympathy persists
between them, so that it is impossible for any one of them to
suffer by itself.   It follows as a natural consequence from this
that sprains can never be the simple things they are usually
considered, or be confined to the mere stretching or tearing
of an isolated ligament.   The immediate effect of an accident
may fall upon the ligaments, or it may not; it can never be
limited to them.   The capsule of the joint is opened up, the
cartilages bruised, the muscles torn, the tendon sheaths
strained, the interior filled with blood, and so much more extravasated into the tissues round that the strain may extend
the whole way up a limb, and may not disappear for six weeks.
Very often, in spite of the popular belief, the ligaments are
the part that suffer least: they certainly never suffer alone.

Even if by any chance they were the only structures hurt
at the moment, it is impossible for the other tissues to remain
unaffected during the changes attendant on their repair.   A
wheel or a band in a piece of machinery may be damaged and
restored without interfering with the other parts.   When a
ligament is hurt a certain amount of blood escapes into the
synovial sac and the spaces round; all the vessels dilate; the
synovial folds become swollen; the joint is tender to the touch;
the temperature of the part is raised; its movements are interfered with; even the external shape of the limb is altered.
Nothing escapes; every structure round participates more or
less.

The same is true of the later troubles that so frequently
impair the freedom of movement in joints long after they have
been sprained.   The stiffness, for example, that is often laid to
the credit of a contracted tendon, or shortened band, is never
due to this alone; nor is the sense of insecurity dependent en-

tirely, or even to any extent, on the weakness of an injured ligament. It is only by taking a wider and more comprehensive view of the structure of joints, and by regarding them as organs of the body, wonderful in their complexity, that a true conception can be obtained of the nature of the damage they suffer in sprains, and of the method in which they should be treated, so as to avoid, as far as may be, the occurrence of permanent injury.

CHAPTER II.

CAUSE AND PREVENTION OF SPRAINS.

WITHOUT going so far as to say that sprained joints can be entirely prevented, there is no doubt that it is possible to avoid and guard against them to a very considerable degree. In some people they are particularly common; and so they are at certain times, and under certain conditions. Others escape in a manner that seems almost marvellous, and possess the power of using their joints in a fashion that would be impossible in the majority.

The Condition of the Muscles.—This depends mainly on the condition of the muscular system. The strength and security of the articulations are assured in proportion to the perfection of its development. Sprains never occur unless the muscles are either weakened and tired out by prolonged exertion, or are caught unawares by some sudden slip, before they can recover themselves. Astley Cooper said of dislocations that it was only possible for them to take place when the muscles were unprepared for resistance; otherwise the greatest force would hardly produce the effect. Without saying so much of sprains, there can be no question that such accidents rarely happen unless the muscles that safeguard the joints are taken by surprise. Ordinarily speaking, they are the result of a sudden twist, so rapid that recovery cannot take place in time, and naturally this is most likely to happen to those who have never accustomed their muscles to much exertion, or who, from fatigue, have lost that instinctive vigilance and power of recovery essential to the safety of a joint.

This, among others, is one reason why sprains, especially of the knee and ankle, are so common among women, and those men who, in their youth, were distinguished for athletic feats. In the former, the muscles are insufficiently exercised, so that they never attain the vigilance and instantaneous power of response necessary to prevent the consequences of a careless step; in the latter, with advancing years and altered modes of life, the muscles fall out of training, without its being perceived, or perhaps sometimes without its being acknowledged. Then some unusual effort, especially a prolonged one, that in days gone by would have been accomplished easily, proves too much for their endurance under the altered conditions, and something gives way. Unhappily, when this has taken place once, the joint often remains, as it were, a weakened spot, and there is always the possibility of the same thing happening again and again, with greater ease each time.

The muscles are really part of the joint as much as the bones or the synovial membrane. It may be more convenient to describe them separately, but the function of a joint is movement, and in considering the way in which sprains interfere with this, the muscles that execute and direct it are as much concerned as the ligaments, which have only the passive duty of checking it when it is excessive. This is true of all joints, but especially of those in which the freedom of movement is greatest, and which on that account are the most exposed to strains and injuries of like character. As Morris has pointed out, the strength of any single joint, and its power of resisting injury, are inversely proportioned to its freedom of mobility.

In the more fixed joints, where there is only an indistinctly marked cavity in the centre of the fibro-cartilage, the muscles are short and broad, with much inelastic fibrous tissue in their composition, and often are so arranged with cross-running and interlacing fibres that while one bone is moving on the other it is held even more firmly in contact with it than when it is at rest. Where, on the other hand, the range of movement is extensive, the security of the joint is often dependent entirely on the muscles. In the shoulder, for example, there is a fibrous capsule surrounding the ends of the bones, and forming the apparent bond of union between them. But it is so loose, and has so little influence in controlling movements, that if the muscles are paralyzed the arm drops down for upwards of an inch. Here in particular, owing to the need of accuracy and delicacy, combined with strength and rapidity, the function of controlling the movements of the joint is assigned almost entirely to those structures which originate them. The muscles take the place of ligaments.

When this occurs their shape and arrangement are modified. They become divided, roughly speaking, into two sets.
Some are short and broad, and immediately surround the
joint. These maintain the proper degree of pressure between
the bones, and keep the action smooth. Others are much
longer, and are attached to distant points by means of rounded
tendons, which lie in grooves lined by a delicate sheath. On
these depend the vigor and rapidity of the movements. They
differ greatly in size and direction, but the connection that
exists between them and the joint is no less intimate; the
same nerve supplies them both. They are really but different
parts of the same mechanism, so closely united together by
the bond of common descent, and so associated with each
other by the identical nature of the nerve supply, that it is
not possible for one of them to be injured and the rest escape.

The same is true of the skin that covers them in and pro-
tects them. This, too, is supplied by the same nerve, and
when the joint or the muscles is injured cannot help being
affected at the same time. Illustrations of this are of common occurrence as the result of sprains. It has often been re-
marked that after prolonged and severe exertion the skin over
the insertion of the muscles, and in certain spots over joints,
becomes exquisitely tender from its sympathy with the parts
beneath. It does not arise from any irritation or inflammation of the skin itself, for nothing has happened to affect it in
any way. Yet the slightest touch gives rise to the feeling of
actual pain. Firm pressure, on the other hand, relieves it,
not, as is often said, because it is hysterical and imaginary,
but because of the numbing effect of compression on the superficial cutaneous nerves. Plainly the skin, which is an exceedingly sensitive structure, is suffering in sympathy with the
overworked organs it is intended to protect.

The Muscles as Ligaments.—The muscles, therefore, must
be considered in a twofold relation to the joints. On the one
hand they are the sole agents for executing movements; on
the other, under all ordinary circumstances, they take the
place usually assigned to ligaments, and act as the main safeguard. So long as the action is confined within moderate
limits the ligaments are entirely unconcerned; they are merely
passive bands of inelastic fibrous tissue, so loose as to have no
restraining power until a certain angle is reached. Then they

suddenly become tight, and bring the movement to an abrupt conclusion. The muscles, on the other hand, are always tense, no matter what may be the position of the limb. No movement, not even the bending of a finger, is so simple that it can be carried out by the action of a single set; the opposing ones must always act with them, so that the movement may be even and steady, not disorderly at its commencement, or brought to a sudden standstill at its close. The firmness and security of the joints—except such as the knee—in all their positions are entirely due to the continuous steady contraction of opposing groups of muscles. They are the agents which prevent movement being carried too far, so that under ordinary conditions strains do not fall on rigid and inelastic ligaments. When from fatigue or carelessness this does happen, the ligament may be strong enough to resist, but more often—especially in the joints with free movement—it stretches or tears, and a sprain of greater or less severity is the result.

Under these conditions the muscles sometimes suffer, while the ligaments escape. The injury may be immediate, or not show itself until some time has elapsed They may be torn or bruised by the violence with which the bones are wrenched apart; or what is, perhaps, more common, hurt themselves by the sudden and almost involuntary attempt at recovery when a slip is threatened. If they escape at the moment they may suffer even more seriously at a later period from wasting, rigidity, or degeneration, so that in severe cases they become converted into dense unyielding bands. This, perhaps, is not a common occurrence when recovery is rapid, though it is by no means unknown; when it is delayed, they rarely fail to show that they have undergone some kind of change, and that they are not so perfect as they were before.

The Effects of Muscular Development.—Besides, however, acting as a safeguard and protection against accidents of this nature, the muscular system is of great importance in another way. The degree of perfection to which joints attain—and naturally they differ immensely in this respect in different individuals—is dependent entirely on the extent to which the muscular system is developed.

Where the muscles are poor and feeble the joints are poor and feeble too, and are easily sprained. The ends of the bones, instead of being angular, with sharply-cut and well-defined

edges, are smooth and rounded. The articular surfaces are
faintly marked, so that they can glide on each other in irregular and unusual directions; the capsule is loose and yielding,
and the ligaments, without the assistance of the muscles, are
unable to withstand the least strain, or even to maintain the
normal relation of the two bones. The action of the joint is
uncertain and often painful, and the loss of power is proportionate. In case of any extra work the bony surfaces glide
irregularly on each other, and move beyond their ordinary
limit. The more often this takes place the more easy it is for
it to happen again. Each time it is always carried a little
farther than it was before, until at length, some day, one bony
prominence is caught behind another over which it has slipped,
or a tendon or disc of cartilage escapes from its bed, and the
joint is locked. Pain and swelling rapidly follow. The patient
may be able to restore things to their natural position at the
first, but more often some assistance is required. The serious
thing is that when this occurs, as it is wont to do more and
more often, the joint never has time to recover its natural
condition, and is left permanently damaged.

The principle that the more a part is used, within, of course,
rational limits, the more perfect it becomes, has long been
recognized in the case of bones. The skeleton of the male is
very different from that of the female; the work is harder, and
the bones become stronger. In the one they are solid, heavy,
and exceedingly irregular, from the development of muscular
ridges; in the other they are lighter altogether, and much
more smooth and even. So with animals that have long been
kept in confinement, the bones, contrasted with those of wild
ones of the same species, scarcely admit of comparison, the
difference is so great. It is the same with the muscles. As
Humphry has pointed out, there is a difference almost of kind
between the slender, compact frame and wiry, active muscular
system of the thoroughbred, and the coarser, heavier, and
more clumsy tissues of the cart-horse.

What is true of the shafts and muscular eminences of
bones is equally true of their articular ends, and of the rough
surfaces to which ligaments are attached. Joints are well
formed and secure from injury, so far as shape can make them,
in proportion to the amount of their use and the perfection of
the muscular system.

Chronic Sprains.—Such a condition as the one I have described above may be almost called a state of chronic sprain. So long as it is slight it does not attract much attention. There are complaints of loss of power, and of twisting or giving way, but, as a rule, the deformity is not conspicuous, and especially as it is most common in children, it is put down to what is called growing pain, a name which has probably done as much harm as any other by the way in which it makes light of what often is the commencement of a serious disease. When it is more severe, or when during some unaccustomed effort the limb fails completely, the joint is generally said to be out. The pain is very severe; swelling soon makes its appearance, owing partly to the unnatural position of the bones, partly to the effusion round; and, owing to the insecurity of the joint, the loss of power is so great that the patient often believes himself paralyzed. It is serious, not on account of the tearing of the capsule or the injury to the parts around, but because the cause is such a persistent one, because the condition of things which has given rise to it is one that requires a long and systematic course of treatment before it can be rectified.

One of the earliest and most characteristic examples I have seen was in a young girl who was brought to me complaining of partial paralysis of the right arm, attended at times with attacks of severe pain. She was a tall, overgrown girl fourteen years of age, employed as a nursemaid, having to carry about a heavy child, and owing to this condition of her arm, which had been coming on gradually for the last three or four months, had lost her situation. She was not aware of having sustained any single severe injury to her shoulder; but stated, of her own accord, that long before it reached its present state it was continually giving way, or, as she expressed it, coming out of joint. On comparing the two sides together, it was evident that the muscles round the shoulder joint on the affected side were smaller than those on the other, though the difference was not equally marked in all. The movements were limited to a great extent by the pain they occasioned, and the general muscular strength was decidedly below normal. The cause was apparent at once; there was a large amount of thickening over the point of the shoulder round the joint, that is to say, between the collar-bone and the shoulder-blade; and the bones were so loosely connected together that the end of one could easily be made to slip backward and forward over the end of the other. When the shoulder-blade was held in position by firm pressure from behind, the movements of the arm could be executed nearly as well as those of the opposite limb, and with nearly as much vigor, while the wasting diminished so much that evidently it was in the main apparent only. As soon as the pressure was taken off, the bone at once underwent considerable rotation, the upper border being so much displaced that a deep hollow made its appearance behind the collar-bone, which slid in such a direction that the two completely lost their normal relation to each other.

The fact that the wasting almost disappeared, and that the movements could be executed with ease as soon as the shoulder-blade was fixed, quite negatived the idea of paralysis. The slight amount of real wasting, affecting only a few of the muscles, could easily be accounted for by the inflammation of and round the joint; wasting much more extensive than this sometimes under these circumstances comes on within a week. There was no history of any accident sufficiently severe to suggest the idea of a dislocation with rupture of the ligaments; the onset of the mischief had been quite slow and gradual, though every now and then the pain—which had, as usual, been called growing pain—and the inconvenience had suddenly become worse. For the same reason it could hardly be termed a partial dislocation; the capsule was not torn, and the whole thing had come on slowly and imperceptibly, so that the patient could assign no date at all for its first commencement. The characteristic features were the weak muscular development, the imperfection in the shape of the articular ends, and the loose yielding condition of the ligaments. So long as no extra strain fell on the joint, the muscles, weak and feeble as they were, were sufficient to maintain the surfaces in contact; a little extra work, slowly and gradually in this case, tiring out the muscles, allowed the strain to fall on the ligaments, until, as ligaments always will when subjected to long-continued tension, they gradually stretched more and more, and became so loose that the end of one bone could slip backward and forward and ride over that of the other.

A similar case, differing, however, in the joint affected, that between the collar-bone and the breast-bone, and in the fact that it was distinctly made worse by one rather severe strain, came under my notice almost the same day. The patient, who was also a girl, aged about 18 years, had suddenly felt a severe pain in this joint two days before as she was trying to lift a heavy weight, and, of course, had been told the joint "was out." At the first glance this did not seem unlikely, for the inner extremity of the collar-bone was much too prominent; but there was very little swelling or tenderness, and no bruising whatever. On further inquiry, too, it was elicited from the patient that for some months past the arm had felt very weak and unsteady in its movements. Examination of the opposite joint showed that it was nearly in the same condition, and, in fact, the bones on both sides were so loose that they could be pushed almost as far backward and forward as they could upward. Clearly, the ligaments were unusually lax, and two days before, when an unaccustomed strain fell on the right joint, it gave way, causing so much pain and inconvenience that the patient was compelled to seek advice.

These two cases are, perhaps, somewhat exaggerated examples, because in both the already loose condition of the ligaments had been intensified by severe strains; the same state, however, exists independently of these, and no joint in the body is exempt. The shoulder, as might be imagined from the description already given, is peculiarly prone to suffer. If the joint is poorly developed, or the muscles on which it depends for its security are lax and feeble, it can readily be made to assume abnormal positions. Sometimes this occurs with any movement, more often only with certain definite actions; in one case, a girl of 16, whom I watched for a long time, whenever in dressing of a morning she placed her hand on the back of her head in trying to arrange her hair, the upper end of the humerus slipped over the edge of its socket, and was caught there. At length she learned by a clever twisting action to bring it into its place again, and even gradually to avoid displacing it altogether.

In the elbow joint, from the shape of the bones, this accident can scarcely happen; but the same condition of things occurs. Examples may often be met with in which the forearm can, without any violence or pain, be bent back to an abnormal extent on the arm; the ligaments in front are so loose that they do not check the movement sufficiently, and the

bones so feebly developed that their projecting extremities do
not come into contact with each other until the normal range
is greatly exceeded.

In the case of the lower jaw it has long been known.
Hamilton described it as occurring in his own person, and,
naturally, with the greatest possible accuracy. He has noticed, also, the curious circumstance that this displacement,
when it does occur, is much more common in the morning than
at any other time of day. Particularly at breakfast the lower
jaw, owing to the looseness of the ligaments that should restrict its action, is apt to become locked when the mouth is
opened at all widely, and some manipulation is required to
bring it back again.

Whether the same thing can occur in connection with the
hip is, I should think, very doubtful. I have seen one patient
who could at will dislocate her thigh-bone by a peculiar twisting of the limb; but in the absence of any history that could
be relied on, and as her other joints gave no sign, which they
almost certainly would have done in such an extreme case, I
should imagine that probably this condition had existed from
birth, by virtue of some congenital defect. In the knee minor
degrees of it are quite common, not only allowing abnormal
movements of the leg upon the thigh, but also giving too wide
a range of action to the semi-lunar cartilages in the interior
of the joint, whereby, perhaps, at length is brought about the
beginning of a most serious affection known as internal derangement.

It is singular that this condition of the joints, which is very
common in slighter degrees, and very striking in the exaggerated form I have described above, should have attracted
so little attention. Sir Astley Cooper has described it in the
case of one joint. Hamilton mentions it from his own personal
experience in another. Malgaigne gives a vague account of
something similar, but although he regards it, quite correctly,
as the consequence of debility, and often determined to one
particular joint by a local trouble, such as a sprain, he does
not appear to recognize it as a general condition, affecting
many joints at one and the same time; and he fails altogether
to separate it from cases in which the capsule or ligament
have been weakened, or stretched by inflammation, or by the
passive accumulation of fluid in their interior. It is even more

strange that he fails to appreciate the fact that the ligaments, though undoubtedly concerned in the production of this condition, are in reality only passive agents, and not in any way the immediate cause. He states that it is due to an essential relaxation of the ligaments, though he fails to describe what this may be. In reality it is the muscular system that is at fault; for on this more than anything else depends the perfection of the joints, and the strength and power of resistance of the ligaments.

The secret of it all is to be found in the feebleness of the muscular system. In the first place the joints are weak, and the ligaments loose, because they have not been properly exercised. Then the muscles are not equal to any amount of work. When a little extra labor falls on them (and very little is needed in cases such as these) they soon become fatigued; the joints lose their support, and either the already feeble ligaments yield slowly and steadily, with a very considerable amount of pain, as ligaments always will yield when exposed to any severe strain; or else, owing to some sudden slip, the weight of the body falls on them before the muscles can save them, and some permanent injury is the result. It cannot be too clearly laid down that not only do the joints depend for their perfection on the degree of development of the muscles, but that, at any moment, the contraction of the muscles round a joint is as essential to its security as the ligaments, perhaps more so. If they yield, the ligaments will never hold for long.

Effects of Age on Joints.—One other feature in the construction of joints cannot be passed over in silence, as it helps to explain why sprains in some people are so liable to be followed by complications from which others are quite exempt. The joints are not alike at any two periods of life. It is acknowledged that they do not attain their highest stage of perfection until adult years are reached, but even after this their most important features undergo continual modifications. In infancy, adult life, and old age there are vast degrees of difference in their structure, due partly to the way in which they have been used, partly to the natural changes that take place in them as age advances, and partly to disease.

Leaving aside for the present this last consideration, the differences that exist between the joints at various periods of life are most striking. In the infant the surfaces and edges

of the cartilages are rounded and smooth, closely fitting together at the centre so as to leave between them merely a
cleft, which widens a little, but very little, at the margin. The
shape of the joint cavity is well defined, regular, and even.
There are no outlying pouches or projecting fringes; everything is as simple as it can be. The fibrous capsule round
presents the same features. It is, it is true, a little stronger
in one part than it is in another, but there are no great accessory bands of dense unyielding ligament. All is soft and delicate in structure, shading off imperceptibly into the surrounding connective tissue, and what is, perhaps, the most important
feature of all, exceedingly richly supplied with blood-vessels.
In the adult these are confined almost entirely to two circles
which surround the ends of the bones, where the capsule is
attached, and send loops into the folds and fringes which
abound there. In the child, and still more in the infant, not
only are they larger and more numerous in proportion to the
size of the parts, but they extend over the whole circumference,
and are not limited to any single region. In consequence of
this, when inflammation arises, no matter what may be the
cause, its course is much more rapid, and the exudation of
lymph infinitely more profuse. In children sprains are attended by an altogether disproportionate amount of swelling,
and probably many of the complications that occur in them
are due, not so much to inherited tendency as to the extraordinary richness of the blood supply, and the rapid and tumult-
uous character of the tissue changes that take place under
such conditions.

All through life, not merely in youth, but even in old age,
this undergoes continual change. The difference is not only
one of size, but of structure, arrangement, and relation. The
cartilage is replaced by bone, with the exception, as already
mentioned, of the layer that directly lines the cavity. The
edges become sharp and well defined, and the surfaces are no
longer moulded accurately to each other. The capsule increases in strength and thickness. Where the strain is great
the delicate connective tissue becomes dense and unyielding
ligament; in other places it forms a close and even membrane
round the central space. But these alterations, great as they
are, are slight when compared with those of the synovial cavity and its delicate lining. This not only increases in size in

proportion to the growth of the joint, but becomes greatly changed in shape. Pouches are thrown out round the bony projections and into the weaker parts of the capsule until in outline it bears scarcely any resemblance to what it was at birth. Accessory spaces, known as bursæ, are developed wherever there is friction, under tendons, for example, or between bones and muscles. These differ in each individual both as regards shape and position. As age advances they become larger and larger, until at length they encroach to such an extent on the lining membrane of the joint cavity that the intervening partition gives way, and a communication between them is established by an opening which grows wider and wider each year.

While this is going on the surface of the lining membrane does not lag behind. It does not remain smooth and regular, merely folded on itself where it is reflected on the bones. Projections grow into the cavity from all sides. Some spring up from the spot where the capsule is attached to the bones, so that these are surrounded by a ring of fringing growths. Others project inward from the ridges and inequalities of the surface or the margins of the openings already mentioned. Some are short and smooth, others long and branched. In some the end expands into a rounded body containing carti-lage corpuscles, while the neck grows thinner and thinner until it gives way and allows it to drop off. Many of them contain loops of vessels, especially when they grow from the region of the vascular circles; other are merely masses of fibrous tissue. There may be only a few scattered about, or the whole interior, especially if examined under water, may be covered with a dense shaggy coating under which it is no longer possible to recognize the polished regular surface met with in youth and childhood.

It is often difficult to tell how far these changes are the result of age, or to what extent they are the direct consequences of disease; the two so often go together hand in hand. The effect is that in no two persons are the joints ever alike; and the older they become, the more work and the harder the work they are called upon to do, the greater the changes and the wider the difference, until at length it is scarcely possible to find a resemblance except in the broad general features of construction.

CHAPTER III.

DIAGNOSIS.

It is not often that there is much difficulty in the diagnosis of a sprain, particularly if the joint is a superficial one, like the ankle or the knee. The nature of the accident, the sudden onset and peculiar character of the pain, the rapid swelling of the part, and the helplessness of the limb, are in general quite sufficient to convince the patient of the misfortune that has befallen him. But as, short of actual dislocation, nearly every kind of injury that can involve either a joint or the tissues in its immediate neighborhood, is called a sprain, this is scarcely sufficiently definite. In no other kind of accident do precision and exactness of diagnosis repay more thoroughly the pain and trouble of careful examination; nowhere is it more essential to form a definite conclusion as early as possible, not only of the kind of hurt sustained, but of its extent and degree. Even then it often happens that constitutional peculiarities, or other agencies less easily controlled, assert their influence, and seriously complicate the progress of the case.

Dislocations, fractures in the neighborhood of joints, and, in the case of children, separation of one of the growing ends of the bones, present the greatest amount of difficulty. In connection with this, there are one or two points which it is advisable to bear in mind. In the first place, in many joints, and particularly in those in which, like the elbow, complicated accidents are of common occurrence, an enormous amount of swelling sets in with such rapidity that all the prominences by which the relative position of the bones is ascertained are buried and lost in a very short time. Consequently, if the diagnosis is not made at once, immediately after the accident, it is necessary either to put the patient under an anæsthetic or to wait without a definite opinion for days, perhaps even for weeks, until the swelling subsides. The importance of this is so great that, especially at the present day, there ought to be no hesitation about the administration of an anæsthetic. In the case of children, it is often impossible to form an opinion without; and even when it is, the risk is so exceedingly slight, the relief from pain so great, and the advantages of being able to examine the joint thoroughly without any muscular rigidity, and to apply the first dressings quietly and systematically, so immense, that they ought to be made use of where there is the least occasion. Nothing is more common than to meet with cases in which, from neglect of this precaution, because the first examination could not be thorough, joints have remained stiff or imperfect in their action throughout the greater part of life.

Further, if there is the slightest question as to the nature of the injury, whether it is a fracture involving a joint, or a sprain, the patient must always be given the benefit of the doubt, and the injury treated as if it were the more serious of the two, with this precaution, that passive motion must be resorted to, and the joint thoroughly worked at a much earlier period than it would be in the case of a simple uncomplicated fracture. It is probable that sprains of the ankle are very frequently confused with fractures of the small bone of the leg, and even with Pott's fracture without displacement of the parts; but as the immediate method of treatment adopted in these instances need not differ materially, no ill result follows, provided passive motion is adopted in time. Stiff joints, whether they are the result of fractures or of sprains, result most often from retaining the part immovable in a fixed apparatus for weeks together.

There is one further caution which it is necessary to observe, one that was originally suggested by Nélaton. It sometimes happens that, even when only a single joint is complained of, one or more of the others in the same limb has sustained some hurt, though of less severity. Consequently it is as well, when examining a sprained limb, always to commence by investigating the movements of the joints which the patient declares not to have been hurt; otherwise they may easily be overlooked, and some time later an aggravating degree of stiffness found that might easily have been avoided by the exercise of a little precaution. There is this further advantage, though it may not be worth much, that the patient, when the joint that really has been injured is taken in hand, knows what is going to be done, and is less apprehensive of any rough movement.

The same thing may happen when one of the bones is broken; a sprain and a fracture may occur in the same limb from the same accident, and owing to the great amount of attention paid to the one, the other may be altogether overlooked. Dr. Bennett, of Dublin, narrates the case of a man who slipped as he was carrying a heavy sack down a sloping plank. His foot was suddenly checked in its slide by some irregularity, and he fell, conscious at the time that something had given way in his leg. Admitted into hospital, as he was unable to bear any weight on his limb, he presented the ordinary features of sprained ankle, without any sign of fracture. The case was treated as a severe sprain, and attracted but little attention for some days, until it was noticed that there were some signs of bruising on the upper part of the leg. On examination, the localized pain, and the crepitus characteristic of fracture, left no room for doubt as to the diagnosis. In addition to his sprain, the small bone of the leg had given way a long distance from the ankle, though he was certain he had not struck it in his fall. The amount of displacement of the broken ends was very slight; the line of fracture was oblique; and there is no doubt it might easily have been passed over altogether. Probably, as Dr. Bennett suggests, accidents of this kind are much more common than is usually supposed.

Swelling.—Much of the difficulty of diagnosis arises from the variety of the symptoms presented by sprains; they are scarcely alike in any two cases. In hinge joints, for example, the mischief falls on the ligaments which oppose a twisting force; in a ball and socket arrangement, the muscles, as a rule, are the greatest sufferers. Sometimes, especially when it is due to hæmorrhage, the swelling makes its appearance at once, and accurately reproduces the shape of the synovial sac. At others the bursæ or the tendon sheaths in the neighborhood are distended, so that this is quite concealed, or there are extensive extravasations into the loose cellular spaces underneath the skin and between the muscles. Or, again, the swelling may commence slowly and gradually, twelve, or even twenty-four hours after the injury, and be smooth and uniform in outline from the very first, owing to the effusion into the soft tissue round as well as into the joint itself.

Very often it is most distinct over the course of the muscles and tendons. The skin, for example, on the outer side of the forearm is raised and puffy over the insertion of the pronator radii teres, or there is a long, low, rounded swelling on the back of the wrist, running obliquely across the joint over the course of the extensor muscles of the thumb. It is quite soft—so soft, indeed, that it can often be appreciated better by the eye than by the finger—never very great, because there is no cavity of any size in which fluid can collect, but exceedingly tender when touched.

Sometimes, instead of the bony prominences being partly buried by the collection of lymph round and between them, the reverse of this is the case. They are increased in size, and stand out under the skin in such a way that there may be some apparent ground for the common conclusion that the joint is out. In the wrist and hand this is a very frequent mistake, and it really is difficult sometimes, when one of these points is projecting beneath the skin, to prove that the bone has not slipped out of its place and been dislocated.

The styloid process of the ulna on the inner side of the wrist is a favorite spot for this. It is often unduly prominent after an attack of gout or rheumatism, and, even when it is certain there has been no injury, it is frequently described as being out. So with the base of the metacarpal bone of the middle finger, which, when the wrist is strongly bent, raises up the skin on the back joint. This often forms a projection, especially in gouty people, varying in size from time to time, and occasionally appears quite suddenly after even slight exertion. Probably it is due to a strain of the tendon attached to this point, and to the amount of effusion thrown out round the bone, but it is nearly always asserted that something is out of joint.

Other parts of the body are not so liable to mistakes of this kind, in all probability because they are not exposed to such continual and minute examination. In the knee and elbow, even, considerable differences are not noticed unless they have appeared suddenly. Natural projections may increase in size, fresh ones may form, or what is perhaps more perplexing still, small ganglions may develop in such places as the outer side of the knee joint, just below the level of the knee cap, and at the same time there may be real impairment of mobility and strength, but unless this happens suddenly, or, what is far more common, is noticed suddenly, little attention is paid to it. When there has been a recent accident the diagnosis is sometimes very difficult, and requires the greatest care.

Staining.—Valuable information may be gained sometimes from the place at which the bruising first shows itself. Blood effused deep down in a limb, as, for example, between the superficial and deep muscles of the calf of the leg, or in the groin, always follows certain well-defined routes, being guided by the anatomical structure and the arrangement of the sheets of fascia. When the limb is bandaged it is often driven great distances by the pressure before it can reach the surface.

Sometimes its distribution is very peculiar. I have seen several instances in which, after a severe injury to the deeper parts of the hand, dark purple crescents caused by blood-staining made their appearance between each of the fingers, just above the web where they divide. Owing to the attachment of the palmar fascia, the coloring matter had soaked through to the skin in a regular and symmetrical pattern.

Pain.—The character of the pain, if the patient can describe it, may be of great help. When the strain falls on the ligaments it is usually said to be sickening, and a patient who has suffered from it once rarely fails to recognize it a second time. It is very sudden, often so severe as to cause the sufferer to faint, and then gradually, if the joint is kept quiet, passes off again, leaving an aching deadness of the limb, but coming back in an aggravated form on the least attempt at movement. This is well marked when a tendon, or one of the internal structures of a joint, slips from its place. So long as the part is kept perfectly still, even if the position is abnormal, the pain is only moderate in severity; it becomes worse and worse as the structure shifts from side to side, until just as it slips back into its bed it is as severe as ever; then it suddenly ceases. The cause at first is the forcible stretching of the ligaments; the later aching seems, in the majority of instances, to be proportionate to, and therefore probably dependent on, the amount of distention of the joint.

Tenderness.—Muscular strains, on the other hand, are distinguished by a peculiar sensitiveness of skin, most marked over the points of attachment to the bones or tendons. These, as a rule, are the weakest spots, where they give way first. If they are even touched the patient shrinks away with the pain; but curiously enough, very often steady, gentle pressure is well borne. The same thing happens when the muscles are overworked, especially during convalescence. At this time the exertion even of sitting upright is sufficient, because the work, trivial though it is, is too much for the muscles in their weakened state.

When a muscle is torn across, either wholly or partially, as in some cases of lawn-tennis leg, the symptoms are of a totally different character. There is a sudden sharp pain, like that of a blow with a whip or a cricket ball, so that the patient turns round to see who has struck him, before he is aware that anything has given way; and then, as the swelling begins, this is followed by a feeling of stiffness and soreness, severe even when the limb is at rest, but so much worse when an attempt is made to use it, that the patient often can hardly be induced to try.

Dislocation of a muscle is not unlike this. There is the same sudden pain, and the part is held fixed in the position of the moment, no matter how inconvenient it may be. If, for example, one of the muscular slips in the neck is displaced by some irregular movement, the head is kept rigid in the position into which it was twisted. It is not possible for a time to bring it straight again, much less to make it face in the opposite direction; only after the first pain has subsided can it be brought round by slow degrees. Even then, as soon as the attention is withdrawn, it quietly, but surely, moves back so long as the displacement is uncorrected. When the parts are restored there is nothing but a sensation of soreness, with a tender spot or line in the neck corresponding to the particular slip displaced.

These tender spots often afford valuable information. They may persist long after apparent recovery has taken place, and they generally point to something which is not quite restored. In a sprained ankle, for example, if one of the lateral ligaments has given way, or has torn off a scale from the bone to which it is attached, that spot remains tender for weeks after. Sometimes they indicate the presence of adhesions, or of tough . contracted parts of the capsule; occasionally they correspond to the situation of synovial fringes, or foreign bodies, or to the

places at which the nerves enter the joint; and in one or two
instances I have known them caused by extravasation in the
substance of the capsule itself.

Allowance must be made for those that are normally present when a joint is hurt. What they are caused by is not
always certain, but as a rule they correspond to places where
the capsule is thin and flexible, and not far removed from the
surface, so that pressure falls on it directly. However this
may be, they are so constant and definite that it is scarcely
possible to mistake them. There is one, for example, nearly
always present on the inner side of the knee-cap, about the
middle of the joint; in the hip it lies behind the projection of
the trochanter, and sometimes there is one also on the inner
side. In the ankle they are not so marked, but there is very
generally one on the front of the joint, rather to the outer side
of the middle line. These are present with such regularity
that they must almost be called normal. When other more
unusual ones are found there is some additional reason to
account for them.

Sprains and Dislocations—the Elbow in Children.—
Sprains and dislocations are sometimes very confusing, even
without taking into consideration the popular view that something is out of joint in every sprain that does not get well at
once. One instance in which there is great difficulty in distinguishing them has been mentioned elsewhere, and it would
be easy to multiply them. There is, for example, a peculiar
injury about the elbow, only met with in children, concerning
the nature of which there is still very considerable doubt. It
is caused by the way in which they are swung round by the
hands, or lifted across a road; and is rarely seen immediately,
for though the child cries out with the pain, there is no distinct or objective sign of anything wrong. Then it is noticed
that the arm is not used as freely as the other; that the child
always cries when it is touched; and that it is held constantly
in one position, the elbow slightly bent, and the palm of the
hand looking downwards. Now, certainly, in the majority of
instances the seat of the mischief is in the elbow joint (J.
Hutchinson, Jun., "Annals of Surgery," 1885); and it is highly
probable that it is due to one of the bones of the forearm, on
which nearly all the weight falls, slipping out from under the
ligamentous collar which holds it in its place. But this view

is not by any means universally held; others, describing the same accident, produced in the same way, causing the same symptoms, and, more than all, cured by the same manipulation, have assigned it to a totally different joint, the wrist.

It is even mistaken for fracture sometimes, for a very simple but altogether insufficient reason. If the elbow is held firmly with one hand, while the forearm is made to rotate slowly from side to side, there is a clicking or snapping sensation, perceptible both to the ear and the touch. Then something is felt to slip, and in general free use of the joint returns immediately. But sometimes this is not so easy; reduction does not take place at once; the peculiar sensation continues, and may even become more plain, until it is really difficult to distinguish it from the crepitus of fracture. It is needless to remark that whatever may be the actual nature of the hurt sustained, it can scarcely be this. If the displacement is rectified, and the arm kept quiet for a day or two, recovery is nearly always complete and thorough, which, under such conditions, would, of course, be quite impossible.

These cases are of everyday occurrence; though there may be minute points of difference, they resemble each other in all important features; the anatomy of the part is thoroughly well-known; the way in which the mischief is produced can generally be ascertained; and there is nothing mysterious, or even unusual, in the manipulation by which the parts are restored. Yet in spite of all this, not only is the actual nature of the injury doubtful, but even its locality is uncertain. When there is no history to be obtained, or only one that is confusing and misleading, and when the limb is stout and shapeless, or so much swollen that nothing can be definitely felt, the difficulty of forming an exact opinion, of making absolutely certain at once that the joint is not dislocated or the bones broken, may be easily imagined.

The close resemblance that exists between many dislocations and some forms of sprains ceases to be astonishing if it is remembered that, as Vidal de Cassis pointed out, they are really the same thing, only that in the case of the former reduction has taken place spontaneously. In the one the articular ends, which at the moment of the accident are wrenched apart, slip back again into their natural position of their own accord; in the other they slip still further aside.

Sprains and Fractures.—Ordinarily speaking there is not much difficulty in distinguishing sprains from fractures. One may easily be overlooked when both are present at the same time, especially if they occur, as they easily may, at the same spot; but in other cases the signs are usually distinctive. The rough grating sensation when two broken ends rub against each other, the undue mobility, deformity, and pain present in most cases of fracture, are nearly always sufficient, though, as will be described later, some of these signs may be imitated exceedingly well by other conditions. If, however, the bones are so driven into each other by the violence of the accident that there is no undue mobility, especially if in addition the line of fracture runs through that part of the bone which lies immediately inside the capsule of the joint, it is not always easy to make a distinction.

In the case of the hip this is well known, but accidents of a similar description, with or without impaction, are met with sometimes in other joints as well.

Sprain Fractures of the Thumb.—The thumb, for example, is liable to a peculiar form of injury, the real nature of which has only recently been explained. It follows in general a severe strain. The ball of the thumb swells up at once, and all power of bending it into the palm of the hand, or bringing it towards the other fingers, is lost. On the back of the bone, just where it joins the wrist, there is a distinct projection, not nearly so large as it would be if the joint were out, and rectified at once by pressure, only as soon as the pressure is removed it returns again, with a visible and painful jerk. If the two hands are compared together the length of the bones corresponds exactly, so that it does not look like a fracture; it cannot be a complete dislocation, and a partial one from the structure of the joint is impossible. In reality the injury partakes of the nature of both. There is an oblique fracture through the base of the bone, where it joins the wrist, splitting off that part which lies deeply buried under the muscles of the ball. It does not involve the back of the bone, so that the measurements are unaltered, but owing to its carrying away with it the projection on the palmar surface that serves to make the joint secure, the rest of the bone slips back and sticks up under the skin. The crepitus, when pressure is made from front to back on the ball of the thumb, and the broken surfaces are rubbed together, can be felt quite easily, and the pain is greatly increased thereby. The ultimate deformity, if the injury is not diagnosed, is not so serious as might be imagined, but the movement of the joint is interfered with for a considerable length of time.

CHAPTER IV.

NATURE OF THE INJURY.

SPRAINS differ a great deal both in the nature and extent of the injury. Sometimes it appears to be quite trivial; there is merely the slipping of a disc of cartilage from between two bones, or the displacement of a tendon from its groove; sometimes everything that holds the two joint surfaces together, with the exception of the skin, is torn and lacerated as it is in a dislocation. In many cases the injury is really as great: the bones are wrenched apart from each other at the moment of the accident, only instead of being caught and held, as they are in a dislocation, they fall back again of themselves into their natural position. Such accidents are always called sprains; but the tissues suffer as much as if the joint had really been put out.

The extent to which the tissues are torn at the moment is not the only thing that has to be taken into consideration. The symptoms and the after consequences are often most serious when this is apparently but slight; and the liability to inflammation, and other troubles, depends a great deal more on the constitution of the patient, and the way in which the sprained joint is treated, than on the number or size of the structures that are torn. So long as the natural process of healing is still in its full vigor, as in children and young adults, injuries, no matter how serious they are, are repaired without the least difficulty. The treatment must be well planned, it is true, and thoroughly carried out; proper care must be taken that the parts are not subjected to too severe a strain before they can stand it; but if this is done, after consequences of any kind are the exception. Unhappily as time goes on the effects of age and of constitutional frailties become so powerful that in many cases, in spite of every care, a comparatively trivial injury often leads to the most serious results, and re-

covery is delayed indefinitely, or remains imperfect perhaps
for the rest of life.

Opportunities for examining joints shortly after they have
been sprained are not very common, though they occur sometimes when a patient has received other and more serious damage in the same accident. By taking advantage of these a
fair amount of information has been obtained with regard to
ordinary cases; and the results have been confirmed by Bonnet, of Lyons, and others, who have made use of other methods.
Many special sprains, however, such, for example, as the internal derangement of the knee-joint, first described by Hey, .
are still involved in a certain amount of obscurity. They are
not uncommon; for years past they have attracted an unusual
amount of attention from the inconvenience they cause, and
the striking character of the symptoms that attend them; but
the joints in which they occur are so complicated, and opportunities for examining them so rare, that there is not as yet
any settled opinion as to what the nature of the accident may
be. It does not seem unlikely that the actual displacement·
varies in different cases, even though the external symptoms
are to all appearance the same.

Generally speaking, the tissues on one side of a joint are
overstretched and torn; those on the other compressed and
crushed together; but there is always so much twisting, and
such a difference in the strength and power of resistance of
the various structures, that unless the part is examined with
the greatest care it is almost impossible to say what actually
has given way. In every case no pains should be spared to
find out the whole of the mischief with as little delay as possible. There are many instances on record in which delayed
convalescence has been due solely to the fact that a displaced
tendon or other structure has not been recognized sufficiently
early. The difficulty increases with every minute. Immediately after a sprain, before the position of the parts has been
altered by attempts at movement, or concealed by swelling,
the nature of the displacement may often be recognized without much trouble. But if the chance is lost, the part begins
to throb with pain, swelling sets in and obscures everything,
and it is often necessary either to place the patient under an
anæsthetic or to wait until the extravasation and œdema have
been dispersed.

Hæmorrhage into the Sac.—Most of the swelling that makes its appearance immediately is due to the blood that pours out from the torn vessels. The central cavity of the joint becomes distended with fluid, which varies in character and amount according to the number and size of the vessels in the injured part, and the length of time that has elapsed since the accident. If the swelling reaches its maximum within the first few hours, it is probably due mainly to blood; if twenty-four hours pass by before this, there is a large proportion of lymph mixed with it, and, at the same time, if the joint is superficial, some heat and redness of skin. The amount is very variable; sometimes it is not easy to detect any increase at all; at others, especially if no steps have been taken to check it, the distention is so great that the outline of the synovial sac may be traced distinctly beneath the skin. The delicate structures lining the cavity are torn and bruised, and the vessels continue to bleed until the contraction of their walls and the pressure of the fluid accumulating round them stops the flow. Probably the blood soon coagulates, as it does when extravasated into other tissues of the body; and at a somewhat variable period becomes liquid again. At least, if a joint is tapped or aspirated a few days after a severe sprain, it is found to contain a fluid, which, though it still reddens on exposure to air, differs from blood in color, and in being turbid from floating *débris*. If left to itself, the quantity diminishes, and it undergoes other changes. The coloring matter slowly soaks into the tissues round, so that they remain deeply stained for weeks; the floating fragments become finer and finer, until they, too, disappear; and at length, though the amount remains excessive for a considerable time, it assumes again the character of the natural synovial fluid.

The rent in the capsule may be almost imperceptible, merely a superficial line, extending across part of the cavity, and only marked by an uneven band of discoloration; or it may stretch right across from one side to the other, and open up the cellular spaces round. It is especially liable to give way along the line of its attachment to the bone, and as this is where the blood-vessels are largest and most abundant it accounts in some measure for the amount of the hæmorrhage. At this point there is a considerable thickness of soft loose tissue with little resisting power, and the fibres are more widely spread out and separated from each other than they are elsewhere, so that when a strain falls on them it attacks them, as it were, in detail, and easily overcomes them. It is very unusual not to find some evidence of violence, some staining or reddening at this point, after a joint has been sprained.

Hæmorrhage in the Synovial Wall.—The extravasation is, however, not limited to the interior. If the cavity is opened there are patches of it, apparently adherent to the inner wall, but really situated within its substance, covered over by so delicate a film of tissue that they can be plainly seen through it. Most of these disappear at length. They merely leave a thickened and discolored spot, which, as a rule, is well out of the way, and causes no inconvenience. If, however, they occur in a part of the joint where the lining membrane is loose and thrown into folds when at rest, or where there are many fringes and outgrowths well protected from pressure, as round the neck of a bone, they sometimes lead to great annoyance. A hard, unyielding patch is formed in the smooth and supple wall; its flexibility is lost, and it cannot yield itself kindly to the movements of the joint, but drags on the other parts, and acts as a continual source of irritation and pain.

These changes are not confined to sprains; they occur after other injuries with almost equal frequency, and may always be suspected when, long after an accident, some particular or unusual spot remains tender, or one special movement is limited in extent. They are particularly common in the deeper layers. The soft cellular pads that are developed in and round joints, for the purpose of filling up spaces that vary in size with every movement, are generally deeply stained with blood. If this is absorbed again no ill result follows; but it often happens, from the soft and yielding nature of the tissues at these places, and from the way in which they are protected from pressure, that when a joint is kept at rest in one position this is never thoroughly carried out. The blood remains for a long time without changing, and then slowly becomes organized into a dense, unyielding mass. The pad which was intended to give way before the faintest pressure, and accommodate itself to every change of position, becomes hard and dense, and moulded to one form. So long as the limb remains at rest it is fairly comfortable; as soon as it is moved there is pain, because the pressure is no longer distributed evenly over the whole surface.

Bursæ.—Changes of a similar character are very prone to occur where there are spaces near joints, in which blood or other fluids collect after injuries. They may be bursæ or mere interspaces in the cellular tissue, without any well-marked limit; some are definite in shape and position, existing, at least in adults, in all alike; but many are accessory, developed here and there by the accidental friction of one structure on another, and, therefore, differing in size and shape and position in each individual. Whatever they are, they act as receptacles for the blood which is extravasated into the tissues after sprains and other injuries. It collects in them and distends them, lining their interior with a layer of false membrane, which slowly becomes organized and makes their wall dense and hard. Then they become tender and painful; their surfaces are roughened and irregular; they obstruct instead of assisting the movement of one part on another; and often, by inducing the patient to keep the part at rest, they lead to other changes, the importance of which is altogether out of proportion to the severity of the original injury.

Some of these bursal swellings are very perplexing. In many cases where there is a large cavity overlying a joint it is very difficult to tell whether the fluid is really in the synovial sac of the joint or outside it. It may reproduce the shape exactly, and by its tension prevent the muscles from contracting as much as if the capsule itself were distended.

In others, especially when the swelling is recent, and there is something firm behind, such as a bone or the wall of the chest, the imitation of a fracture is surprisingly good. There is a sensation of crackling, when the part is handled, closely similar to that produced by rubbing together the two ends of a broken bone. It is really due to the dense fluid being pressed through the meshwork of connective-tissue interspaces which make up the interior of most of these; and it may nearly always be distinguished (independently of the absence of the other signs of fracture) by the difficulty there is in eliciting it a second time, until either the fluid is driven back again or some more allowed to accumulate. There is no difficulty in feeling it once, but it is very hard to demonstrate it to another person.

When extravasated blood collects in the space between the shoulder-blade and the back the sensation is most deceptive.

I have known many instances in which a mistake has been made through relying on this, fractures of various parts of bone having been diagnosed, in spite of the absence of displacement and of tenderness on pressure. This occurs, too, in other situations. In one case in particular the patient, who had on a previous occasion suffered from several fractures in different parts of his body, was so firmly convinced that his collar-bone was broken that nothing could make him believe the contrary. He had sustained, certainly, a severe fall on his shoulder, and was badly bruised; there was great difficulty in raising his arm from the side, and the whole region was much swollen; but there was no displacement of any kind, and the tenderness was general, not limited to any one definite spot, as it would have been in the case of a fracture. On manipulation, however, the most distinct crepitus would be obtained, especially when the arm was lifted up, and the shoulder grasped firmly from before backward by the finger and thumb; and it was so definite in character, and so perceptible to the patient, that he was absolutely sure that it came from his collar-bone. Not until ten days had passed, when he could use his limb freely in all directions without pain, would he admit that the fracture (if it was one) had united very much more rapidly than those he had sustained on a previous occasion.

In this case there was undoubtedly a large extravasation of blood into the bursa which covers in the shoulder joint. Very likely its walls were torn, or crushed and bruised with some of the muscular fibres lying over it. Raising the arm pressed its sides together, so that the fluid was driven from one part to another, and squeezed among the irregular meshes that lined the interior. Later on this was absorbed; the staining made its appearance in the usual situation, under the borders of the deltoid, and as there was no permanent thickening or rigidity of the walls, movement was completely regained. All cases are not so fortunate. It is not uncommon to find the interior of this bursa lined in all directions with shaggy villous projections, hanging down in the cavity, the result of repeated injury or inflammation, and the cause of constant inconvenience and even pain.

The Ligaments.—The extent to which the ligaments are injured varies quite as much. It is no uncommon thing to find the strongest in the body, such as the internal lateral ligament of the knee or ankle, completely torn across, and the joint as full of blood as it can be; or, on the other hand, there may be scarcely a bruise or tear. They are really part of the capsule uniting together the ends of the bones. The structure is the same in all essential particulars, and they are practically continuous; only the arrangement is different; in the one, the fibres are scanty and weak, with many and large inter-fibrillar spaces; in the other, they are arranged in closely woven bundles, parallel to each other, and so tense as scarcely to admit of any elongation by sudden violence. They may tear, especially small portions of them here and there, so that the whole thickness is not broken across at any one spot; but they will not stretch. It is true that under certain conditions they do become elongated, but this only happens when the strain is continuous, and lasts for some considerable time. A slight degree of inflammation sets in then, and under its influence the fibrils soften until they yield

Sometimes ligaments give way in the middle, but it is more common for them to separate from the bone, or to wrench from it a small thin scale corresponding to their attachment. This is due in part to the arrangement of their fibres. In the centre they are woven closely together, and form a rounded bundle of great strength; at the ends they spread out like a fan, so as to secure a wider attachment. By this their mutual support is lost, and the course of the fibres is altered, so that the direction of the strain no longer coincides equally well with that of all the strands. Owing to this they give way much more easily. A ligament that can resist successfully a straight pull of great violence yields at once to a twisting force of much less severity, because this falls on the fibres unequally, one by one, and tears them from their attachment.

Intra-articular Ligaments.—Some of the structures that lie in the interior of joints occasionally suffer in a peculiar manner. Inter-osseous ligaments, formed of very short numerous bands of fibres connecting immediately two roughened bony surfaces, rarely give way, owing to their great strength, the bone yielding instead; but the discs of fibro-cartilage, which are interposed in places between the bones for the purpose of deepening the sockets, and modifying the effect of shocks, are very liable to suffer. Sometimes they are bruised or crushed; more often they are torn from their attachments and displaced, so that they interfere with the working of the joint. Or, without being actually separated, they may be so stretched that the result is much the same. This is best known in the knee; in other joints in which discs of this kind are found they are so much smaller and so firmly fixed that they rarely give rise to any inconvenience. In the knee they are very large; their normal range of movement is very considerable, and they are so loosely held that displacement is not only easy, but, when it has once been produced (owing to the feebleness with which repair takes place), is always liable to occur again.

The Knee.—I am not aware that there has ever been an opportunity for examining the interior of a knee joint shortly after this had happened for the first time, and before the disc has been replaced. Indeed, from the nature of the accident, it is scarcely likely there could be such, except under the strangest coincidence; but on several occasions the joint has been opened and the displacement verified after it has occurred repeatedly. And often the patient is aware of a projection from the side of the knee, caused by the displaced disc. There is, therefore, no question as to the nature of the accident, but, as has been already mentioned, it is by no means certain that this explanation serves for all the various forms of internal derangement that have been described, even when full allowance is made for the different directions in which it may take place.

The Fingers.—The finger joints, again, are the seat of a peculiar kind of injury somewhat similar to this. They all of them belong to the class of hinge-joints, admitting free movement so far as flexion is concerned, but exceedingly little in any other direction. On the under surface of each there is a plate of fibro-cartilage, similar in structure to the discs in the knee joint, and, like them, helping to deepen the socket in which the head of one bone rotates. In fact, this is the chief bond of union between the bones, but while it is so firmly united to one that it is almost impossible to tear it off with any reasonable degree of force, the fibrous tissue that binds it to the other is soft and flexible, so as not to interfere unduly with the action of the joint. Sometimes it happens in severe wrenches, especially when the finger is forced backward, that this plate of cartilage is torn from its attachment, and slips

up between the bones, so that when the force is past they cannot resume their natural position.

Mitchell Banks has shown how this occurs in the joint between the index finger and the hand, in which it is most common; and I have met with several instances, not only there,
but in other joints also.   It is an exceedingly painful accident,
often causing fainting and sickness.   The deformity is very
conspicuous, especially in the back of the joint, though it is not
so great as that of a true dislocation or when a bone is broken.
The finger is kept slightly bent.   By using the other hand the
patient can move it through a considerable angle, but he cannot either straighten it out or bend it thoroughly into the palm.
No amount of force produces any effect in the displacement; it
is due to the cartilage which has slipped between the ends of
the bones and prevents them moving freely on each other.
Until this is released from its position the deformity must
remain unrelieved.   If left to itself the finger generally recovers a good deal of its power, but the appearance is very
unsightly.

The Muscles.—The muscles round joints rarely escape when
the sprain is severe, though the injury may at first be masked
by other symptoms.   Sometimes it is very serious, but this
depends probably on their condition at the moment of the accident.   If they are firmly contracted and ready to resist, the
joint does not suffer unless they are overcome, and then the
injury is generally too great to be called a sprain.   Most often
they are taken by surprise, and are hurt more by their own
sudden and spasmodic effort at recovery than by anything else.

The weakest part of a muscle varies a good deal according
to its shape.   When they are short and broad, with wide attachments to the bones and firmly bound down by sheets of
fibrous tissue, there does not seem to be any definite rule.
Probably the part that gives way first is determined mainly
by individual peculiarities of structure; but when they are of
considerable length, and attached to distant bones by rounded
tendons, the weakest part is the line of junction between the
muscular fibres and the connective tissue.   It is at this point
that they tear, causing a great extravasation of blood, and
giving rise to a swelling which at first is soft and fluctuating,
but which soon becomes hard and solid, and may persist in that
condition for an almost indefinite period.

This often happens when the fibres are torn across, while the dense unyielding sheath that surrounds them remains intact. The extravasated blood is tightly bound down, and forms a hard resisting nodule, the nature of which can only be ascertained by the rapidity with which it occurs and the way in which it is confined to the limits of the muscle. I have recently had under my care a patient with a nodule of this kind in one of the muscles of the neck just where the tendinous and muscular fibres meet. It made its first appearance quite suddenly during a violent effort, with all the characteristic signs of muscular rupture, more than a year before, but in spite of energetic treatment by massage and other methods it was nearly three months before it finally disappeared.

When a muscle gives way completely, it is usually at the same spot. A curious instance of this is not uncommon among butchers. They occasionly lose the last joint of their thumb by catching it in a hook and tearing it off. The skin and the ligaments give way at the seat of injury, but the tendons of the muscles retain their connection with the bones. The long flexor is pulled out of its sheath for five or six inches, one end remaining attached to the bone, the other bringing away with it torn shreds of the muscular fibres that have given way above the wrist.

Rider's Sprain.—Sometimes the muscles are torn and strained without the joints being hurt at all. Those, for example, that lie on the inner side of the thigh occasionally give way under the semi-voluntary grip by which a rider secures his seat when his horse swerves or bolts round. There is a sudden sharp contraction, a sensation of something giving way, and a feeling that the hold on the saddle is gone. A dull aching pain sets in at once, and grows worse and worse with every attempt to proceed; the part begins to swell as the blood pours out from the torn vessels; a peculiar warm trickling sensation is felt down the inner side of the leg, and, as a rule, the rider is compelled to dismount. When standing, the symptoms are not quite so severe, but the least attempt to bring that group of muscles into play again, or to remount, makes them tenfold worse.

The kind of injury is well known, and is usually recognized at once. It is due to the rupture of the tendon that stands out under the skin on the inner side of the thigh; sometimes it

gives way near the bone, so that the gap can be felt, but more
often the muscular fibres are torn away from it without leaving any distinct interval. The extravasation is often very extensive, and it may be weeks before the last traces of the
staining finally disappear. Every endeavor must be made to
keep it as much as possible within bounds. A stirrup leather
may be tied tightly round the part as a temporary measure;
but a much more effectual method is to buckle a long strap of
webbing round the thigh, outside the breeches. It must be
well padded, on the inner side, over the point where the muscle
is torn, and coming up in front and behind, should cross over
the hip and be carried round the waist. Where the laceration
is complete, some such appliance may be permanently required.

Rider's Bone.—A long slender spine of bone which is occasionally met with in connection with these tendons probably
has its origin in the same kind of injury. It is known as
rider's bone, from its being found chiefly in those who have
spent a large proportion of their lives in the saddle. Sometimes it causes a good deal of inconvenience by the way in
which it interferes with the flexibility of the part; but more
often its existence is hardly known, as it lies buried in the substance of the tendon itself. If the history is inquired into, it is
always said to have developed after one single severe strain;
but comparing it with similar formations in other tendons, it
seems more probable that it is due to the constant bruising to
which the muscles are subjected. Probably it is formed from
the organization of lymph thrown out from time to time.

Rider's Bursa.—Other troubles also are produced in this
way. A soft fluctuating swelling sometimes makes its appearance underneath the tendon, high up in the groin. So
long as the muscle is in action it is tense and firm, as soon as
it is relaxed it becomes soft and flaccid; but it cannot be dispersed, or even reduced in size, by pressure. In one case under
my care, considerable improvement was effected by rest and
blistering, but I am afraid it was not permanent. The patient
was a man who had been accustomed to a great deal of rough
riding, and it seemed to cause him considerable annoyance.
The thing of which he complained most was a sensation of
weakness, similar, apparently, to that which is so often experienced in the hand when there is a ganglion on the back of
the wrist; but it was doubtful if there was any actual loss of

power. The swelling had made its appearance slowly, and was still increasing when he came to see me, so that it evidently was not due to any extravasation. Most probably it resulted from the effusion poured out after repeated strains; and, as he could not give up his occupation, it is certain to increase, until it ends either in inflammation and suppuration or else in the formation of a bursa.

Lawn Tennis Leg.—Lawn tennis leg is another instance. This was a well-known form of accident long before lawn tennis was ever played; but it has become so much more common, as the game has grown popular, that perhaps the name is not inappropriate. It is most frequently met with in men, especially in those who, as youth passes by, are beginning to increase in weight, and whose muscles are somewhat out of training; but not improbably there are other causes too. It is decidedly rare, for instance, among the laboring classes; I am not aware myself of having seen any example among the out-patients at hospitals; and, whether it is worth anything or not, it is certain that in a very large proportion of the cases some evidence of gout may be found, not necessarily of any very acute attack, but merely of those indefinite forerunners which are often quite as distinctive. Generally speaking, it occurs during some sudden and violent effort, a sudden spring forward to take a ball, for example; but the merest slip is enough. Indeed, in some cases it is so difficult to obtain a definite history of such an accident that I am rather sceptical as to its really being required. I have known at least one in which it occurred while the patient was walking along a level road, on which there was not even a projecting stone.

The symptoms are exceedingly characteristic. All of a sudden there is a sharp stab of pain in the calf of the leg; the patient stops instantaneously, lifts his foot from the ground, and nearly always looks round to see if some one has not struck him a violent blow with a stick or a stone. Rest his weight on the leg he cannot; the pain, it is true, does not continue with the same intensity, but the recollection is such that nothing will induce him to try. When the part is examined, there is generally nothing to be seen; but there is an exceedingly tender spot in the substance of the calf, and sometimes a slight depression can be felt. Later on, marks of bruising make their appearance, yellow at first, but gradually becoming darker as the coloring matter approaches the surface, and, generally speaking, most plain toward the lower part of the leg, even when the painful spot is nearer to the knee. This, however, is liable to be modified considerably if the part is well bandaged. In one or two cases I have noted a slight degree of puffy swelling behind the ankle, and it is said that occasionally the foot is deflected somewhat from the straight line; but this I have never seen myself, and I should feel inclined to assign it, when it is present, to secondary changes taking place in the smaller joints of the foot, consequent on the very unequal and unfair degree of strain thrown on them.

The usually received explanation of this very striking accident is that it is the result of the rupture of an exceedingly small muscle, known as the plantaris, situated in the substance of the calf of the leg. The muscle itself is in many respects most peculiar; it is very deeply placed, lying under the largest muscle of the calf, is itself exceedingly short and weak, being rarely three inches long, and is provided with a prodigiously long tendon, which either joins the tendo Achillis at the back of the heel, or else is attached to the bone in close proximity to it. Whether rupture of such a structure can take place or not is almost impossible to prove; the fact is commonly asserted, and it is usually admitted as an explanation of the symptoms, but I am not aware of any instance in which it has been actually shown. It is quite certain that the same effect may be produced by other causes.

This explanation, for example, does not answer when the same accident occurs twice in the same leg at different places. A striking instance of this recently came under my notice, the interval between the two occurrences being only a few weeks. On the first occasion the middle of the calf of the leg was the part involved; on the second it was at least four inches lower down, and nearer to the ankle. Nor was this to be explained as the rupture of muscular adhesions that had developed during the period of convalescence; for not only had there been nothing to occasion them in this locality, but recovery was practically perfect, so that the patient could walk without inconvenience, and without any apparent limping. The second accident was precisely of the same nature as the first; there was the same sharp stab of pain, with tenderness, and a slight amount of swelling, and the same feeling that it was impossible to place the foot upon the ground; but clearly it could not be due to the tendon. This, if it had united at all, could not have been sufficiently firm to withstand a strain that compelled it to give way at another part. The scar could not have been so strong as the original structure.

W. Hood (Lancet, 1884) considers that it is the result of the rupture of some portion of the muscular or tendinous structure of the calf, without specifying it more particularly; and no doubt this is correct in many instances, especially when a depression can be felt by the finger where the fibres have given way. Rupture of the plantaris, which is comparatively a deeply-seated muscle, could never cause this. I would venture to suggest, however, that, in those cases at least in which the amount of blood extravasated is considerable, the cause is connected with the condition of some of the deep intermuscular veins. In many instances they are unusually large; they become varicose, nearly to as great an extent as the superficial ones, and there is no doubt that sometimes they give way, or become blocked by the development of coagula in their interior. This naturally causes very severe pain, owing to the way in which the nerve-fibres are stretched or compressed; and unless absorption is completed very soon, is sure to leave behind a considerable degree of stiffness. The degree of pain that is caused by the rupture of a small vein, especially when the extravasated blood is bound down by surrounding textures, is something surprising so long as it lasts.

The method of treatment to be adopted in these cases is admirably described by the same writer. He recommends that as soon as possible after the accident the patient should be placed in the recumbent position, with the injured leg raised above the level of his head, and should be kept in this position for five minutes. This is very important for two reasons. In the first place, the leg is emptied at once of all superfluous blood, so that the swelling soon goes down. When a limb is raised in this fashion the artery contracts; much less blood flows to it, and the veins are so rapidly emptied that if a superficial one has given way this alone is sufficient to stop the bleeding. The calf, which is enlarged and hard, returns to its normal size, and the patient at once obtains relief from the distressing feeling of tension. But besides this, if the elevation of the limb is neglected, the plaster next to be described is

loosened by the subsidence of the swelling, and requires to be
replaced in a few hours. He then advises that while the leg
is still raised strips of adhesive plaster, each an inch and a
half in width and of length adapted to the size of the limb,
should be applied from two inches above the ankle joint to
above the thickest part of the calf, somewhat as strapping is
applied in the treatment of chronic ulcers of the leg. As soon
as it is applied the patient should be directed to walk about
the room, and to place the heel firmly, or at least fully, on the
ground at each step. For the first dozen steps he will probably hesitate, and will retain more or less of the limp with
which he entered; but after a short time, finding that his pain
is diminished or possibly removed, he will gain confidence, and
will walk with a pride in his own performance which is very
interesting to witness. This description is exceedingly accurate:—" Until this point is reached he should not be suffered
to depart; for, if he does not walk properly before he leaves
the surgeon, he will hesitate still more when alone, and will
be likely to return to the ungainly progression which he ex-
hibited at the commencement of the interview. Success in
walking, in the first instance, will depend largely upon the
temperament of the injured person. A resolute man, who believes in his doctor, will walk at once, while a more timid
patient will require coaxing and urging. The chief trouble
will be with the sceptical man, who has his own ' views ' about
the injury, and who will express them in such questions as,
' Well, but do you not think there is a risk of inflaming my
leg ? ' 'Shall I not make the internal wound larger ? ' and so
forth. With reasonable care neither to jerk the leg nor to
twist the ankle on uneven ground, the patient, as soon as the
plaster is applied, may walk about as usual. By the third
day the plaster will be somewhat loose, and the patient will
say that he is not quite so comfortable as before, and is less
inclined to trust his leg. The strapping should be reapplied,
and he will at once feel more secure and better able to walk.
Four days may elapse before the next strapping, which may
be left untouched for a week, but the application should be
continued at intervals until the patient is quite convinced of his
ability to do without it. On the first occasion very little
pressure is desirable, and mere laying on of the plaster will be
sufficient. Subsequent strappings should be tighter, but never

so tight as to produce a sense of unpleasant constriction, a rule which must be especially borne in mind in applying the first and last piece. The amount of walking should be increased daily, and after the third day the patient should go up and down stairs freely in the usual manner. Until then his ascents and descents may be infantile."

I would only add that in those cases in which I believe the real cause to have been the rupture of some deep-seated varicose vein, I have found the above-mentioned method of treatment as successful as when the muscular fibres were plainly torn. In other parts of the body partial rupture is equally common. Sometimes only the sheath of fibrous tissue that surrounds the muscles gives way; the soft tissue is squeezed out through the rent, and so tightly constricted at the opening that it becomes forced into the shape of a mushroom. I have seen this in the extensor muscle on the front of the thigh. It was attributed at the time to the fact that the patient received a violent blow on the spot from a blunt piece of iron at the moment of vigorous contraction. The symptoms, however, were not well marked, and as recovery was complete without further inconvenience than a small depression in the substance of the muscle, nothing further was seen of it.

Many other tendons occasionally give way during great exertion. Even the stoutest, such as the tendo Achillis, may be torn across, though it is more common for the bone or the muscle to yield instead. I have in my possession a shoulder joint in which the long tendon of the biceps has been ruptured about an inch and a half from its attachment to the bone, so that the end projects into the cavity of the joint. The other part has formed for itself a secondary attachment on the floor of the groove in which it normally lies. Similar changes have been described from time to time in connection with many others.

Dislocation of Tendons and Muscles.—When the injury falls short of actual rupture it may still be very severe, and lead to a great deal of after trouble. Tendons, for example, where they cross a joint or run over a projecting process of bone, lie in grooves, which are lined with a delicate sheath similar to that in joints, and this rarely escapes. In slight cases it is merely bruised where the tendon presses against it, but it may be filled with extravasated blood, or be torn open

down the whole of its length, while the tendon escapes and
lies displaced among the adjacent tissues.

  In the Back.—Both muscles and tendons may be dislocated
in this way. Callender and others have shown how this happens where long and slender slips lie embedded among shorter
and stronger ones, as in the back and some parts of the limbs.
The muscles are closely packed together, surrounded, and at
the same time separated from each other, by fibrous tissue,
which is dense and firm toward their ends, soft and yielding
at their centre. In all ordinary movements, carried out in
an orderly fashion, with a definite object in view, the action
spreads, as it were, from one muscle to the next. Very few
are carried out by the contraction of a single one. Nearly
all involve not only those immediately necessary, but those
also by their side, which are more or less parallel in their
course. The shape and consistence alter together, so that
their mutual relations remain unchanged. When the contraction is sudden and spasmodic, it sometimes happens that one
of these slips from its bed between the rest, tearing its fibrous
sheath, and becomes displaced or dislocated. Probably this
is due to the irregular and disorderly fashion of the contraction. There is a sudden pain, quite local, but made worse by
any movement that would call that muscle into play, sometimes so severe that such movements cannot be executed at all.
The surface of the skin is slightly raised if it is superficial, and
nearly always there is considerable local tenderness.

  These symptoms are, it is true, very nearly the same as
those of partial rupture, which is a great deal more common;
but there is no question that dislocation does sometimes happen, as complete and almost instantaneous recovery takes
place as soon as it is reduced. In some instances the patients
have actually felt the muscle slip back into its place again;
and in a few it has been known to slip in and out again and
again, owing to incautious movement at a too early period.

  The Sartorius.—Large muscles, too, are occasionally displaced. A remarkable case has been recorded in which the
sartorius was detached from its position on the inner side of
the knee by an accident of this kind. Just before its attachment to the bones of the leg, this muscle gives off from its
border a tough fibrous expansion to the capsule of the joint.
This was torn across, and the muscle itself displaced. The

accident befell a man who was squatting on the floor of a
wagon in the position assumed by tailors. A companion tripped over him and fell across his knees; something was felt to
give way near the ham, and on examination the above mischief
was made out. In another instance under my own care, after
a somewhat similar accident, there was much tenderness, and
a soft ill-defined swelling over the inner side of the knee for a
considerable time; and all the movements that require the
assistance of this muscle were very painful, as if some of its
fibres had been torn across.

Peronæi Tendons.—The tendons of the peronæi muscles,
again, are not unfrequently displaced from their position behind the outer ankle. The sheath that confines them in their
groove is torn down its whole length, and they slip forward
on to the bone. In the two examples that have come under
my immediate notice, neither of the patients was sufficiently
trained in accurate observation to give a reasonable account
of the way in which the accident occurred. It is not hard,
however, to conjecture the direction in which the foot must
have been twisted for such displacement to be produced. One
of them had sprained the same joint already several times before, and although the tendon had never been completely displaced, it is by no means improbable that the constant repetition of the injury had caused the sheath to stretch until it
became too weak to resist. It is possible, too, that the groove
in the bone had become partly filled up by the lymph thrown
out. In neither was there the least difficulty in reduction; but
while this was successful and permanent in the case of the
one, in the other the least movement caused them to slip over
the bony margin again, confirming my suspicion that the mischief was not due to one accident only. Bandaging, strapping with pads in all positions, fixed apparatus of many kinds,
complete rest, with the foot kept at a right angle for weeks
together, all were of no service. Gradually the inconvenience
became so much less that the patient would not submit to any
further treatment. At first, each time they slipped forward
there was the peculiar sickening pain common to all overstretched fibrous textures; but soon this, too, ceased to be felt,
and the patient having had no arch to his foot for some long
time before, the comparative loss of these muscles was not so
serious to him as it otherwise would have been.

On the Hand, etc.—Other tendons do not so often suffer in this way. Paget has described displacement of some of the extensor ones on the back of the wrist; but though a slight degree of slipping and yielding at this point is very common, complete dislocation rarely happens, probably because the direction in which they run deviates so little from the straight line. In bad cases of knock-knee, the knee-cap lying in the tendon of the great extensor often slips to the outer side of the joint when the limb is straightened; and the same thing sometimes occurs during flexion, from defective development of the lower limb, associated with a peculiar kind of deformity; but neither of these can be fairly regarded as dislocation of a tendon due to injury

Biceps.—Whether the long tendon of the biceps can be displaced from the groove in which it lies seems still not quite certain. I have seen one case in which this peculiar injury was diagnosed, and although verification was not possible, I think there can be no doubt not only that the tendon did actually slip out of its bed, but that by twisting the arm round, which the patient could do by means of his other hand, it could be made to slip in and out again at pleasure. No snap could be heard, it is true, nor was there any distinct difference along the front of the arm when the two sides were compared together; but the inability to raise the arm from the side at one moment, and the comparatively free range of action after reduction had been effected, left little doubt that it was a genuine example. Passive motion was fairly good, as it was in the case described by Hamilton, only somewhat painful. There was no undue prominence on the front of the shoulder, possibly because of the recent date of the accident. The case, it is admitted, is incomplete, and as the patient was under my observation only a short time, I cannot give any account of the subsequent progress. It does not agree in all respects with those recorded; but as Hamilton has shown by actual dissection the possibility of such an accident, and as I cannot understand what other displacement in the region of the shoulder could have produced so peculiar a train of symptoms, sometimes well marked and definite, and then all of a sudden disappearing for a time, I think it must be allowed. In old cases of rheumatic gout it is not at all uncommon to find the groove filled up, and the tendon flattened out over some adjacent part of the head of the bone, but there was no evidence of disease in the present instance.

Ruptured Veins.—The presence of varicose veins is often a serious matter when the ankle joint is sprained, particularly in the case of a person who is advanced in life; and in this respect minute vessels, which give rise merely to a mottled bluish appearance of the skin, are, perhaps, more to be apprehended than when one or two of the larger trunks only are involved. The actual amount of blood lost may not be so great, but the tissues do not seem so well nourished, and absorption is much more slow. It must not be forgotten either that the deep intermuscular veins are often as much dilated as the more superficial ones, and that when they give way a very large quantity of blood may be effused into the deeper strata of a limb before making its appearance on the surface. The inconvenience that results from this is very serious, and convalescence is much protracted; for until the whole of the blood thus effused is absorbed the muscles do not recover their freedom of action, or the subcutaneous tissues their normal supple feel. Rigidity and œdema, worse when any exertion is made, may persist for months solely owing to this.

Injury to Bones.—This even does not exhaust the list of structures that may be injured. The bones themselves are frequently bruised, especially when, either from delicacy of constitution or other causes, such as disease, their substance is soft and vascular with an undue amount of fat in their composition. It is true these injuries are not often demonstrated, though I have sometimes found dark stains, due to hæmorrhage, deep in their substance; but inflammation is sufficiently common to make it unreasonable to doubt that they too meet with their share of damage. Diseases of the spine, hip, and other joints in children may be due, in great measure, to some constitutional taint, though it is open to question whether the influence of this is not overrated; but it is quite certain that the immediate starting-point in nine cases out of ten is some chance sprain, often so slight as scarcely to have been noticed at the time.

CHAPTER V.

INFLAMMATION AND THE PROCESS OF REPAIR.

THE changes that take place in the tissues after the immediate effects of the injury have disappeared cannot be allowed to pass without some degree of notice. It is true that there is little that is special or peculiar about them; they are in nearly all respects identical with those that follow fractures or other injuries; but, for some reason or other, it is the popular impression, one that is shared, too, by not a few medical men, that these accidents are almost invariably followed by acute inflammation. Imperfect recovery is, I admit, exceedingly common; it is the frequency of it which makes sprains so serious; but, rightly or wrongly, inflammation is nearly always regarded as the cause. If it is the case, it is only reasonable that it should be allowed a certain amount of influence on the kind of treatment adopted.

At first sight, I am bound to confess, much apparently may be said in favor of this opinion. There is nearly always present in these cases a cavity of some kind or other, whether it is a joint, sac, bursa, or tendon sheath; and this is certain to be distended under considerable pressure by blood or lymph, which, unless active measures are taken, is very slowly removed by absorption. The quantity that may collect in a few minutes is enormous; I have on many occasions seen the wrist double the circumference of its fellow within half an hour of an accident. Naturally the degree of tension is very considerable; the sensory nerves are stretched or compressed; the part begins to throb; the skin becomes hot and red; and, to all appearance, there is the commencement of an attack of acute inflammation.

Now, there is no question that if this is allowed to continue unchecked it is very likely to be followed by this result; but if due and proper precautions are taken against it there need not be the least fear. When inflammation breaks out, it is either the consequence of neglect, maltreatment, or some peculiarity of constitution, such as gout or struma, so marked that the least accident is sufficient to precipitate an attack. The changes that take place in the tissues after sprains are merely those necessary for the repair of the damage; it is only when they are encouraged beyond measure by other causes that inflammation is likely to break out.

Hyperæmia and Softening.—As soon as the bleeding is checked the vessels all through the injured area dilate, and their walls become relaxed and softened. The volume of blood circulating through the part is immensely increased; a much larger amount of liquid plasma pours out through the walls into the tissues round, mixing with the blood that has already been extravasated. All the interstices are filled with it, and become distended more and more, until the joint swells up and the skin becomes tense and shining from the way in which it is stretched. The different tissues are affected, of course, in different degrees; the capsule itself, owing to its delicate construction, very soon becomes thickened and softened; the loose tissue round it is affected even more quickly; the ligaments, from the way in which their fibres lie close set against each other, resist much longer; but they, too, at length, if the process continues unchecked, undergo a similar change, so that the softening and distention become general.

Effusion and Distention.—The fluid pours at once into any natural spaces, such as tendon sheaths or bursæ, that may be present. These and the synovial sacs of joints are the first to become distended, so that for some time the shape of the swelling follows distantly the natural contour of the part. Later, when the connective tissue round becomes softened and the swelling more general, this is lost, and the outline is rounded and uniform. At this stage the skin may be whiter than natural, though the temperature when the hand is laid upon it is higher than that of the corresponding point of the opposite limb; the superficial parts are so tensely stretched that the blood-vessels are emptied by the pressure, but the sensation of warmth is still transmitted from below.

Very little of this, of course, is to be seen post-mortem. No hyperæmia can be found then, no matter how great it was during life. It disappears with the vitality of the part, and its extent and degree can only be conjectured from the few signs it leaves behind. Minute extravasations may be found here and there, especially among the softer parts; and the fluid in the cavities may be stained with blood in different de-grees, or, it may be, turbid from shreds, and flakes of fibrin or mucus floating in it; but apart from the actual lacerations, nothing further can be seen in the earliest stages.

At a later period the changes are better marked. The smooth glistening polish on the inner lining of the joint is gone; in its place there is a dull and lustreless surface, stained and discolored by the blood, and coated over with a deposit similar to that which makes the fluid in the interior turbid. In recent cases this may be washed off; after a time it appears to be incorporated with the wall itself. The two cannot be separated, and if a small portion is removed and examined under water, a number of little gelatinous processes float up from the surface, so that it looks something like a piece of coarse velvet. This is particularly marked over the softer parts of the capsule, where the synovial membrane is thrown into folds, or where masses of delicate and vascular connective tissue project into the interior for the pupose of filling up the irregularities between the bones. On the other hand, where the ligaments directly bound the cavity, merely covered by a layer of cells, with no soft intervening stratum, hardly any such change is to be seen. So it is with the cartilage that covers the bones; it scarcely shows a trace; even the blood stains cannot penetrate beneath the surface.

Organization.—The softer and looser the tissue the greater the effect. Round the edge of the joints, so to speak, outside the line of pressure, where the fibrous capsule is attached to the bones, and where the synovial membrane lies folded on itself, and, as age advances, becomes covered over with fringes and villous processes, the bruising and softening are most conspicuous. It is not the surface, or the lining membrane only, that shows the change; the whole thickness of the cap-sule is affected, and where it is thin and delicate, or where, owing to the shape of the bones, there are hollow spaces round on which pressure never falls, the tissues outside suffer too. In more than one example I have seen this extend long dis-tances by the side of the bones; and it is, I believe, in great measure owing to this that many sprains, apparently trivial at the outset, are followed by such impairment of mobility. Unless measures are taken to prevent it, the whole of the fibrous structures at this part, the folds of the synovial membrane, the capsule, and the loose tissue outside it, appear to be lost in a soft, gelatinous mass of lymph, in which a few fibres here and there can still be found. If the joint is allowed to remain unmoved this fills up the entire hollow between the bones. Then, after the effect of the injury has passed off, when the hyperæmic stage is becoming less marked and repair is carried on more actively, it becomes organized, and converted into dense, unyielding, fibrous tissue, which ties the bones together, and to a great extent cripples the joint. It is not the fault of the synovial membrane alone, or the capsule, or the soft and loose connective tissue on the outside; they all play their part, though the share each of them takes may show a certain degree of difference in different cases.

In Joints.—In the shoulder, for example, stiffness of this description is of common occurrence, and may lead to serious inconvenience. At the lower and inner part of the joint the capsule is very thin, and has round it a large amount of loose fibrous tissue, so soft and delicate that it is thrown into folds when the arm is hanging by the side. No pressure falls on it so long as the limb is in the natural position; as it is raised from the side the folds are gradually straightened out, until they are put upon the stretch by the pressure of the head of the bone. Now, when the joint is sprained or hurt, this part of the capsule, owing to its softness and vascularity, is exceedingly likely to be injured; and unless active measures are taken to prevent it, the whole of it is very easily converted, first into a mass of soft, vascular lymph, and then into dense and unyielding fibrous tissue. There is nothing to prevent it. There is no pressure to close the vessels and limit the amount of lymph thrown out, or to help on the process of absorption; the folds are never opened out or separated from each other; if the joint is in the least degree painful it is kept at perfect rest, owing to the presence of others close by ready to undertake its work, and all the time without the patient being aware of it. When he is directed to raise his arm sideways from the body, he imagines he is using his shoulder joint, while, as a matter of fact, the whole of the action is being carried out by others; and this goes on until, by degrees, organization com-

mences, and the part quietly becomes stiff and rigid. The surfaces of the folds become adherent to each other, and incorporated with the tissue round; and instead of a soft and flexible capsule, there is a mass of shortened, rigid, and unyielding
fibrous tissue, matting everything together, and not only by
its strength preventing proper movement of the bones, but,
by the pain it causes when any attempt is made, preventing
any vigor being thrown into it.

Between Muscles.—Similar changes take place in the
planes of the soft, cellular tissues that surround muscles, lying
between them and other structures. The blood, escaping into
these from the torn vessels, makes its way along the line of
least resistance until it reaches some part where there is no
pressure or movement. Here it remains, passive and unchanged, for a considerable period; but at length it slowly becomes organized, and by gluing together the different strata,
gives rise to the stiffness and loss of power that are so common after severe muscular strains.

In Bursæ.—The effect produced by large bursæ has been
already mentioned in speaking of joints. Many of them are
merely open spaces in the connective tissue, lined by a single
layer of cells, and, in ordinary circumstances, contain merely
sufficient fluid to enable one surface to glide freely and smoothly
on another. In reality they are formed, as required, out of
the intercellular and interfibrillar spaces that exist everywhere
in connective tissue. After sprains they act as receptacles
for blood and lymph, and often become immensely distended.
If the fluid is quickly absorbed again there is no ill result; the
walls contract, and the cavity resumes its former size and
shape; but if there is any delay when at length absorption
does take place, the softened and relaxed walls are thrown
into folds, so that the sides grow together and become incorporated with each other. Instead of there being a thin-walled
sac, assisting every movement by diminishing friction, there
is a rigid mass of tissue, stiffened, irregularly thickened, and
adhering to everything round it, the seat of constant pain and
tenderness. When this change is established, restoration is
much delayed. The progress at first is often rapid, the later
stages are sure to lag behind; and the longer the thickening
and infiltration of the tissues have lasted, the greater difficulty
there is in getting rid of them.

Inflammation.—These changes are not due to inflammation. Pilcher, in describing the consequences of sprains affecting the wrist joint, has shown the difference between them
with admirable clearness. It is perfectly true that the parts
are swollen from the extravasation of blood, and the effusion
of lymph; that the skin is sometimes reddened, and the temperature raised, owing to the increased amount of blood circulating in the vessels of the injured area; and that there is
tenderness and pain, partly because the nerves are torn across,
partly because the sensitiveness of the skin is heightened; but
this, though it may end in it, does not make up inflammation.

The increase in the flow of blood is the natural outcome of
the injury. A certain amount of repair is always being carried
on, in correspondence with the ordinary wear and tear of
everyday life. At times, from accidents or other causes, this
work undergoes an immense increase; then, in accordance with
the physiological laws which control all parts of the body, a
much larger amount of blood flows through the part, and a
greater quantity of reparative lymph is poured into it.

So long as the skin remains unbroken, it is altogether unusual for injured parts to become inflamed. Except under
such circumstances as blood-poisoning (when any injury leads
to abscess), or where from some accidental cause, such as the
rupture of a large artery, a high degree of tension is set up in
the tissues, inflammation following a subcutaneous injury is
the exception, not the rule. Fractured bones, when the skin
is unbroken, hardly ever excite inflammation; contusions and
bruises may more often, because it is more common in them to
meet with tension from fluid that is allowed to accumulate;
sprains form no exception. Inflammation may set in from
maltreatment or neglect; from peculiar conditions of the blood
(such as gout or rheumatism) in which inflammation of joints
sometimes occurs without any injury at all; or if a large
amount of blood is allowed to accumulate, just as it sometimes
does after a bruise; but under ordinary conditions it is not a
necessary consequence, and may nearly always be prevented.

This is of material importance in the question of treatment.
As regards the time at which this should be commenced, most
people are agreed; and the methods adopted for the earliest
stage have (most of them) something to be said on their be-
half; but when the second stage is reached, as Pilcher, Hood,

and many others have pointed out, the mistaken notion of inflammation being a necessary consequence, has given rise to
a plan which is not only directly opposed to all that is rational,
but which, as might be expected of anything of which such a
statement can be made, is to be regarded as the immediate
cause of many of the troubles of later times. Small blood-
vessels are always torn across when such accidents happen;
sometimes the number is considerable; a certain amount of
extravasation necessarily follows; this must be absorbed, and
the injured tissues repaired or replaced, before the part can
be said to have recovered, but it is always effected by perfectly
natural means. The amount of blood that circulates through
the part, and the quantity of lymph that is poured into the
tissues, are increased in proportion to the work that has to be
done. The softening of the intercellular substance is to facili-
tate this. It is only when the process passes beyond what is
needed for the purpose, and becomes continuous and progressive, that it deserves the name of inflammation.

It does not do, however, on this account to run to the other
extreme, and declare that inflammation never occurs. If a
large amount of blood escapes from the vessels into the tissues,
or if from using the joint too freely or too soon after it has
been hurt, the hyperæmia is not allowed to subside, it is almost
certain to do so. Anything that causes a high degree of tension is sufficient to induce it; the part begins to throb; the
temperature rises; the swelling increases more and more until
it may declare itself at any moment. It is more likely to
break out in certain constitutions, and in certain joints; but if
any synovial sac, or bursal space, is allowed to become distended, it follows as naturally as it does elsewhere. Only, so
long as the amount of effusion is confined within due limits,
so that the tissues can deal with it with a little assistance,
without being overtaxed, inflammation is the exception, always
provided there is no constitutional predisposition to bring it
on.

Absorption.—These are the changes that take place in one
direction. Side by side with them, commencing more slowly,
it is true, but steadily progressing until it gains upon, and
finally overtakes them, is the process of absorption. The
sooner it begins, and the greater the activity with which it is
carried on, the better the prospect of speedy recovery. When

it is incomplete, the consequences are always serious. As already mentioned, inflammation may set in and end in grave disease; the synovial cavity of the joint may continue distended with fluid until the capsule loses its elasticity and cannot contract again; the ligaments may be stretched and softened; there may be hard, unyielding masses of old blood clot lying among the tissues, and causing pain by pressing upon the nerves; or bands of lymph, converted into fibrous tissue, may pass from one bone to the other across the joint, making it stiff and rigid, and preventing free movement. Sometimes (after a sprained ankle, for instance) the soft tissues behind the bony prominences remain swollen and puffy for years, getting better from time to time, and then, again, especially of an evening or after any exertion, swelling up more than ever. At others, the nutrition of the part does not recover, and it remains cold and stiff, with a look of utter helplessness about it. Whenever, in short, recovery after a sprain is incomplete, and no actual displacement or other gross lesion can be found to account for it, the real fault is that absorption has never been thoroughly carried out, and that the circulation is not restored. The perfect recovery after these injuries is, however, of so much importance, and is so intimately bound up with the question of treatment, that it must be dealt with by itself.

The track of the extravasated blood, as it is absorbed, is easily made out. The red blood corpuscles break down, and are destroyed; their coloring matter dissolves in the fluid, and soaks into the tissues along the easiest routes, marking its path by the staining of the skin. The distance this spreads, and the length of time it lasts, may give some idea of the slowness with which absorption is carried on, even when the area is extensive. It is no uncommon thing for the bruising of a sprained ankle to reach the knee; and it may be many weeks before the last trace has vanished. Even then it disappears from the connective tissue interspaces outside the joint more rapidly than it does from the synovial sac within, or the bursæ and tendon sheaths round. In the one case it is widely diffused among the fibres, lying actually in the little interstitial spaces, out of which the absorbent vessels spring; in the other it occupies a cavity, only part of the wall of which possesses any absorbing power, and that not in a very high degree. Sometimes, owing to this, a few days after a sprain, the joint appears larger in proportion to the parts round than it did shortly after the injury.

Gradually the semi-fluid material between the cells and fibres diminishes in amount, and becomes firmer in consistence; the surplus lymph, not needed for the repair of the tissues, is carried off, taking with it the remaining *débris* of the red blood corpuscles; and the nutritive plasma circulates again in normal amount, and at its normal rate, through the tissues.

Effects of Pressure.—It is worth noting how immensely these changes are assisted by the judicious use of compression. The extravasated blood betrays its presence everywhere by the stains upon the skin. In nearly every case it follows defi- nite directions, being guided along certain strata either by the arrangement of the stronger sheets of fibrous tissue which surround and separate groups of muscles, or else by pressure applied from the outside. Where the bones lie immediately under the surface, so that the skin and subcutaneous tissues are firmly compressed when a bandage is applied, the color remains white and unstained. In the hollows between the bones, or behind eminences, which protect the soft parts, the tissues are swollen and puffed out, and may be jet black for a time. So it is with the effusion of lymph at a later period; only owing to there being here no alteration of color, the signs are not so conspicuous. The swelling always disappears first from those parts on which the pressure falls; it persists long- est in just those places where it effects most mischief, in the little irregular hollows that lie between the bones, especially,. as has been mentioned already, in the case of the shoulder, on the side where the tissues are softest and most yielding.

As the tissues shrink to their former size, the lining mem- brane of the joint cavity slowly resumes its natural appear- ance. Granulations cease to form on the inner surface; the latest formed cells, instead of dropping off into the fluid, be- come firmer and flatter, and are held together better by the cementing substance, so that they reproduce the glistening surface of the synovial lining. The fluid becomes more clear again, and its normal color and consistence return, though the quantity may continue excessive for a very considerable time.

Permanent Changes.—The fringes, and the tissues at their base, retain their altered character the longest. Often, indeed, they never quite regain their former size or texture. They

become firm and hard, and more opaque from the organization of lymph in their substance. Sometimes the larger ones
become vascular, a loop of blood-vessels growing down into
them from the base; and then they are practically permanent.
If a joint has been sprained more than once, their presence can
nearly always be detected in certain favorite localities, as, for
example, on either side of the knee-cap. Owing to the synovial
membrane being so superficial here they can be felt quite distinctly, even when they are still small, rolling between the
finger and the bone. So long as they remain small they
scarcely give rise to a sensation of inconvenience, but when
they reach any size they act to all intents and purposes as so
many fixed foreign bodies. Owing to their position, well out
of the way of the bones, they do not often get caught between
them, or they would prove a grave source of danger; but even
though they escape this, they keep up a continuous if slight
amount of irritation; the hyperæmia and effusion never quite
disappear; the capsule and the ligaments become involved
more and more, and the strength and security of the joint at
length are seriously impaired.

Length of Time.—Where ligaments have been torn, whether
they are completely separated in two, or, what is more usual,
have merely sustained a number of small lacerations in their
substance, it is, of course, a matter of some considerable time
before perfect repair can be effected. So it is when muscles or
tendons are torn, or if the sheath in which they lie is widely
rent; and above all, if, before the parts are firmly united another undue strain falls on them. When this occurs, not only
is the whole of the original mischief reproduced, but the degree is, generally speaking, more severe; for, owing to the
vascularity and softness of the part at the time, the hæmorrhage and laceration are nearly always more extensive than
they were at first.

It is impossible to lay down any precise rule as to the length
of time required for the repair of these more serious hurts.
Each case must be judged on its own merits. The amount of
injury, not merely that sustained at the moment, but the subsequent damage often inflicted in ill-advised attempts at treatment; the kind of tissue that has suffered most; the extent of
the extravasation; the particular kind of joint, whether in the
upper or the lower limb; the age, and above all, the constitu-

tion of the patient; the care he will take of himself; all these
things have to be considered with many others before an esti-
mate can be given.   All that can be said is that a severe sprain,
tearing a strong ligament, or wrenching it from the bone, takes
quite as long before union is perfect as a fracture through the
bone near it.   The patient may be able, probably will be able,
to make limited use of the limb much earlier, especially if he
is careful to avoid any movement calculated to throw a strain
on the injured part (which, of course, in the case of a fracture
is rarely possible); but recovery takes at least as long, and
perfect convalescence, with perfect movement, often much
longer.

CHAPTER VI.

IMPERFECT RECOVERY.

ONE of the most annoying things in connection with sprains is the frequency with which they improve up to a certain point and then come to an abrupt standstill. It is not merely that convalescence is protracted, it is delayed so long that it becomes a question if the joint is ever to recover. For the first few days, perhaps, everything progresses as well as it possibly can. The patient is wise enough to recognize the situation, and to reconcile himself to the necessary confinement, though this, as only those who have suffered themselves know, is very often far from being an easy matter. The dread of inflammation passes off, the swelling begins to diminish, the color of the skin changes from black and purple to green and yellow, the tender points can be touched again, and a certain range of movement is permitted once more, though in a tentative and cautious manner. With moderate good fortune this continues, until at the end of two or three weeks the injury is repaired, and the joint as sound and as trustworthy as it was before. Very often, however, it happens, as time goes on, that the improvement becomes more and more slow, until, perhaps, it comes to an end altogether, and the joint is left stiff, painful, it may be, and almost useless. The tissues seem to have been repaired, but freedom of movement does not return.

The extent to which this suffers differs very considerably. As has been mentioned already, the joint may be merely a little weak and unsteady, not quite to be relied on, perhaps, when called upon for any special effort; or it may be so stiff and rigid as to give rise to the suspicion that the bones are grown together, and the cavity completely obliterated. It may be perfectly free from all uneasiness in ordinary circumstances, or it may be the seat of constant aching, with frequent sharp twinges of rheumatic pain. In many cases it may be moved without inconvenience up to a certain point, but the

least attempt to carry it beyond this is stopped at once by
pain, and a sense of resistance. Yet, in spite of this, the skin
may be quite cool, and the tissues of the joint, to all appearance, perfectly sound. Sometimes, in cases such as these, it is
possible to find a definite reason; a tendon may be displaced
and have been overlooked, or one of the internal portions
thrown out of gear; secondary changes, such as wasting or
spasmodic rigidity, may have made their appearance in the
muscles; or the capsule may be so relaxed that it is unable to
maintain the necessary degree of pressure on its contents; but
such as these, for this reason, must be dealt with by themselves. Those to which I wish to refer at present are altogether different; no definite lesion is to be found in them; they
do not seem to have been severely injured; there is no evidence
that the amount of laceration was extensive; yet they remain
so stiff and painful as to be almost useless, without any apparent cause.

The severity of the sprain has nothing to do with it. It is
quite as common after slight injuries as after severe ones.
Indeed, it very rarely follows complete dislocations, in which
the laceration is most extensive of all. It may even come on
without injury if the joint has been inflamed; no matter how
slight the attack, it sometimes leaves behind it a degree of
stiffness that lasts for years, long after all trace of the exciting cause has passed, and without there being any gross
change to explain it.

General Appearance.—There are certain features about
these joints by which they may usually be recognized. If it
is a superficial one, like the knee, the skin is reddened, but not
with the bright flush of inflammation, or the ruddy glow of
use; it is dusky and bluish, and if the finger is pressed upon it
so as to drive the color out it is very slow in returning. Often
it is cold to the touch; the patient may declare that it feels
warmer than the rest of the limb, and even complain of a constant burning pain, but as tested with the hand, or, better still,
with a surface thermometer, it is decidedly cooler. Sometimes
the skin is smooth and gloosy, sometimes wrinkled, but it does
not fall into the natural folds of the part, or glide evenly over
the bony prominences beneath. It seems too tight, as if it
were shrunken, and it cannot be pinched up, or made to glide
from side to side Frequently one or two spots are exquisitely

tender, not merely when firmly pressed upon, but even if a finger touches the

The tissues round are wasted; the shape of the bones stands out too distinctly; the hollows are not filled in by muscles or by fat as they are in normal health. Even in joints so well covered as the hip and shoulder something of this can generally be made out by the eye, though measurements may fail. Occasionally, however, this is concealed by the swelling of the subcutaneous tissue round, especially in the case of the ankle joint, if the leg has been allowed to hang down for any time before it is examined.

Impairment of Mobility.—The most prominent feature, however, in connection with these joints is the interference with their movement. The limb in most may be bent more easily than it can be straightened; but it is seldom that it can be moved to its full extent in either direction. It is stopped abruptly as soon as a particular angle is reached; the check is so sudden and so firm that the bones seem locked together, and any attempt to force it further only causes intense pain shooting through the joint, often most severe where the skin is so tender to the touch. Generally, though there is a sense of discomfort and apprehension the joint can be moved up to this point without much distress, but occasionally even this is not possible. The pain is so severe, and the dread so great, that before the part is touched the muscles contract and hold it rigid, almost in spite of the patients' will. It is literally beyond their power to allow the movement to take place; the pain is to them so intense that their will is overcome and control over their actions lost

Muscular Rigidity.—In these cases it is impossible to form an opinion without anæsthetics. When the muscles are relaxed so that their action is eliminated from the question altogether, and there is no longer any fear of causing pain, the part may be examined thoroughly, and it is easy to ascertain whether the check is entirely the result of muscular rigidity or whether there is some other obstacle in addition. Such cases are not uncommon. Brodhurst mentions one in which the joint was so stiff and motionless as to give rise to the suspicion that the bones had actually grown together; when the patient was under an anæsthetic, movement was almost as free as it is naturally.

It is true that a good deal of information may be gained, especially in children, by diverting the patient's attention from the part, and carefully manipulating it at the same time. When this can be done, it is often discovered that the actual range of movement is a great deal wider than it appeared to be; but, in the first place, this is not always possible; and then, though the information is undoubtedly of very great service, it is never quite enough. It shows beyond question that the rigidity is due in some degree to muscular contraction; but it entirely fails to show how much. It is only possible to make certain of this when the muscles are in some way completely relaxed, so that they no longer enter into the question.

Creaking.—Creaking or grating, as the surfaces move on each other, is always present in these joints. It may be but the faintest sensation of friction, only to be perceived by pressing the hand firmly on the part, as if two smooth silken surfaces were being rubbed together; or the noise produced as the fluid is squeezed from one side of the joint to the other may be distinctly audible to those around. This, of course, depends on the condition of the lining membrane of the cavity, whether it has merely lost the polish from its surface or is covered over with folds and fringes, which project from all round the margin into the interior.

Bands and Adhesions.—It is a matter of popular belief that there is in these joints a band of some kind, passing across the cavity from one side to the other, independently of the lining membrane. When at rest this is quite loose; as the limb moves it suddenly becomes tense, and stops it abruptly, causing very severe pain by the way in which it is stretched. It is possible, of course, that a structure of this kind is developed sometimes; but I have never found such a one myself in a joint, nor am I aware of any case in which such a phenomenon has been recorded. Its presence would undoubtedly furnish a very simple explanation of symptoms that are often obscure; but it possesses the objection of being almost too simple. It explains all the facts at once, in such a plain and straightforward manner, that in the absence of all corroborative proof, one cannot but feel a certain degree of scepticism and reluctance in accepting it.

At the same time it cannot be denied that the evidence on which this opinion is based is very striking, and is sadly in want of an explanation. A joint has been sprained some long time before, and for years has remained painful, and, comparatively speaking, useless; it has been rested, and bandaged, and blistered over and over again without the least benefit; any attempt to move it is stopped at once by the pain; every time it is tried it becomes swollen, hot, and tender; and apparently drifts down into a worse condition than it was before. All of a sudden, something gives way, perhaps with an audible snap; there is a moment's intense pain; but movement is regained, and recovery is perfect from that instant, without after trouble or ill consquence of any kind.

A good many cases such as this have been recorded from time to time, among others by medical men, from their own personal experience. Sometimes they have been cured by a designed plan of manipulation, sometimes by an accidental fall. There is, however, a certain amount of suspicion that they are not quite so common as is generally believed, for it is in the nature of people to spread abroad as widely as they can everything that savors of the marvellous. I have myself met with very few that could be called in any way typical, though, of course, instances of joint disease, in which great improvement has resulted from vigorous passive motion, are common enough. One instance was very characteristic. The patient was a strong, healthy man on active service, who had been invalided home owing to the condition of his knee. (I may remark that a very large proportion of the more striking cases occur in connection with this joint.) He had sprained it severely some months before in a fall from his horse, and as it was considerable time before anything could be done for him the swelling became enormous. Then it was kept absolutely quiet in a straight position for three weeks. Cold was applied, but not compression. At the end of that time the joint was exceedingly stiff and painful, but still he managed to get about upon it, and it improved gradually, up to a certain point. It could be straightened out fairly well, but could only be bent through about twenty degrees; as soon as this angle was reached it came to a dead stop, and any attempt to carry it further only caused the most intense pain and made the swelling worse. At the time that I saw him he was so disabled that he was only able to go upstairs with difficulty. The joint was very slightly swollen; so far as could be detected nothing was out of place. All that could be found was a very tender spot on the inner side of the knee-cap, where the pain was always most intense. Circumstances at the time rendered it unadvisable that an anæsthetic should be administered, and a few days after he was completely cured by an accident. Coming downstairs he tripped suddenly, throwing involuntarily the whole of his weight on the affected limb, felt something snap, and fainted away from the pain. When he recovered the joint was a little tender over the old spot, but it could be moved as freely as the other. There was no increase in the amount of the swelling, and the pain was gone, nor did it return. (Strange cures of this description are not limited to sprains, as the following extract shows:—"Persons given to meditation must often have found ample material for speculation in endeavoring to imagine what train of thought could have prompted the introduction of certain surgical procedures, or led to the first trial of this or that therapeutical agent in the treatment of a particular disease. What, for example, could have stimulated the first idea of curing sciatica by stretching the sciatic nerve; certainly the task of finding a train of thought which should conduct to that conclusion would be a severe one. Many such methods have doubtless been suggested by a real or fancied analogy between them and certain natural accidental occurrences, and in this sort of observation charlatans in all ages have shown themselves singularly apt. We may quote a couple of instances of recent occurrence, where the cure was effected under circumstances which must have suggested to bone-shakers their violent and unscientific, but occasionally successful manipulations. In one case the person had been almost bedridden for many weeks from sciatica; still suffering acutely from the attack, but a trifle less in pain, he hobbled forth to get the benefit of a little fresh air; at a crossing he was roughly pushed by a passing vehicle, and after a desperate but unavailing effort to preserve his equilibrium he fell on the road in the midst of a fairly dense traffic. It was only when he had regained the sidewalk that he began to feel astonishment at the, in him, remarkable agility shown in jumping up and running to a place of safety. The sciatica had quite disappeared, and had not returned four years later. In case number two a strain had been followed by severe pain on movement over the outer condyle of the right elbow, which

lasted for several months, almost incapacitating the sufferer
from pursuing his occupation as a hairdresser. There was no
obvious lesion, but no treatment was attended with any benefit. One night, on leaving work, he had to find his way along
a dark passage, in which the cellar door had inadvertently
been left open. Against this he struck himself violently on
the painful spot, giving rise to such pain that he nearly fainted.
Within a day or two, however, as the effects of the bruise disappeared, the other pain was now noticed to be absent. The
facts are rather curious, although it must be confessed it is
not easy to see how to formulate any practical rules of treatment as a deduction therefrom.")

It certainly seems possible that in this case a band was developed in connection with the joint during the long period of
repose, but I am not prepared to assert that it was in the interior of the sac. The tissues were very much swollen for a
long time after the accident; the joint was never moved; a
great deal of effusion was thrown out; the soft folds that exist
round the knee-cap were immensely thickened, so that it is
possible they gradually formed a connection along the interior
of the capsule with those of the opposite side; as organization
proceeded the union gradually increased in strength, until it
was firm enough to check the movement of the joint; straining on it caused severe pain by the way it dragged upon the
softer tissues; the sudden violent jerk tore it in two, and restored free movement. But it must be admitted that this does
not rest on any direct or certain evidence.

Changes in the Tissues.—Opportunities for examining the
interior of these joints must, from the very nature of things,
be quite exceptional; and the difficulty of explaining the symptoms is not diminished by the fact that when one does occur
the result is not always unequivocal. In a large proportion
there is nothing to be found post-mortem; the structures appear as sound and as healthy as could be wished; and even
where there is something definitely wrong, it is often so slight
that it is impossible to believe symptoms of such intensity could
be due to it alone. Clearly, the conditions upon which they
depend must, in the majority of cases, be such that they come
to an end, and disappear with the life of the part. Nor is it
difficult to imagine of what sort and kind they must be.
Changes in the circulation or nutrition of the tissues, for ex-

ample, often leave no trace behind, and yet may cause the
most serious interference with the way in which the work is
carried out.   It is quite enough if the part is imperfectly supplied with blood so that the muscles are overloaded with waste
products, and the nerves enfeebled and unable to play their
part with sufficient energy.   There need be no actual change
apparent to our present methods of investigation; the tissues
may be merely stiffened from disuse and badly nourished, unable to move freely, or accommodate themselves to each other;
there is no need of more, it is quite sufficient, without having
to invoke the aid of conspicuous alterations in structure.

The Interior of the Joint.—Sometimes there is an excess
of fluid in the interior; more often, especially if the joint has
been kept at rest for long, the quantity is diminished, and it is
nearly always thin and serous in character, a little turbid, and
not so oily as it should be.   The cartilages are never much
affected, the part they play is too passive, only in old and long-
standing cases they lose the glistening polish from their surface, and are a little thinned.   The capsule, with the loose tissue round, as a rule, shows more; instead of being soft and
flexible, so that it falls into folds as the joint moves in one
direction, and opens out again as it moves in the other, it is
stiff and unyielding.   In other cases it is irregularly thickened,
with its inner surface marked by folds and ridges, in which
are little elevations of the lining membrane; or at the point
where it is attached to the bone, and the fibres diverge somewhat from each other, there is an accumulation of lymph holding them together, and as it becomes organized making one
part drag unfairly and unevenly on the rest; or, again, there
is an old extravasation of blood, the remains of some larger
quantity, of which part has never been reabsorbed.

Old Extravasations in the Wall.—In one case, at least,
I think I could attribute the whole of the symptoms to a cause
of this kind.   The patient was a man of more than middle age,
who came to me complaining of an exceedingly painful and
tender spot over the inner side of the knee joint, about half an
inch from the margin of the knee-cap.   There was a history
of his having struck the joint against a sharp piece of furni-
ture on this particular spot some weeks before.   The skin itself
was freely movable, but appeared slightly raised and puffy;
there was no dislocation at the time that I saw him, and it

was doubtful if there had been any—at least, the patient had not noticed it. The pain on touching it was intense; steady pressure could hardly be borne at first, but seemed to relieve it afterward; walking, particularly going upstairs, and setting the extensor muscle of the leg in action, were both very painful. With the joint itself there seemed to be nothing wrong; there was no appreciable excess of fluid, and the tender spot was so fixed, that, almost certainly, it had nothing to do with the formation of any fringes or foreign bodies in the interior. The suggestion was that either some of the fibres of the muscle inserted into the capsule had given way, or that there had been a small hæmorrhage into the substance of the capsule itself. I had the opportunity of examining the joint at a later period, and was able to verify the diagnosis; so far as I could ascertain the muscular fibres were intact; in the substance of the synovial membrane, corresponding to the painful spot, there was a small hard mass projecting further into the cavity than it did on the exterior, probably because there was least resistance in this direction. It seemed to be the residue of an old extravasation; the blood had been effused between the fibres of the capsule; some of it had been absorbed; the rest, owing to the protection it received from the side of the knee-cap, escaping all pressure, had become organized and formed a small hard nodule. Probably this happens in many cases without material consequence; most likely in this particular one it implicated in some way or other a nerve filament, and, like the little peculiar tumors known as painful subcutaneous tubercles, when it was touched it dragged or pressed on the nerve and gave rise to stabs of acute pain.

Dry Synovitis.—Barwell has described under the name of dry synovitis, another condition which may exist in some of these cases, and help, in a measure, to account for the symptoms. There is, according to him, a deposit of fibrinous material on the inner surface of certain parts of the lining membrane, probably derived from the fluid which collects in the joint when it is inflamed. During life these spots are so painful that the patient will hardly allow them to be touched, and can scarcely be persuaded to move the limb. Sometimes the pain is paroxysmal, and often periodic in character, and it is always severe to a degree which bears no comparison with that of ordinary synovitis.

Neuralgia.—Occasionally the pain and loss of power are caused by a kind of neuralgia, which attacks joints and seriously interferes with their freedom of action, without leaving behind any visible evidence of its existence. These may be recognized by the peculiar periodic character of the pain, and by the way in which it is limited to certain spots, which correspond fairly well to the places where the nerves penetrate the fibrous capsule. The skin immediately over them is exquisitely tender to the touch, and sometimes puffy, or slightly swollen; and movement is limited, because, as the joint bends, the capsule is exposed to different degrees of tension, and in certain positions the affected nerve is pressed upon or stretched. The check, however, in these is rarely so abrupt as it is in the others. In one case under my care it appeared to alternate with supraorbital neuralgia, the pain sometimes occurring in one locality, sometimes in the other, but scarcely ever being present in both at the same time. The patient, who was thoroughly overworked, was readily cured by rest and change of scene.

Tissue Starvation.—In a large number, however, this explanation fails as well. There is no evidence of neuralgia; there is no gross lesion to be detected anywhere; no increased effusion, thickening, or adhesion; the tissues simply are wasted; the muscles have lost their power, and the joint is so stiff and painful that it is almost useless. The real reason is the prolonged want of use. The tissues are starved and badly nourished. During life they are surrounded and bathed in a nutritive fluid, which pours out through the walls of the vessels and permeates them in all directions. It spreads everywhere in the interstices, giving up to the structures with which it comes in contact the material they require for their growth and action, and taking away whatever is worn out. The surplus is drained off by a special system of vessels, the absorbents, so that it may never remain stagnant. The rapidity of its flow is entirely regulated by the activity of the tissues. If they are in constant use, a larger amount of blood comes to them; more of this plasma passes through the walls of the vessels into the spaces round; the supply of nutritive material is greater, and the waste more rapidly carried off. If, on the other hand, the part is kept in a condition of absolute repose, the plasma lies stagnant round and between the tissue elements, so that when they are suddenly called upon for active work they are unfitted and unable. Until the free current of the plasma is thoroughly re-established once more, recovery of power is impossible. When this is effected the parts regain their strength and vigor almost of themselves.

Even a healthy joint that is kept absolutely at rest may be so badly nourished that it becomes stiff and unfitted for work, especially if the demand is urgent or severe. If it has been injured or inflamed, so that there is a larger amount of waste and greater need for repair, and is then kept motionless, this result is almost certain to occur.

It is a common thing to call such joints as these hysterical, merely because there is no evidence of any gross or conspicuous lesion; nothing, for example, is out of place, and no band or adhesion can be detected. But it is more than doubtful how far this is correct. When a joint becomes stiff, and the muscles wasted because they have been disused and are not properly nourished, it ceases to be purely and simply hysterical. It is true this may have been the starting-point, because of this the joint may have been kept at rest or prevented from enjoying its full range and freedom of action; but when changes of this description have once made their appearance there is something above and beyond mere hysteria. There is a local affection which can only be cured by local measures, and which must be cured before the hysterical condition can disappear. So long as it persists the patient is convinced, and quite rightly convinced, that the joint cannot be used freely as it ought to be. It is quite true that it cannot, and until it has regained its freedom of action, and the muscles their strength, it is hopeless trying to convince the patient that it can. Happily in many instances the changes are so slight that the joint recovers if it is only used in a moderate degree; if, for example, under the influence of change of air, or change of interest, the patient's attention can be diverted from it. Often, however, this is not enough, and then measures must be taken, first to give back to the joint its complete range of movement, and then to restore the nutrition of its tissues so that they may regain their power and activity.

CHAPTER VII.

TREATMENT. COLD. HEAT. PRESSURE.

It must be admitted there is something very unsatisfactory in the results obtained by the ordinary methods of treatment. Even when the greatest care is taken, when every precaution is used, tedious convalescence is the rule, rapid and perfect recovery the exception, and often, owing to carelessness or delay, the joint never recovers at all. It is left weak or tender, not so trustworthy as it was; prone to swelling with the least exertion, and sensible to every change of weather, so that there is an end once and for all to the healthy unconsciousness that such a thing as a joint exists.

The reason is not far to seek. In a large proportion of cases the measures adopted are altogether insufficient; in some they are absolutely wrong, when, for example, a joint is kept perfectly quiet until it becomes hopelessly stiff; while in nearly all the time that is of the greatest value, that which immediately follows the accident, is allowed to pass by without anything being done, and completely wasted.

Whatever plan is adopted it is essential to begin at once. Every moment lost makes a serious difference. The injury is not confined to the instant of the accident. The blood keeps pouring out from the wounded vessels and accumulates in the synovial sac and the interstices of the tissues, until if left to itself it causes such an amount of pain and tension that inflammation is bound to follow. If recovery is to be speedy or sound this must be stopped at once, or, at any rate, confined within the narrowest limits. When once it has left the vessels, and become extravasated, it serves no useful purpose, whether it collects in the cavity of a joint or spreads itself through the loose tissues of the limb. It separates the ends of the torn ligaments; it distends the synovial sac until it becomes stretched out of all proportions, and when it is absorbed it leaves the capsule loose and flaccid, so that the joint feels weak and powerless.   If it remains, the consequences are worse still; either it breaks down and forms an abscess, or; as already described, becomes organized into a hard unyielding mass, which interferes with the action of the muscles and compresses the nerves so that free use of the limb is rendered impossible.

The first thing to be done then is to check the bleeding into the tissues, and to spread out over as large an area as possible the fluid that has escaped already.   Then, as reaction sets in, as the part becomes warm and red, and as the quantity of blood circulating through the uninjured vessels begins to increase, steps must be taken to keep this well within bounds. There must be a certain increase; it is essential for repair; the injury entails more work; there is a larger quantity of worn-out material to be removed and replaced, and more blood is required for it.   Only it must be kept strictly within limits, and not allowed to run on until the synovial sac and tendon sheaths become distended or inflammation itself sets in.

If this can be done little further is required.   All that remains is to assist the circulation through the tissues in every way, to maintain the nutrition at its highest level, and by gentle passive motion prevent the limb becoming stiff.   Repair takes place with very different rapidity in different people and in different ages, but ligaments that have given way, or that have sustained many small injuries in their substance, naturally cannot in any circumstances be repaired at once.

Cold.—When the matter is thought out there is something almost ludicrous, if such serious consequences did not follow, in the general way in which, as a matter of routine, a wet bandage is applied to a sprained ankle.   For the moment it is cool and pleasant, and with the folds and turns lying evenly and smoothly on each other, looks exceedingly neat.   The uniform pressure does give relief at first, but in a very few minutes the coolness disappears and the temperature is as high as that of the joint beneath.   In a few more it begins to dry, and as it dries it becomes loose, so that the pressure (which never at any time falls quite in the right part) disappears altogether.   If the bandage is removed and the limb examined it is smooth and round, with the hollows quite filled up.   The bandage, of course, passes over them without pressing upon them, reserving this for the bony prominences which

do not require it. The soft tissues are swollen and œdematous, and the synovial sac and the tendon sheaths distended
with fluid. ' Applying it again in the same fashion does no
good, nor is it of any use keeping the bandage wet. The principle is correct, but the method of application altogether a failure. Neither the cold nor the pressure is applied effectually,
and the result of this method of treatment may be seen in the
fullness and swelling that persist round ankles for years after
they have been sprained.

The fault is not that of the cold. This is one of the most
useful and satisfactory applications known. It may be dry or
moist; it does not matter how it is obtained. The limb may
be surrounded with ice or cold spring water poured over it, or
it may be immersed in the water, or any other method adopted
that suggests itself at the moment. The important point is
that it should be applied at once, and that the limb should not
be allowed to recover its temperature until a more permanent
application is ready. Used in this way, as a first agent, cold
is simply invaluable. It is always at hand, any one can apply
it, and it fulfills every indication. The blood-vessels contract
at once, the skin becomes white, the bleeding is checked, the
sensitiveness to pain is diminished, and the tendency to swelling very much lessened.

If, however, it is used in a hap-hazard sort of way, as it is
under a wet bandage, if the limb is allowed to grow warm from
time to time, the whole of the benefit is lost. Reaction follows
as the effect passes off; the blood-vessels dilate again until their
diameter is much larger than it was before. More blood flows
through the skin and the adjacent parts; a larger quantity
pours out where the vessels are torn; the temperature rises;
the sensitiveness of the skin is increased; it begins to glow,
and the patient becomes conscious that the joint is increasing
in size. In reality more harm is done in this way than if the
the part is left entirely to itself. In some people who are more
than usually susceptible, it is enough to produce results of
exactly the opposite character to those intended, and in the
later stages of sprains, when the joint is cold and powerless,
it is used in this way for this very purpose. The alternate
action of cold and warmth is one of the most effectual measures known for stimulating the circulation through a part,
and if employed soon after the infliction of such an injury as

a sprain, before the ends of the vessels have had time to close, certainly does more harm than good.

As a Temporary Application.—It is equally important that the application should not be continued too long. As an immediate and temporary expedient cold can scarcely be surpassed, but after a time a condition of passive congestion sets in. The nerves and the delicate muscular fibres on which the contraction of the vessels depends become paralyzed; the part becomes red and swollen, in great measure from the blood that lies stagnant in it; the skin is anæmic, shrunken, and rough from the upstanding papillæ; the amount of blood and lymph in the tissues is sufficient, but it is never changed; the vitality of the part is lowered; the nutritive changes on which repair depends are carried on more feebly, and if the process is continued may stop altogether, so that the part either actually perishes or is attacked by a low form of inflammation. Even when the effect falls far short of this, long-continued cold brings about a state of things in the tissues that is by no means favorable to the repair of injury.

Method of Application.—Cold may be applied in a multitude of ways, but as a rule the simpler the method the better. It may be dry or moist. In the former case it acts by conduction only; in the latter by evaporation as well, but it is possible this advantage is more apparent than real. It is much more important that time should not be lost, and that the injured limb, especially if it is the ankle, should not be allowed to hang down, as it nearly always is. In some parts of the body, such as the hip, there is no doubt of the superior comfort of the dry method; in others the position in which the limb must be placed, and the facility with which the cold can be applied, form the best guide.

Cold spring water is nearly always at hand. It may be either poured freely over the injured part, or this may be immersed in it. The former plan is the more efficacious; independently of the fact that fresh quantities of water are continually being brought into contact with the skin and abstracting heat from it, and that a certain amount of evaporation can take place as well, it is probable that the actual impact of the falling water, perhaps by the shock and the influence it has on the nerves in making the vessels contract, perhaps by the force of its fall, is of great assistance. As soon as the joint ceases to swell and the skin is beginning to look dull and livid, the maximum amount of benefit has been produced. It is rarely advisable (at any rate, if pressure can be applied) to carry it any further.

The same effect may be produced by immersion, but unless the water is very cold it is much more slow, probably because the layer next to the skin is soon warmed to the temperature of the body. If ice can be obtained at once in sufficient quantity, the result is as rapid, but there is the disadvantage that it is nearly always necessary to allow the limb to hang down, a position which should always be avoided, as it tends to increase the amount of blood in the part, and sometimes makes it much more painful.

Continuous Application.—A few days after the accident, if by any mischance inflammation does set in, cold may be applied continuously, but then the reason is not the same. In these circumstances it may be kept up for an indefinite length of time. The object is to diminish the amount of blood circulating through the part, and so to lower the temperature and reduce the inflammation. But in sprains, ordinarily speaking, there is not any inflammation to reduce. As Hood and many others have pointed out, there is absolutely no reason why, when a sprain occurs in a healthy person, and is treated with a reasonable amount of care, this complication should set in more often than it does in the case of simple fracture.

The most convenient fashion for its continuous application is by a set of Leiter's coils. They may readily be improvised out of India-rubber tubing (the best is that which has an internal diameter of about one-third of an inch and moderately thin walls), or better still from composition gas-piping, which has the advantage of retaining the shape to which it is bent. They may be applied to any part of the body, coiled round a limb, for example, without the circles being in any way fastened together, or wound in a flat spiral and rested on the part, as in the groin, or pressed into the shape of a low cone and arranged to fit the shoulder. All that is necessary is that there should be two buckets, one containing water of the desired temperature placed on a stool a little higher than the limb, and connected with one end of the coil by means of a piece of tubing; the other, on a lower level, empty, and connected with the other end. As soon as the current is started from one to the other the flow is continuous, and may be regulated with the greatest accuracy. It is not essential that the cold should be confined strictly to the part actually inflamed. If an ice-bag is laid on a limb over the course of one of the main arteries it causes a very sensible diminution in the temperature of the part below by the constriction it induces, and by the proportionate diminution in the amount of blood.

There are other methods as efficacious, but less convenient. One depends on the well-known fact that if a skein of wool is allowed to hang over the edge of a vessel, so that one end dips in the fluid inside and the other hangs over the edge, a continuous stream of drops will come from the dependent half until all the fluid is gone. A drip pot of this kind, or more than one, suspended over a limb and filled with evaporating lotion reduces the temperature quite far enough. Iced water, or a lotion containing chloride of ammonium in solution, answers very well, but if the full effect is desired there is nothing to equal lead lotion mixed with spirit, and containing a few fragments of ice. The effect is greater in proportion to the amount and strength of the spirit. It may be allowed to drip on to the skin directly, or this may be covered with a single thickness of lint, so as to avoid splashing, and to carry off the surplus fluid. If the lint is folded even once, so that there are two layers, evaporation is checked to a considerable extent, and a great deal of the effect lost.

Arnica, which is frequently recommended in the early stages of sprains, is worse than useless. The sole merit that it possesses is due to the spirit that is mixed with it, and it has the very serious defect of exciting in many people (especially when it is not very much diluted) a peculiar form of inflammation of the skin, which is not only very difficult to distinguish from erysipelas, but which is very likely to run on into it. Aconite, too, may be mentioned here as occasionally of service when one or two small spots are exceedingly tender, but care must be taken, especially when it is mixed with chloroform, that it is not applied over too large a surface.

A still more simple way of applying cold is to fill an India-rubber bag (or where this is not handy an ordinary bladder answers all the purpose) with small fragments of ice, or with ice and salt, and to allow it to hang over the joint so as just to be in contact with it. A double fold of lint, or a thin pocket-handkerchief, must be placed underneath, lying on the skin and changed occasionally, as it soon becomes wet from the condensation of moist air on the outside of the bag. This plan is particularly useful when it is desirable to produce an effect on deep-lying structures, or to keep the cold up for a considerable length of time, as it is very effectual, may be graduated exactly, does not want watching, and makes no mess.

Cold is most successful in sprains of large joints when the swelling comes on rapidly. If twelve or more hours pass by before this makes its appearance, pressure applied early answers a great deal better, though even then, if a joint such as the knee or ankle has been bandaged carefully, an ice-bag laid on it makes its influence felt, and helps to relieve the feeling of tension and throbbing. When the brunt of the injury is borne by the muscles it is not nearly so serviceable. In the aged, in the very young, in those subject to local congestions such as chilblains, and in the rheumatic, it must be used with great caution, and the skin, if it is moistened, must be dried with the greatest care; otherwise it may happen that the depression due to the cold insensibly shades off into an attack of inflammation, the very thing it is intended to prevent.

Heat.—Heat may be employed in many cases in which the use of cold does not seem advisable. Its value as an immediate application depends on the fact, which is not so widely known as it might be, that hot water, if the temperature is sufficiently high, is as effectual in stopping bleeding as ice. The skin becomes cold, the vessels in it and in the layer immediately beneath contract, and the circulation in many instances almost stops. In the case of the fingers, where in proportion to their thickness the extent of surface is very great, I have seen complete blanching and numbness produced by dipping the hand into very hot water, and have known it last even in the hot days of summer for many hours, longer than if it had been due to the application of ice.

To produce such an effect as this the temperature of the water must be as hot as can be borne. It cannot, therefore, be kept up for more than a few moments, for fear the skin may be injured; and for the same reason it cannot be employed, as cold is, to diminish the calibre of the vessels in the deeper-lying structures. Its value is greatest when the injured part lies near the surface, particularly in the case of tendons, which, like those on the back of the hand, run a long distance down into the fingers, lying immediately under the skin the whole way. In the ankle and elbow, also, it succeeds fairly well, but the difficulty of application in the case of other joints is so great that it is generally better to rely on cold.

The temperature of the water requires a good deal of judgment, especially as different people, even different parts of the body, vary very much in their degree of tolerance. With children, it is particularly necessary to be careful, as their skin is so delicate. Happily in them joint sprains are not so common as they are in adults. The fingers can stand a higher temperature than the hand, and this, again, a much higher one than the elbow; indeed, the point of the elbow is, so far as heat is concerned, one of the most sensitive parts of the body. The extent of surface immersed has to be considered, too. It must not be forgotten that the sensitiveness to heat increases with the area exposed. It is not a bad plan to place the limb in hot water, and then raise the temperature rapidly by adding more, until it is as high as the patient can stand, taking care to stir it round all the while, so as to distribute the heat evenly through the whole. Two or three minutes ought to be sufficient; often the full effect is gained at the end of the first.

Heat used in this way has a wonderful power of relieving pain. The skin may not be blanched, but its sensitiveness is lowered; manipulation is more easy, and displaced tendons or other structures can be restored to their position without the sickening sense of over-stretched fibrous tissue. It is worth noting, moreover, as another point in its favor, that the effects are more lasting than those of cold, and consequently time is gained for the application of other and more permanent measures, such as massage and bandaging.

Sometimes, after prolonged overwork or severe strains, the bony prominences to which the muscles are attached become sore and tender, or the tendon sheaths seem to be roughened and uneven, so that perfect smoothness of motion is lost; or in certain classes of work, where without the actual exertion being great, rapidity and delicacy of movement are carried to a very high pitch, the nerves become painful, and the muscles liable to sudden and spasmodic contractions. When this occurs the prolonged application of warmth may generally be relied upon to give relief, at any rate for a time. A moderate temperature usually suffices. The object is not to numb the sensibility of the part, but rather to relax the walls of the vessels and relieve the tension, so that blood may circulate more freely through the tissues, and the delicate fibres, in which the nerves end, may no longer be kept upon the stretch. This holds good even when some of the muscular fibres have been torn across or rent from their attachments.

Later, when the joint is beginning to recover and movement is returning, heat is of value both for its own merits and as a preliminary to massage. There is then no limit to the length of time it may be applied. The hand, for example, if it is stiff from the effects of some old sprain, may be kept soaking for hours in water as hot as can be borne with the greatest benefit. The tissues become soft, everything is supple and flexible, the constant aching disappears, and movements which before were out of the question are executed with ease and freedom; only, unfortunately, it rarely happens that the whole of the improvement is retained. So far as stiffened joints, at least, are concerned, it does not seem improbable that the reputation enjoyed by many of the foreign baths is due more to the temperature of the water and the length of time the limbs are allowed to steep in it than to anything else, though it is not denied that in other respects they may be of considerable service.

Besides these there are other methods, less general in their application, which are better described in the treatment of special sprains. Ironing, for example, is often of great use where large masses of muscle in the loins are stiff and painful from overwork or cold, so that the patient cannot move with freedom or even hold himself erect; and hot vapor or mud baths, where the limbs are stiff and crippled from old attacks of inflammation, frequently procure great relief from pain; but remedies of this description must be dealt with by themselves. As a rule, they are used in conjunction with others, and do not depend for their merit on heat alone.

Heat and Cold Alternately.—Later still, when the repair of the tissues is perfect, but full use is not restored, nothing can be more successful than the alternate action of heat and cold. Some weeks, perhaps, have passed since the joint was hurt; all fear of inflammation has been dispelled; there is nothing out of place; no bands or adhesions to hurt the movement; no very tender spot, though the whole may ache, especially after it has been used; but there is no power in it. The joint is colder than its fellow; the skin is livid and wrinkled, fitting closely on to the bones, and often slightly swollen where it stretches over the hollows between them; the position of the parts is natural and good; one bone can be moved upon the other, though, perhaps, not quite to its full extent; but the part looks and feels as if it were only half alive, able to put out half the energy it should. Sometimes, it is true, this is the result of defective energy and will in the great nerve centres, but often the fault lies in the part itself. The tissues round the joint have been at rest so long, have been so long without doing anything for themselves, that they have almost lost the power. The circulation through them has been at its lowest ebb for such a length of time, that when a sudden demand is made upon it it is unable to respond. In these circumstances the shock of alternate heat and cold acts as a most powerful stimulus, especially when used in the form of a douche, projected with some force and suddenness against a part which has been allowed to soak in hot. water. The skin, of course, receives the greatest amount of effect, and sometimes, especially with the needle douche, a great deal more has been done than was desirable; but the whole circulation through the part is quickened; the volume of blood increases; the nutrition of the tissues is carried on more as it is in normal health, and the muscles and nerves begin at once to regain their power. Aided by galvanism and other measures, it is surprising how this method of treatment restores tone to the muscles, and causes the absorption of chronic exudations that perhaps have remained passive and unaltered for years; only, partly from the very ease with which it may be applied, it is not advisable that this line of treatment should be carried out without suitable supervision; or more harm than good may easily be done.

Pressure.—This is not the only plan which illustrates the value of a time-honored practice, when carried out thoroughly, and its worthlessness as usually employed. Bandaging for sprains is almost universal, and well deserves its reputation; only it must be carried out systematically and rationally, with

a proper regard to the structure of the joint, the arrangement
of the parts round it, and the movements it ought to perform;
and this implies anatomical and surgical knowledge of no mean
order.

Heat and cold are only of temporary use; their influence
on the vessels is exerted through the nerves and muscles, and
after a time these, like other vital structures, become tired out,
relax, and give way. Both of them when continued too long
help to produce the very effect they are intended to prevent.
The tissues become congested; the circulation is checked,
though the actual amount of blood in the part may even be
greater than normal; the cavity of the joint is distended; and
the soft tissues round and between the bony prominences are
filled with exudation, which becomes organized, develops into
tough and unyielding fibrous bands, and cripples the movement of the joint in all directions.

As compared with these the action of pressure is entirely
mechanical; the measure may be graduated according to the
needs of each case, and it may be kept up at any required degree for an indefinite period of time. When carefully and
methodically applied, nothing can be more efficient for stopping
bleeding, or for insuring the absorption and dispersal of blood
that has escaped already. It controls the hyperæmia and
checks the dilatation of the vessels, so that the outpouring
of the plasma into the tissues is restrained within proper limits.
It prevents the accumulation of fluid in the synovial cavities;
assists the absorption of plasma from protected spots, so that
it neither runs on to inflammatory exudation on the one hand,
nor becomes organized and leads to stiffening of the joint on
the other; and above all it relieves pain in the most wonderful
way, whether it is the sharp and acute kind that comes on
immediately after an accident, due to the stretching and tearing of the nerves in the ligaments and fibrous structures, or
the dull aching afterward caused by the continued tension on
the capsule. In the majority of instances, if compression is
properly applied, the swelling disappears by the next day, and
the joint may be moved through nearly its whole range without more than a sense of discomfort.

Method.—To bring about this result, however, the compression must be applied with a definite knowledge of what is
desired, and how it is to be obtained. Merely putting a band-

age on a limb that has been sprained is only liable to perpet-
uate the very evil it is intended to prevent.

It may be commenced at once, as soon after the accident
as practicable, or heat or cold, as the case may indicate, may
be applied for a short time first. Probably in most cases
the latter plan is the better; heat or cold requires less skill,
and relief from pain is attained more immediately, while, if
carried out effectually, time is not really lost. Besides, before
a bandage can be applied, it is necessary to make perfectly
certain that there is no displacement of any kind. If there is
anything of the sort it must be made out and rectified before
further steps are taken; it is hopeless trying to cure a sprained
joint if any of the structures belonging to it are out of their
natural position. How far it may be advisable in these circumstances to make use of massage as a preliminary, is a
question that is best dealt with by itself.

The method of application is all important, though the
rules that guide it are sufficiently simple. The joint must be
fixed in the most suitable position, not necessarily the one selected by the patient. For example, in sprains of the ankle the
foot should be at right angles with the leg; when the knee is
injured the joint should be slightly bent, though not nearly to
the degree in which the patient is almost sure to place it, and
the arm should hang by the side when the shoulder is involved.

The pressure must be applied so that it falls only on the
parts that require it, not on the bony prominences, that is to
say, but over the tendon sheaths, and on the masses of soft
and delicate tissue that fill up the interspace between them
and the bones, especially on the inner side of the limb. It
must be smooth, even, and well graduated, commencing from
below, and working upward toward the trunk, and it must
possess a certain amount of elasticity, so that as the swelling
diminishes under its influence the bandage may still keep up
some degree of compression.

For this purpose there is nothing more suitable, and, fortunately, nothing more easily obtained, than ordinary cotton
wool. Pads may be made of this to fit into any depression,
no matter how small, and, if not too firmly compressed, they
keep up an even and equable amount of pressure, even when
absorption underneath has effected a considerable difference
in the size of the limb. Failing this, the next most useful sub-

stance is a firm and fine-textured sponge. This may be made
into pads which admit of the most perfect adjustment as regards size, shape, and thickness, and it is more easy to keep
them in their proper place when the limb is being bandaged.
Many other substances, however, serve on special occasions;
dried moss, for instance, forms a capital substitute, and I have
known even seaweed tried with success. Some of the thicker
and softer kinds of felt make admirable pads, firm and soft,
yet quite elastic, and capable, if several layers are sewn together, of being modeled into any shape. Sometimes this
firmness is of especial service. I have employed them with
great advantage in sprains of the extensor tendons on the
back of the wrist, when the distention has not been very great,
but where there has been a large amount of creaking or grating on movement. It is difficult here to adjust pads of cotton
wool sufficiently accurately, while the felt is easily shaped to
suit the varying thickness of the soft parts. The pressure is
distributed evenly over the whole length; the tendons are kept
at rest; and the firm compression insures the rapid disappear-
ance of the exudation.

Pads of sponge or felt may, moreover, be soaked in lotions,
if it is considered advisable, without altogether destroying
their elasticity. I have not found much occasion to put this
into practice, but once or twice, when the pain over small
joints was very severe, the application of a lotion containing
a solution of morphia afforded great relief. Of course, a certain amount of caution must be used. A thick felt pad, covered
on the outer side with a layer of some waterproof material, is
capable of taking up no inconsiderable quantity, but the area
of the pad is generally small, and the condition of the parts
beneath is not one adapted for rapid absorption. If there is
the least abrasion this caution is particularly required.

It is impossible to be too careful in molding the pads to
the proper shape of the limb. In the case of the ankle, for example, where the joint alone is involved, the swelling shows
itself on the front, lifting up the tendons that run down to the
toes, and behind on either side of the tendo-Achillis, filling up
the natural hollows there, and reaching up the leg higher on
the inner side than the outer. Over the malleoli, of course,
there is none, and, unless the injury has been so severe as to
tear the ligaments, scarcely any is perceptible along their

lower border. This may be complicated by the distention of
some or all of the tendon sheaths that run down on either side;
and if some few hours have been allowed to pass by, there is,
in addition, a great deal of thickening in the loose and delicate
tissue that fills up the interstices between the skin and the
tendons, and the tendons and the bone. The swelling may
reach down far on to the foot, and almost to the knee. All
this must be made out; and the natural contour of the limb
seen, as it were, through the swelling, before the pads can be
shaped and the bandage adjusted.

Sometimes pads of this kind may be made to serve in the
place of splints. In the knee, for example, a bandage, as usually applied, is of very little use; nor is it much better if a
horseshoe-shaped cushion is adjusted around the knee-cap.
But if this is combined with a firm elastic pad of felt in the
popliteal space behind (I have known, when nothing else could
be obtained at the moment, a small folded pocket-handkerchief
answer admirably), the compression is spread over a larger
surface of the joint, better resistance is given for the bandage
in front, and an admirable splint is applied to the knee joint,
keeping it nearly straight, and possessing the great advantage
over an ordinary back splint that it is not so absolutely and
uncomfortably rigid.

Sometimes it is one's misfortune to meet with a case in
which the limb (generally the forearm) seems to have been
sprained, as it were, all round, the swelling and pain are so
universal. For such as these I have used with success what
may be considered a distant imitation of Guérin's treatment
of wounds; that, at least, first gave me the idea. The limb is
to be well padded first, according to the anatomy of the part,
and lightly bandaged; then, commencing from the fingers, between which small cushions are placed, it must be wrapped in
sheet after sheet of cotton wool until it is three or four times
the natural size; finally, it must be bandaged from below upward as firmly as possible. If the cotton wool is sufficiently
thick it is impossible to exert too much pressure. It must be
admitted that the application is exceedingly hot; but it certainly relieves pain; and such is the elastic tension of the wool,
that the limb, when exposed on the next day, is almost its
natural size. The comfort is greatly increased by dusting the
limb over first with violet powder.

Bandages used for sprained joints need not be of any special kind so long as they lie evenly and smoothly on the limb and do not stretch. India-rubber ones, or those made of woven elastic, are strongly recommended by some; but, it seems to me, without adequate reason. They keep the limb very hot; the solid ones, at any rate, retain the perspiration so as to be sometimes unpleasant; and it is very difficult to apply them sufficiently firmly without making them too tight and converting them into a species of torture. While the limb is being bandaged the pads may be secured in position by means of common elastic bands passed round the limb, an excellent method suggested by Dacre Fox.

Starch bandages and other fixed appliances, such as gum and chalk, plaster of Paris, or silicate of potash, can only be recommended under special conditions. They are certain to be left on too long, and that is a fatal objection. Bandages, as a rule, should be changed every day. The limb no doubt feels fairly comfortable so long as it is encased and kept motionless. But every day it is growing more and more stiff, and when it is released the least attempt at movement is attended by pain. This is not due to straining or tearing of the union between the ends of the torn ligaments; no strain falls on it. Ligaments may be tense, but they are not stretched unless movement is carried beyond what is natural, which, under proper management, never should happen. It cannot, therefore, be due to this. In reality its persistence and severity are regulated more by the amount and duration of the swelling than by anything else. Of course if ligaments have been torn from bones, or muscles have been strained or lacerated, the skin over them is tender when it is pressed upon or tightly stretched, but the pain that is ordinarily felt when a sprained joint is first used is scarcely noticeable if exudation is prevented and passive motion begun early enough. Neither of these conditions is likely to be carried out properly if the limb is encased in a fixed bandage.

How long the limb should be bandaged is a question that can hardly be answered until the effects produced in joints by prolonged inaction have been taken into consideration.

CHAPTER VIII.

TREATMENT.—REST.

NOTHING is so difficult in the treatment of sprains as the question of rest— how long the joint should be kept quiet, and when the patient may use it with safety as he likes. It is the first thing asked, and a definite time is usually wanted at once, utterly regardless of the fact that it is impossible to return more than a general answer in the majority of instances. Each case must be judged on its own merits. On the one hand, if the joint remains long unused, there is the possibility, almost the certainty, of its becoming stiff and crippled, so that it is years before it regains its natural freedom, if it ever does; on the other, there is the dread of exciting inflammation, and the risk of reproducing by some momentary slip the whole of the original mischief. Between these it is necessary to hold a middle course; leaning too much to either side inevitably brings after it delayed convalescence in some form or other and much discredit.

There is no doubt that in the majority of cases sprained joints are kept at rest much too long. It is imagined that if anything, it does not matter what, has happened to a joint, it cannot be wrong to rest it, and that no harm can possibly follow from its being kept quiet. The dread of inflammation is allowed to overshadow everything else. It is forgotten that the function of a joint is movement; that this is the reason for its existence, and that if from any cause it is kept absolutely at rest it loses the power of working, just as an eye accustomed to long-continued darkness becomes unable to bear the light. It is forgotten that prolonged rest does produce changes, and very definite ones, too, in the structure of joints, even when they are healthy, and that these are tenfold more likely to occur after injury. And so the part is kept perfectly quiet until it becomes stiff and rigid, and every attempt at movement causes pain.

Effects of Prolonged Rest on Healthy Joints.—Some of the effects stated to result from this cause are of a very striking character. Duverney and Petit have described cases in which they found the synovial sac and the spaces round it enormously distended with a serous effusion; and others in which there were adhesions passing across the interior from one bone to the other, so that the joint was almost crippled. Teissier has given an account of one in which the adhesions were so dense and numerous that the cavity of the joint was entirely obliterated, and the bones so tied together that one could not move in the least upon the other. In others he found the synovial sac distended with blood, the lining membrane thickened, and more vascular than natural, and the inner surface coated over with a recent deposit of fibrinous material, which was rapidly being organized into dense unyielding bands. In many the cartilages were swollen and thickened at the margin, softened in the centre, and even eroded on the surface, while the synovial fringes were almost uniformly converted into tough fibrous bands that limited the fredom of the joint in all directions.

Some doubt, it is true, has been thrown upon his explanation, owing to the fact that in all the cases the limb had been severely hurt; and the suggestion has been offered that these changes are really due to inflammation, which spread from the seat of injury to the affected joint; but it is admitted that there is no evidence that anything of the kind had occurred. According to Teissier, unbroken rest can be the only cause; and in this he is strongly supported by Bonnet of Lyons, who came to the same conclusion after a series of experiments expressly bearing on this point. It is admitted that the position in which the limb is retained is of some importance; that some joints are more liable to be affected in this way than others, those farther from the trunk more frequently than the nearer ones, the fingers, for example, more often than the wrist; and, further, that the changes are most conspicuous in the aged, or in limbs that have been paralyzed; but the main fact itself, according to them, admits of no dispute.

Even supposing the consequences of long inaction are not so extensive as this, they may still be sufficiently serious to lead to grave discomfort and suffering. It is certain that, in old people at any rate, a rest of comparatively short duration is enough to cause great stiffness, especially when the wrist and fingers are concerned. These show the effect more rapidy than other joints, possibly because the movements they execute are so numerous and complicated; even in a few days the power of bending them may be completely lost; they remain rigidly extended, and the least attempt at forcing them, no matter how gently it is done, gives rise to severe pain, and meets with a sense of resistance which is not due to muscular contraction.

It is often said when this occurs that the patients are gouty or rheumatic, and that the stiffness is due to their diathesis; but there is no evidence of it. It comes on without aching or pain, that is not felt until after manipulation; the skin is not hot; there is no swelling or sign of inflammation; the onset is imperceptible; and the patient is unaware of anything being wrong until the hand is released from confinement and some attempt made to move it. There does not seem any other reason possible but the want of use and the prolonged rest in the straight position.

Changes in the Tissues Due to Prolonged Rest.—When the time is short these are not very conspicuous. There is less fluid in the joint, and its quality sometimes appears to be altered; it is not so viscid as it ought to be; but it is rare to find anything more. The tissues themselves do not seem to be affected as they are at a later period, and recovery is generally rapid. Afterwards there are other alterations; the loose and delicate connective tissue that fills up all the irregularities and interspaces becomes affected. In some parts it is compressed until it becomes dense and hard; in others it is filled with fluid, and becomes soft and pulpy. Then, as the bones and muscles move, and the pressure shifts from one point to another, the uneven tension causes pain. Instead of the tissues yielding smoothly and evenly, accommodating themselves to each other so that no unfair pressure falls on any part, some are hard and resistant, having completely lost their flexibility; others are swollen and distended, so that they cannot give way. The effect, if force is used, is much the same as when a ligament or any other band of connective tissue is stretched beyond its natural limit; the part swells up and becomes painful; the temperature rises; and if the attempt is repeated sufficiently often, the changes become more and more marked until they insensibly pass into inflammation.

In some of the older cases the results are even more serious. The capsule shrinks, and becomes rigid; or, owing to the relaxation of the muscles, loses its tone, and is unduly stretched; the secretion of the synovial membrane is completely altered; the softened parts in the tissues, where there has been no pressure, become, as it were, accustomed to the increase in the size of the space in which they lie, and fill it up entirely; those, on the other hand, that have been compressed, waste away, so that when the two surfaces of the joint are moved apart there is nothing to fill up the interval, unless the surrounding tissues are crushed in by outside pressure. The cartilages grow thinner and thinner; the ligaments shorten, and hold the bones in rigid apposition; the muscles degenerate, and, accommodating themselves to the fixed length at which they are kept, either contract and become converted into a kind of fibroid tissue, or waste and stretch. The tendons, too, at length become glued to their sheaths, and refuse to move; the skin loses its elasticity and suppleness; there is a blue congested look about it; it does not move freely or easily over the structures beneath, but seems shrunken on to the bones, as if it were too tight, and all the soft tissue underneath had gone. Even the bones waste, and become so thinned that a comparatively slight degree of violence may cause them to give way.

In the Fingers and Ankle.—This may happen when the joints are perfectly healthy in all other respects. The fingers have been already mentioned. There is scarcely a fracture of the arm or forearm in which a certain amount of stiffness is not left afterwards. It is not that they have been hurt in any way; they have merely been kept confined in a straight position, under pressure, without being allowed to move, and when released they are found to be stiff and rigid. The same thing occurs in the ankle joint when a patient is confined to bed during the course of a prolonged or exhausting illness. The foot is kept constantly pressed down by the weight of the bedclothes into the same straight line as the leg, and at last becomes fixed in that position; the muscles on the back of the leg become rigid and shortened; the ligaments on the front of the joint are elongated and stretched; and when the patient begins to get about he finds that he is unable to place the sole of the foot flat upon the ground, and, not unfrequently, is compeled to undergo a long and tedious course of treatment before the displacement can be rectified.

Not the Result of Injury or Inflammation.—It is quite true that this condition is more common after injuries than anything else; but it must be recollected that they are by far the most frequent cause of confinement in one position. It certainly may occur independently of them, as well as of inflammation; and it cannot be considered a peculiarity of old age, for though it is more often met with in people who have passed middle life, slight degrees of it, sufficiently severe to cause considerable inconvenience, though they yield more readily to treatment, may be found in all periods. ·

Faulty Position.—Malgaigne has offered the suggestion that stiffening of joints from rest alone is due not so much to confinement in one position (for then it would be more common even than it is in cases of fracture), but to the fact that the position is unsuitable, and, therefore, hurtful. In his opinion, unbroken rest, combined with extension in the straight line, is the immediate cause. The natural position of repose, in which the ligaments are relaxed, lies between the extremes of flexion and extension; if a joint is kept for any length of time rigidly straight some of the ligaments are loose, others are in a state of constant tension. The former gradually shorten, and become rigid and unyielding; the latter stretch, and grow weaker and weaker, or even at last become inflamed, owing to the unnatural condition in which they are maintained. In either case, the suppleness and flexibility are lost, and when an attempt is made to move the joint, pain is caused owing to the fact that the tension falls unfairly on them.

It is not unlikely that this is correct in the main, and that if a joint is perfectly healthy there is not much fear of its becoming stiff, unless the limb is kept in such a position that unfair traction is maintained continuously on ligaments which are not suited to resist it. The important fact is that it may occur—indeed, that in some circumstances it will occur—even when a joint is absolutely sound. If it has been sprained, if the ligaments and the capsule are softened by exudation, and by the changes in the circulation that of necessity take place after injuries, continued rest is almost certain to produce it in a very severe form. The length of time need not be great; very few days are sufficient; and the actual alteration in

UNIVERSITY OF
HISTORICAL ... COLLEGE
LOND ...

structure need not be of great extent; a fold of the capsule may be thickened, or some of the synovial fringes matted together, or there may be merely some induration in the soft tissues, or filling up of the bursal spaces on the outside of the joint, a state of things that may be produced in a few days at the most; it is quite enough to prevent the free action of the joint and to give rise to severe pain if the attempt is carried too far.

In the majority of instances joints that continue stiff and crippled for such a length of time after being sprained show nothing more than this, and it does not appear to be much. There is no heat or redness of skin; the swelling is only such as would be accounted for by the extravasation of blood at the time, and the amount of exudation that is needed for repair afterward; there is none of that throbbing, burning pain which can rarely be mistaken; and there is no sign of inflammation. The reason that makes it so serious is, that when once this condition is set up, unless proper steps are taken to prevent it, there is a constant tendency for it to grow worse and worse. The adhesions and contractions that develop during prolonged immobility cause the softer and more delicate structures to be strained and bruised whenever an attempt at movement is made. Probably, if they are forced to give way once for all, the good that is done far exceeds the harm; but this rarely happens. Much more often either the sufferer does not move the joint at all, so that it is kept rigid longer still, or, if he has sufficient fortitude to persevere, makes matters worse by half measures. The shortened structures are merely stretched and strained, the part becomes swollen again, a fresh amount of exudation is thrown out, the adhesions grow thicker and stronger, and the joint is doomed to a further course of rest under the impression that it is inflamed.

Movement and Inflammation.—On the other hand it is urged, even by those who admit that inflammation is not an absolutely necessary consequence, that it is almost certain to be produced if the part is moved too freely or is used too soon. They agree that, unless there are other causes at work, sprains are not more likely to set up an attack of inflammation than simple fracture or any other form of subcutaneous injury; but they insist that it is absolutely necessary to keep the part at rest for fear of its setting in. It seems to me, however, that in laying down a rule of this kind it is advisable to be more precise with regard to the extent and character of the movements executed, and the object with which they are performed. The danger of inflammation does not arise from slowly and carefully moving an injured joint once or twice a day; the liability to its occurrence is not increased in the least by this. An attack may be brought on by some peculiarity of constitution, such as gout or rheumatism, or by some morbid condition of the blood, inherited or accidental; or it may be caused by tension if blood or any other fluid is allowed to collect unchecked in the synovial spaces or the tissues round; but it is scarcely possible to imagine that, once or twice in the course of a day, slowly and firmly straightening out a joint that has been sprained could produce any such result.

It is not intended for a moment that anyone should be allowed to do what he pleases with his limb. There is a popular idea that injuries of this kind can be walked off, that only provided the joint is not allowed to rest for some considerable time no ill result will follow; and there are always to be found people ready to declare that they themselves have done it time after time without hurt of any kind, and that they have recovered more quickly in consequence. Sprains that admit of being cured in this way can clearly be only of the very slightest description; for such as these it may answer well enough, but it would scarcely be advisable to try it where the tissues have been seriously injured, or where the swelling and extravasation are of any extent. It is impossible to imagine that the repair of a ligament that has been torn in two or wrenched from its point of attachment to the bone can be assisted by such a proceeding. It may be of service where the strain has fallen on the muscles only and has not been sufficiently severe to tear any of their fibres, or where the effusion is limited to some of the muscular interspaces outside the joint; in others it is a method of cure which is only too likely to end in disaster.

Passive Movement.—It by no means follows, however, that the extreme opposite course should be adopted and the limb maintained in a state of absolute immobility. It is quite possible to move a sprained joint sufficiently to prevent the occurrence of stiffness or the formation of adhesions without causing the least pain or suspicion of inflammation. The first thing is to check the swelling of the part; if this can be pre-

vented passive movement may be carried out with no more
than a sense of inconvenience. The pain, throbbing, and risk of
inflammation are due to the distention of the joint and tissues
round, and to the continued traction exerted on the nerves. If
this is stopped at the first the joint may be quietly, but firmly,
flexed and extended without causing anything deserving the
name of suffering, and without any fear of reproducing the
original accident.

Movement undertaken with this object must be passive,
not carried out by the patient. Active movements are effected
by the contraction of the muscles, acting in their ordinary
course, and are executed for some purpose, or in opposition to
some resisting power; passive ones, on the other hand, are
carried out by some other force, as when one person bends and
extends the limbs of another who exerts no strength himself;
or when the finger joints of one hand are worked by means of
the other. The bones are moved one on the other; the tendons
play backward and forward in their sheaths; the folds of the
synovial membrane and of the capsule are alternately
straightened out and compressed; the pressure points in the
tissues are shifted as they are in normal action; and, what is
especially important for maintaining their vigor, a certain
amount of traction is put upon the muscles and nerves; but
no work is done. The joints are treated as complicated pieces
of machinery, each part of which is moved by some external
force, in a direction, and with a range, that can be limited with
the greatest nicety. If one of the restraining ligaments is
torn or hurt, no stress need fall on it; if the soft tissues on one
side are bruised, they need not be pressed upon; and if a
muscle has been ruptured, its ends are not more widely separated from each other. Everything can be regulated with the
greatest accuracy.

Time for Movement.—The sooner this is begun the better.
It is very rare for the tissues on both sides of a joint to suffer
to the same extent. Those on one aspect may be torn, those
on the other bruised, from the way in which they are crushed
together when it is twisted; but the latter recover long before
the former, and are capable of carrying out all their ordinary
work at a time when a comparatively slight strain would tear
the others in two again. As a rule, passive movement may
be commenced from the second day with the certainty of pre-

venting adhesions, and without the least fear; it can be regulated much too well to allow any tension to fall on the injured
part.

This answers especially well when the ligaments have suffered most. As a rule, these structures cannot stretch; their
function is solely to prevent movement being excessive or passing some definite limit. So long as the range of action is kept
within its normal bounds no strain falls on them; they are
merely straightened out or unfolded, as it were. When a joint
is sprained the movement is carried beyond this, and the ligaments, unless they are strong enough to resist the momentum,
yield and give way; but even after this has happened, if the
part is prevented from swelling, it may be made to execute all
ordinary movements without fear of hurt, provided it is
handled carefully by one who knows how much may be done.

It need not be said that hap-hazard or careless movements
must be absolutely forbidden. The most accurate diagnosis
is necessary to make certain what structures have suffered
and what have not; and there must be a thorough and exact
acquaintance with the action of the joint, so that the right
kind and right degree of movement may be selected; but provided this is done there is no reason why the joint should not
be worked in this way from the very first. If it is carried out
thoroughly adhesions cannot form.

If a tendon has been dislocated, and the sheath of fibrous
tissue which maintains it in its groove torn open, or if one of
the cartilaginous discs which exist in some joints, such as the
knee, has been displaced, the part may be exercised without
fear of reproducing the dislocation or of delaying the union of
torn fibres. In the ankle, for example, it is not uncommon for
the tendons on the outer side to be displaced forward on to
the bone. They are, ordinarily speaking, held firmly down by
a fibrous sheath thrown over them, and lined with a delicate
synovial membrane; sometimes this is torn, and the tendon
escapes from its bed. When this has once taken place a single
incautious movement on the part of the patient, before the
sheath has had time to repair itself, may tear it open again
and reproduce the dislocation; and if this happens more than
once it is not improbable that repair never will be carried out;
that the sheath will remain loose and yielding, allowing the
tendons to slip backward and forward with the slightest

twist until the use of the corresponding muscles is practically
lost. But if passive motion is employed systematically and
carefully by some other person, who knows what the injury is,
and how best its ill-effects may be avoided, the joint may be
exercised thoroughly, flexed and extended as far as is desirable,
and the nutrition of the muscles permanently maintained without the least fear of this untoward complication.

Even in the most severe sprains, when the staining due to
the extravasated blood reaches, as it often does, nearly up to
the knee-joint, it is advisable to begin on the second, or, at the
very latest, on the third day. All that is necessary is that
the whole of the swelling should have been dispersed by careful bandaging, or by other means. The foot is then to be released from all constraint, the skin and the subcutaneous tissues thoroughly kneaded, and the joint quietly, but firmly,
flexed and extended several times as far as it is ordinarily in
walking. This should be repeated every day until recovery is
perfect, the limb in the meantime being as carefully and
methodically bandaged as it was at first.

At first, no doubt, there is considerable apprehension on
the part of the patient, and probably the muscles are unconsciously kept rigid and resisting; but this is easily overcome
by kneading and steady, gentle pressure. Gradually, as the
fear of being hurt diminishes, the movements become more and
more free until all that is wished can be executed without distress. Pain ought scarcely to be felt. Of course, if a ligament
has been torn off the bone, and direct pressure is exerted on
the spot, it is felt acutely; but these are the places that should
be carefully avoided, especially at first. After a little manipulation the tenderness generally diminishes considerably. If
the swelling has been thoroughly dispersed, so that there is
no tension on any part of the capsule or the tissues round, and
if care is taken not to move the joint, so far as to put undue
strain on a ligament that has been stretched or torn, the
nerves are not dragged upon or compressed, and the movement is practically painless.

The ankle joint, owing to the plan of its construction, is
peculiarly well suited to this method of treatment. Sprains
are nearly always caused by the foot being suddenly twisted
to one side or the other, so that the greatest strain falls on
ligaments, which in all ordinary movements, are only moder-

ately tight. The slightest attempt at bending the foot later-
ally, in the direction of the original twist, causes the most intense pain, and all the muscles round become involuntarily
rigid. All ordinary movements, on the other hand, are allowed
to take place from the first, without the least resistance, after
the natural feeling of apprehension has been overcome.

I have repeatedly seen the most severe cases treated in this
way recover so completely in the course of a few days, that,
unless there was an exceptional amount of walking to be done,
the patient could follow his ordinary occupation without danger
and without pain. Of course, if a ligament is torn across, a
certain amount of time is required before it can unite, and still
more before it can be firm; but the position in which the
structures are placed by this plan is unquestionably the most
favorable for speedy recovery. The ends lie in close apposition to each other; no external force is allowed to separate
them, and, what is much more important, the synovial cavity
of the joint is not allowed to remain distended with fluid, keeping the torn surfaces continually apart. If this is carried out
fairly and consistently from the commencement, it is impossible for the joint to become stiff. Adhesions between contiguous
surfaces are effectually prevented by the passive motion. The
free manipulation renders any rigidity or contraction of the
capsule impossible. Unless there is some other predisposing influence, inflammation is equally out of the question. There is no
tension to excite it, and, if the compression is properly carried
out, there can be no dilatation of the blood-vessels to pave the
way for it; nor need there be any fear that afterward there
will be that peculiar sense of weakness and insecurity which
is so common as a consequence of sprains. In by far the majority of instances this is due to distention of the capsule or
yielding of the ligaments; or, when this does not occur, to the
fact that the muscles, from being so long unused, have become
stiff or rigid, and do not respond as actively or as vigorously
as they ought.

CHAPTER IX.

FORCIBLE MANIPULATION.

FEW modes of treatment have had a more curious history than forcible manipulation as applied to stiff joints. Often, for years together, in the greatest disfavor, owing, it must be admitted, to indiscriminate application, and almost discarded, it has always managed to retain a foothold in some part or other; and every now and then, when its mishaps have been forgotten, has sprung up again into notoriety, under, perhaps, some change of name. Very few minor operations are capable of giving such instantaneous and striking relief. It often happens that, as a result of some simple manipulation, a joint that has been crippled and the seat of pain for weeks and weeks is suddenly and completely released; but, at the same time, it must be remembered that, unless proper care is taken in the selection of cases, very few operations can do more harm, and also that it is not always easy to lay down rules by which the choice is to be guided.

Adhesions must be Divided or Torn.—If a joint is stiff and rigid from shortening in the fibrous tissue round it, there is only one thing to be done, only one plan of treatment that holds out a reasonable prospect of success: the contracted tissue must be either divided or stretched. Nothing else is of any avail. Baths, whether hot, or cold, or douche; galvanism, massage, friction, counter-irritation, blistering, and the numberless other remedies so often employed, are of little or no service. It is true that the circulation and nutrition of the part improve under their use; the muscles recover their tone and firmness; the skin becomes more healthy in appearance, and the general aspect of the joint is altogether different; but if, when the muscles were relaxed, the movements were stiff and constrained, they will continue in this condition, no matter how energetically these methods are carried out. They are necessary as accessories; in fact, they are almost indispensable as a means for educating the muscles and nerves, so that they can exert their power again as soon as freedom of movement has become possible; but of themselves they can do little or nothing toward getting rid of the stiffness when there is the least degree of change in the fibrous tissue.

This has been learnt by dint of experience of the roughest kind. The strange idea that sprains are nearly always followed by inflammation (though it is admitted that it rarely results from any other form of subcutaneous injury), and the dread of causing a fresh outbreak by rough handling, have, to a great extent, deterred those who felt the responsibility from adopting more active measures. At least, this seems to be the most reasonable explanation of the fact that, at the present day, though means for making an accurate diagnosis are so much better than they were, and though it is so easy to avoid the infliction of pain, so little is accomplished by this method, and so many people are content to get about, as best they can, with joints which, at the most, have only partially recovered. Even then it is not easy to understand why there should be such objection. Supposing for an instant that inflammation were a much more common consequence of sprains than it really is, it is very unlikely that an attack would be caused by moving a stiffened joint within its natural limits, especially when every precaution is being taken to prevent its occurrence. The popular treatment is absolute rest; but though this, as already mentioned, is necessary under certain conditions, it must always be remembered that a joint can never become healthy so long as it remains unused.

Division.—Of the two methods I have mentioned, the first, division, is very rarely required in the case of simple sprains. Sometimes, it is true, the muscles on one side of a limb become so hard and rigid from long disuse that they refuse to yield to any reasonable amount of force, and then something of the kind must be done; but this is not common. It may occur in the ankle, when a patient has been for some time confined to bed, with the weight of the clothes resting on the front of the foot, constantly pressing it into the same straight line with the leg. When this happens, the muscles at the back of the calf grow more and more rigid, until, if proper steps are not taken to prevent it, they become permanently contracted. If an

attempt is made to move the joint against them, it feels as if
two bony surfaces were being driven against each other; it
does not yield in the least; the foot is hopelessly fixed, and
there is no alternative but to divide the tendon.

Structures that require division are rarely situated close
to a joint. As a rule, they have little or nothing to do with its
synovial lining, or even with the loose fibrous tissue outside
the capsule. For the most part they are attached to distant
points, and are either thickened portions of the fascia, which
have undergone passive contraction, or tendons of muscles
shortened from disuse. These have to be divided before any
thing further can be done; but though this is not unusual after
a joint has been inflamed, it is rare to find such extensive
changes after mere sprains. In any case it is necessary to
examine the limb thoroughly beforehand while the patient is
under an anæsthetic. It very commonly happens that what
is apparently absolute rigidity disappears at once when the
muscles are relaxed.

When division is required it must be carried out in accordance with the ordinary rules of tenotomy. A preliminary
course of kneading is frequently of great benefit; it loosens
the subcutaneous tissue, and makes the skin more supple and
yielding; but care must be taken to give the part a complete
rest for at least two days before. The fewer the number of
punctures, and the smaller the size, the better, so long as it is
done thoroughly. Very often, after beginning, it is found that,
independently of the superficial bands, there are deeper ones
beneath, the presence of which could not be ascertained before;
whenever it is safe, they must be treated in the same manner.
In all cases the punctures must be allowed to heal before the
least degree of extension or manipulation is attempted, for
fear of tearing the skin, as this is often exceedingly thin over
such parts. In general, four or five days are sufficient. Then,
if firm pressure is made with the thumb over the point of section, while the part is being manipulated, the newly-formed
fibrous tissue between the deeper structures is easily made to
yield without fear of injury to the rest. Failure of union, when
a tendon or a band of fascia is divided in only one place, is
quite exceptional.

Manipulation.—Manipulation is much more useful than
division; it can be employed for such a variety of purposes. In

the early stages it prevents the occurrence of stiffness or the formation of adhesions. Later, when the swelling and heat have disappeared, it is no less successful in restoring freedom and ease of movement, and afterward, when all mechanical obstructions have been cleared away by its use, it is one of the most effectual methods known for bringing back the circulation and nutrition of the part, and giving again to the muscles and nerves the energy which has so long been wanting.

When the object is to set free a stiffened joint, it may be applied in one of two ways. The first aims at breaking down all obstacles at once by a few vigorous but well-directed movements; the second merely attempts to stretch the contracted tissues, little by little each day until they cease to act any longer as an obstruction. The principle is quite distinct. Each plan has its own advocates, but it is especially urged against the former that it is a rough and hap-hazard method of proceeding, likely to excite inflammation, and always liable to do more harm than good.

Rapid.—In certain cases no doubt this may occur. There are plenty of instances on record in which limbs, and even lives, have been lost by reckless manipulation. But this is entirely due to the fact that the cases were unsuitable, and that sufficient precautions were not taken.[1] When carried out properly and scientifically, rapid manipulation is not only more efficacious, but is more free from risk than the slow and tedious process of stretching the opposing tissues little by little.

Strange as it may seem at first sight, there is scarcely anything in the proceeding itself that can cause inflammation. Tearing across bands of fibrous tissue is no more likely to produce it than breaking a bone or dividing a tendon. There is little that is different and nothing that is exceptional in the nature of the injury. A certain amount of blood is extrava-

---

[1] The following instances in which manipulation was either attempted or proposed are mentioned by the author of one of the most recent and complete works on Diseases of the Joints (Howard Marsh) as having occurred under his own observation:—Malignant tumor of the thigh; malignant tumor of the shoulder; disease of the spine; three cases of scrofulous disease of the knee-joint; hæmorrhoids; and a case in which, after the hip-joint had already been excised, it was gravely declared that the bone was out, and must be replaced. The list could easily be extended.

sated; the vessels dilate; more lymph is poured out to repair
the damage; but unless there is some grave constitutional
affection present in addition, or it is followed up by serious
maltreatment, this is no more likely to excite inflammation
than a single bruise or subcutaneous laceration in any other
part of the body. The capsule of a joint is always extensively
torn in dislocations, but they are never followed by inflammation unless some similar cause is present, and it is difficult to
understand why it should be so much feared when the injury
is so much less.

Slow and Gradual.—Repeated straining, on the other hand,
constantly attempting to stretch the contracted tissues, is
one of the surest ways of exciting it. It does not matter how
carefully it is managed. Each time a stiffened joint is gently
worked the fibrous bands that check its movements are
stretched, and very likely slightly torn; each time, in short,
the tissues are sprained again, so that they become more and
more tender and swollen. One of two things then must happen. Either the interval before the next attempt is not long
enough for them to recover, the heat and swelling never have
time to subside, and the joint becomes inflamed, though it does
not regain its freedom, or for fear of such an untoward occurrence manipulation is abandoned for a time, thorough rest en-
joined, and all the improvement lost; the bands regain their
strength, and the stiffness becomes worse than it was before.
One method aims at restoring perfect freedom at once with
a single risk; in the other the danger is incurred again and
again, each occasion being worse than the one that preceded
it, without the chance of recovery being nearly so good

Accidental Bone-setting.—I must not be understood to
advocate indiscriminate employment of forcible movement in
all cases alike; it is just this which has brought it into such
disrepute, and caused such an amount of opposition; only
where other things are equal, adhesions in connection with
sprained joints are far better broken across, once for all, than
repeatedly strained and stretched. There is no difficulty in
supplying examples in proof of this. One I have mentioned
already while describing the changes that occur in the tissues
round a joint after injury, and it is by no means a solitary, or
even an unusual, case. A very similar one was narrated to
me a short time since by another patient. According to his

own account, he had fallen down, with his arm outstretched, some time before, and (as was very probable) had dislocated his shoulder. It was reduced by a surgeon, but, for fear of reproducing the dislocation, the arm was kept bandaged close to the side for nearly six weeks. At the end of that time he could scarcely move it, and was almost convinced from the stiffness of the joint that the dislocation had never been reduced at all. It got better, however, by slow degrees, until he was able to move his arm in all directions, except upward and outward; the least attempt at this was stopped at once by a sharp stab of pain on the inner and under side of the joint. This continued until one day, about four months after the original accident, falling down again in much the same way, he felt a sudden snap, which hurt him intensely for the moment. Probably this was due to the rupture of a band, or of some contracted portion of the capsular tissue; at any rate, he found to his astonishment that his arm was from that moment practically free. Nothing afterward could turn him from the belief that the same kind of fall had both dislocated and reduced his shoulder joint. It was certainly wonderful that he did not dislocate it a second time.

In the ankle, when it is left stiff and painful after a sprain or fracture, manipulation carried out in this way is always worth trying. The particular kind of case in which it is likely to be successful can often be recognized at once. The skin over it is red and shining, as if it were stretched too tight; the color disappears readily when it is pressed upon, but is very slow in returning; firm pressure often causes it to pit, especially where there is a large amount of subcutaneous tissue; at the same time it feels cold to the touch. There is no displacement or dislocation; the outline of the bones is quite natural, though all the depressions are partly filled up, and the prominences rounded off; and the tendons can, generally speaking, be traced to their grooves. The position, however, is awkward, so that when standing upright the sole cannot rest flat upon the ground; movement is limited, and exceedingly painful at certain spots; and there is constant aching, especially at night or after any exertion. In several cases such as this, by putting the patient under an anæsthetic and working the joint thoroughly, I have succeeded in restoring perfect freedom of movement, sometimes at the first attempt.

It is essential to recollect in dealing with this part that though the original injury may have appeared to be confined to the ankle, the other joints of the foot rarely escape entirely; and that even if they are so fortunate, they have been kept continuously at rest as much as the ankle, and have undergone similar changes. For want of this precaution, I have seen more than one case fail at the first, and only succeed when the manipulation was extended to the others too.

Sprains of the wrist, again, often leave the fingers stiff and rigid for weeks, long after all heat and swelling have disappeared. In a case recently under my care the patient had fallen, about three weeks before, down a flight of steps, bending his right wrist-joint beneath him. According to his own account, he lay for some time (how long he scarcely knew) unconscious; and on coming round found that his arm was intensely painful, and that there was an enormous amount of swelling over the back of the hand and wrist, extending some distance along the forearm. This was reduced by careful bandaging, so that when I saw him it had almost disappeared, though there was evidence in the staining of the skin by the elbow how severe the injury had been. The hand was quite cool and painless so long as it was left alone, but he had not the least power over his fingers; they lay nearly straight, not apparently hurt, slightly swollen it is true, so that the shape of the joints was too rounded and uniform, but with nothing else about them to show that they had been injured. With the aid of the other hand he could almost bend them down into the palm, though it gave him a considerable amount of pain; but as soon as they were released they sprang back again almost mechanically. He was directed to have the part thoroughly kneaded and steamed for a few days; and at the end of the week was placed under an anæsthetic, and every joint in the fingers and wrist systematically worked through its full range. The next day the hand felt very sore, and was slightly more swollen, but this soon disappeared under massage. Movement was slow, and executed with great deliberation, but the range was much wider, and he was encouraged to use it freely. Two days after full power had nearly returned, and he was able to resume his work.

Where Rapid Manipulation is Suitable.—The joints in which this plan of treatment is most successful are those which are cold, but not much wasted, where the adhesions are still recent, and especially where, from the pain and tenderness being constant at one spot, there is some probability of the contracted tissues being limited in extent. Hinge joints, in which the movements are, comparatively speaking, simple, and take place only in one plane, can be treated much more easily than ball and socket ones, or those in which the variety of movements is more extensive.

An anæsthetic should always be given unless there is some special reason against it. Not only does it render the operation painless, but by insuring that the muscles are relaxed, it enables the maximum result to be obtained with the least degree of violence. In many cases, indeed, it is necessary, in order to make the diagnosis exact; so long as the muscles are contracted, it is often impossible to give an opinion either as to the strength or the extent of the adhesions. The obstruction itself may be of the slightest description, and the limb so rigid as apparently to have lost the joint altogether. No ordinary degree of force may produce the least effect; but as soon as the contraction of the muscles is done away with, the mere weight of the part is sufficient to separate the adherent surfaces, and restore perfect freedom.

Preparation.—When some time has escaped since the accident, and the circulation is feeble, or when the skin and the subcutaneous tissues appear thin and shrunken, it is not advisable to attempt this without a certain degree of preparation. The joint should be well steamed, or douched with water from a jet of moderate diameter, commencing with it fairly warm, and finishing up with cold; or it should be thoroughly kneaded every day, for a week or a fortnight, to loosen the skin and bring back the circulation. No pains should be spared to insure this. Great stress is laid by some on the use of oil, which is to be well rubbed in; and certain kinds are much more highly recommended than others; but in all probability the beneficial effect is entirely due to the friction. A small quantity of oily matter is no doubt absorbed, but it is impossible to imagine that its action under these conditions is mechanical, as this would imply.

The operation itself is not so simple as might be imagined. It is true that occasionally the most extraordinary recoveries are effected by falls or other accidents; but it must always

be remembered that these are only heard of when they are
successful; and that, very probably, they are quite the exception.   In the majority of cases failure is much more likely, unless a definite and well-ordered scheme is followed out.

Method.—The chance of success is greatest when the obstruction can be accurately localized. No pains should be
spared to effect this. The joint must be thoroughly examined
in every position it can be made to assume; any spot that is
tender must be marked beforehand; the movements that
cause an increase in the pain must be noted, both as regards
direction and extent, as well as the least irregularity or un-
evenness as one part glides over another. It is entirely owing
to their power of appreciating minutiæ of this description that
some persons have acquired such a reputation for the treatment of these cases.

The patient must be placed so that the portion of the limb
between the affected joint and the trunk can be fixed securely
by an assistant while the lower part can be freely moved by
the operator. In the case of the larger joints, one hand should
grasp the limb immediately below, so that the thumb may
press firmly on any spot that is tender; the other must be
sufficiently far off to secure a proper amount of leverage. All
rapid movements should, so far as possible, be in the direction
of flexion, combining with it abduction, adduction, or rotation,
according to the case, so that the tension may be directed to
the required spot.

To carry this out effectually two things are needed beyond
all others. The one is a sense of touch so delicate that it can
appreciate the least resistance or irregularity of movement;
the other an accurate knowledge, not merely of the ordinary
anatomy of the part, but of the different degrees of tension
that fall on the ligaments in every position of the limb.

Each joint requires a different kind of manipulation according to its construction. In the case of the shoulder, for example, the elbow must be bent so that the forearm may be
used as a lever, and the arm rotated first to one side then to
the other, bringing it across the chest and carrying it round
behind the back before any attempt is made to raise it from
the side. Bringing it up at once would very likely dislocate
the joint. For the knee Hood recommends the foot of the
affected limb to be held by the operator between his thighs,

so that when flexion is accomplished by the hand it may serve as a lever for rotation. This, however, can be effected by the hands alone if the muscles have been relaxed by an anæsthetic. The smaller hinge joints can be managed even more easily, flexion being combined with lateral or rotatory movements so far as the shape of the bone will allow.

There should be no jerking. The movements must be vigorous and forcible, but perfectly smooth; and they must be carried out thoroughly, the joint being moved to its full extent in all directions that are natural to it. Each kind of action should be combined successively with the rest, one by one, so that the tension may fall in turn upon all the different parts of the capsule.

Movements which are especially restricted or painful of course require most attention, but the others, though they may not be affected to the same extent, are not to be neglected. It sometimes happens if these are dealt with first that a considerable proportion of the main obstruction is cleared away, as it were, by side attacks, so that when its turn comes it yields more readily than it otherwise would.

Recent slight adhesions give way at once without a sound, though the sensation is generally conveyed to the hand. When they are older the noise may be as loud and clear as when a bone is broken. Probably in many cases this is due not so much to the actual tearing of adhesions as to the sudden separation of two synovial surfaces that fit accurately into each other. The noise that can be produced in this way, especially if a table or other structure is made use of as a sounding board, is well known.

The after treatment of these cases should be in all respects the same as that of a recent sprain, only if passive motion at an early date is advisable to prevent the occurrence of stiffness in the one, it is absolutely necessary in the other. The joint must be worked systematically every day from the first. If the adhesions have been thoroughly broken across, and if swelling is prevented by compression, it is almost painless. In exceptional cases it may be necessary to administer an anæsthetic the first few times.

Manipulation as an Exercise.—This, however, is not the only use for forcible manipulation. Even when all adhesions have been broken down and the action of the joint thoroughly

re-established, voluntary power is often slow in returning.
The joint itself may move with perfect freedom, but the muscles, and even the nerves, seem to have lost their power. It
is so long since they have done any work that they have become unable to do any. They are wasted and shrunken in
size; the circulation in them is defective; possibly their structure, even, has undergone some alteration. Whatever it may
be there is no question that, when a case has lasted any time,
their strength and vigor become seriously impaired. The
joint cannot be considered cured merely because the mechanical obstacles to its action have been removed; something
more than this is required. Recovery is not complete until the
natural condition is restored, and the joint is able to undertake active work again.

Exercise, of course, is the most effectual remedy for this.
When it can be carried out the cure is rapid and certain, but
in many cases it seems impossible. Sometimes there appears
to be an actual inability to make use of the muscles, as if the
power of the will was unable to reach them. Sometimes the
sense of insecurity is so great that the patient cannot be persuaded to place sufficient trust in them. Whatever the cause
may be, forcible manipulation is of the greatest service in
these cases, especially if it is helped by massage and galvanism. The way in which it is used is, of course, very different
to that already described, and the object is different; in the one
its purpose is to tear across adhesions, in the other to rouse
latent muscular activity, but if used systematically, success,
though, perhaps, not quite so conspicuous, is equally sure.
Elaborate accounts have been written from time to time of
what has been called the movement cure, and many varieties
of manipulation have been described in connection with it, but,
so far, at least, as the treatment of sprains is concerned, it
does not seem clear that they possess any great advantage
one over the other. The principle in them all alike is to exercise the muscles according to their strength, to stretch them
out, and manipulate them without fatigue. In most cases the
greatest amount of benefit appears to be obtained by making
use of the different plans successively, beginning with that
which calls for the least effort on the part of the patient.

Simple extension, gradually straightening out the muscles,
one after the other, with some degree of force, until a distinct

sensation of resistance is experienced, is especially useful in the earlier stages, immediately after the adhesions have been broken down. Sometimes the muscles are irritable, and inclined to painful spasmodic contraction; or hard knots form in their substance, possibly due to rupture of a few of the fibres; or a certain degree of soreness and tenderness of skin makes itself felt over them. Whatever may underlie them, these conditions are often relieved by slowly but firmly extending, one after the other, the various groups of muscles that lie round the joint, and applying firm and even pressure.

What are known as resistive movements are of much wider application. In these the patient either carries out a definite course of action against the resistance of the operator, who is able to select any particular group of muscles, and regulate exactly the amount of work, or the latter makes use of his strength to oppose some voluntary action on the part of the patient, compelling him to give way. The former of these methods is by far the most useful of the two. The secret is to keep the opposing force well within the limits of the patient's strength, making use alternately of flexion or extension, or of rotation inward or outward, as the case may be. Exercise of this description certainly possesses wonderful influence on the nutrition and activity of the tissues, not the muscles only; and with a reasonable amount of care it may be kept up for a considerable time each day without overfatigue. The other plan tires out the muscles at once, and is too exhausting to deserve strong recommendation.

In some cases it is possible to substitute for the hand of the operator mechanical contrivances, arrangements of wheels and levers adjusted to resist any individual movement that may be wished, and capable of being graduated exactly by the patient to suit his own strength. The action, however, is not quite the same. The resistance of a spring or an elastic band cannot be graduated like that of human muscles, guided by an experience of what is required; and unless very carefully superintended the progress of cases treated in this fashion is apt to be very uneven and irregular.

CHAPTER X.

MASSAGE.

MASSAGE, again, which is a most valuable remedy in the treatment of sprained joints, has a history as strange as that of forcible manipulation. It has never been altogether forgotten; some people have always practiced it, more or less carefully, and with a varying degree of knowledge and skill; but at certain times, and in certain countries, it seems to have acquired an extraordinary reputation, and then, again, almost capriciously to have been as strongly condemned. Possibly fashion may account for it in certain measure, for this exerts an influence in the use of remedies just as it does over everything else; but something, at least, must be attributed to the indiscriminate and unscientific manner of its application by unskilled persons in all cases alike, whether they could or could not be benefited by it. Like many other things it has been destroyed by its own popularity.

It is certainly not a novelty; in most countries there has been handed down by tradition from unknown ages a custom of treating injuries of joints and muscles by friction or manipulation, and in some places this has been considered a special prerogative of certain families or individuals, who, by dint of long practice and a certain delicacy of touch (perhaps inherited), have attained no inconsiderable degree of skill. The modern plan is simply the scientific outcome of this; the working has been studied more accurately; its action on the tissues better considered; and certain rules laid down for guidance in the selection of cases.

At one time, for example, Beveridge's rubbers were well known in Edinburgh, and the success that attended their treatment (which was carried out very thoroughly and methodically) had a marked influence on the practice of the Continent. Then the process was almost forgotten, or, at any rate, was rarely employed, except in country districts, where rubbing is often used, in a rough sort of way, without skill of any kind other than that derived from custom. Lately, again, owing in great measure to the exertions of Dacre Fox, in England, and Graham, Norström, Metzger, and others, abroad, it has been placed on a scientific basis, and received once more into favor. Even at the present day, however, there is too great a tendency to consider it a quack remedy, and to hand it over to persons whose chief recommendation is that they act as untiring rubbing machines, without following any definite rules or guidance.

It is often said against it that those who take it up abandon it again as soon as they have had sufficient experience of its results; they find, so it is alleged, that not only does it require a large amount of patience on the part of the sufferer, as well as the operator, but that it is only beneficial to those who would recover as soon without it, and that in some cases it is actually injurious. As a rule, and so far as sprains at any rate are concerned, this arises from the inability to distinguish massage from mere unskilled rubbing. In reality there is nearly as great a difference between them as there is between painting the wall of a house and the work of a skilled artist. The one requires a certain amount of muscular strength and manual dexterity, the other only comes to those who are by nature fitted for it, as a result of teaching and experience. It may or may not be true that it requires two years, as Dr. Murrell states, to learn the process; that depends on the person and on the previous training; certainly many do not acquire the art even in that time.

As a general application massage is very widely used. There are many descriptions copied from travelers' works of its employment in one form or another among most of the races of mankind. It was largely practiced by the ancients; the Turks and Africans at the present day make use of it; even among the Siberians and Laplanders it may be found in a form modified by the exigencies of climate; while the "lomilomi" of the Sandwich Islanders is spoken of in terms of enthusiasm by nearly every one who has written of them for its power of relieving the stiffness and soreness of excessive exertion, and procuring rest and sleep. The effect is described as most luxurious; the process is neither kneading, squeezing, nor rubbing, but now like one, now like the other, each muscle is manipulated in its turn, beginning with the head and working down slowly over the whole body, until in half-an-hour the weariness has quite disappeared and given place to a most refreshing sense of ease and comfort.

Like many other words that have crept into science from popular usage, massage has scarcely yet acquired a precise or definite meaning. It has been used for every kind of manipulation, whether applied to joints alone or to the whole surface of the body, with the hands only, or with the assistance of instruments. All varieties of friction, pressure, kneading, percussion, and even passive motion, have been included in it at one time or another; and the description of the manner in which it is carried out, and the rules by which suitable cases are selected, are proportionately vague and uncertain.

For all practical purposes, so far, at least, as concerns the treatment of injured joints and muscles, the various processes that have been enumerated may be grouped under the three heads of friction, percussion, and kneading. Passive motion differs to such an extent in its object and method of application that it seems unwise to include it.

Friction.—Of these friction is by far the most simple, and the easiest and least fatiguing to carry out; but its power is very limited, and it has scarcely any direct influence, except on the most superficial structures. It consists merely in a succession of strokings with the hand (using as much of the surface as possible, and fitting it into all the inequalities) from the extremities toward the trunk, commencing lightly at first, and gradually increasing in strength as the part becomes accustomed to it. The knuckles even may be used where the tissues are very deep-seated, or unusually firm. The skin soon becomes red and warm; more blood flows through it, the temperature rises, and, after a few days' treatment, a distinct change may be noticed in the nutrition of the part. Instead of being hard and unyielding, tied down, as it were, to the subjacent tissues, the skin becomes soft and supple, the natural appearance returns, the folds become visible again, and the superficial tissues begin to regain their firmness and elasticity.

Besides this, however, friction exerts considerable influence on the nerves distributed to the skin, and indirectly through them on internal organs, especially on other parts of the nervous system. The medium through which this takes place is not accurately known. It is possibly the result of the increased activity of the circulation, but more probably it is due to the peculiar sympathy existing between different parts of the nervous system, by virtue of which one cannot be stimulated or excited without influencing the rest. However this may be, of the fact itself there can be no doubt; friction, especially along the back, is often of the greatest service in relieving irritability or sleeplessness.

Combined with baths, and applied generally over the surface of the body, it is of excellent service when the limbs are aching and stiff from over-exertion or exposure to cold. It allays the sensitiveness of the skin, leaves behind it a feeling of well-being and comfort, and does away with the sensation of fatigue. In sprains, however, and injuries of like character, its application is more limited. In recent cases, where there is no extensive laceration of ligaments, and where it is thought advisable to begin massage without delay, it may be used as a preliminary to allay the sensibility of the skin, and accustom the patient to firmer kneading. In old chronic cases, too, where the joint has not been moved for some length of time, it is of undoubted use in restoring the natural tone to the skin before more active measures are undertaken. In other circumstances it is rarely employed for injuries of joints, though it is highly recommended as part of general massage for other disorders.

Percussion.—Percussion, too, whether carried out by means of an instrument or with the hand, is of very limited use. Unless applied with such force as to cause actual bruising, it has no direct influence on any structure deeper than the skin and the subcutaneous stratum of muscles. On the former it produces the same general result as friction, though without its soothing influence; on the latter it acts as a local stimulus, causing each time a single contraction of the fibres beneath, varying in extent and vigor according to the condition of the muscles. To produce the full effect, the movement must be rapid and short, the pressure being raised at once. The weight of the blow must be regulated by the depth of the structure. Great stress is laid by some on the number per minute, when percussion is used for the relief of pain or neuralgia; but, so far as the muscles are concerned, this does not seem material, though it is as well the strokes should not be too rapid.

The effect is most marked when the muscles are in a state of tension, though the actual shortening produced in these circumstances may be less apparent. When, for example, the lumbar region is being percussed, the patient should stoop forward, so that the muscular slips lying along the side of the spinal column may be placed upon the stretch, and receive the full effect of the vibration. Otherwise a considerable amount of the benefit is lost before the muscular substance is affected at all.

Massage.—Massage, in the strict sense of the term, is a great deal more efficacious, especially with older sprains. Its action is not limited to the skin and superficial structures. These undergo immense changes, it is true; they become softer and finer while under manipulation; their strength and elasticity increase, the extreme tenderness diminishes, and the natural appearance and texture return. The surface loses its dry harsh character and becomes warm and moist again; the livid bluish color gives way to a brighter hue, and the deeper layers of fibrous tissue yield and stretch, so that the hide-bound shrunken condition that is often present after long disuse gradually passes off. But the good effect is not by any means limited to, or even most conspicuously shown by this. When properly carried out massage exerts a simultaneous influence on muscles, nerves, and vessels, in fact on all the tissues within its reach.

The circulation is the first thing to feel its power. It has already been explained how, after prolonged rest, the blood, as it were, lies almost stagnant in the tissues, slowly circulating through them, and neither giving them sufficient for their nutrition, nor removing from them the waste products of their action. This is changed at once. The life of the part is quickened. The veins and absorbents are emptied first, and the fluid they contain driven on to the heart, which fills more rapidly, and contracts more vigorously and firmly. Then the pressure falls on the smaller vessels, and the tiny irregular spaces, full of lymph, which extend in all directions through the tissues. These, in their turn, are compressed and mechanically emptied, their contents being driven on into the empty vessels, from which any backward flow is prevented by the valves. The circulation becomes more rapid; nutrition is carried on with greater energy, and the actual amount of blood in the tissues at any one time so much increased that they become full and soft to the touch and regain the even and rounded contour of active health.

Next to the skin the muscles seem to experience the greatest amount of benefit. Even after a single application they are capable of doing a great deal more work with much less fatigue. It has often been shown that a muscle, exhausted by lifting a heavy weight many times in a minute, scarcely regains any of its power if it is merely allowed to rest a quarter of an hour. It remains stiff and weak, and liable to irregular and spasmodic contractions. If, on the other hand, it is treated by massage for the same length of time, its strength returns, so that it is able to do as much again with even less fatigue than it felt before.

At the same time the sensitiveness to electric stimuli is increased. Murrell has shown that a current, too weak to cause any response when applied to the motor point of one of the muscles of the arm, is able to produce vigorous contraction after a few minutes' massage. The excitability of muscles, and the amount of energy they are capable of putting out, are regulated—other things being equal—by the way in which they are supplied with food, and the rapidity with which the waste products are removed. This, in its turn, is dependent on the circulation. Each muscle and each bundle of muscular fibres is surrounded by a sheath of fascia, to all intents and purposes quite inelastic; under this is collected the fluid plasma which is the immediate source of the nutrition of the tissues. So long as the muscle is at rest this remains unchanged; when it contracts, so that the shape and consistence are altered, or when the muscle itself is thoroughly and systematically kneaded, the fluid is driven onward into the lymphatics and at once renewed from behind. It is for this reason that massage, so far from causing fatigue, is of such service in relieving it.

The good effect does not pass off at once. If the treatment is continued and a proper supply of food maintained there is a lasting increase in the size and condition of the muscles. Instead of being soft and flaccid or stiff and unyielding, with hard and tender nodules in their substance, so that they rather

impede movement than otherwise, they become firm and elastic
to the touch, ready to respond at once to any stimulus, and
able, when called upon, to put out a much greater amount of
energy.

It is hardly fair, however, to attribute the whole of this improvement to the condition of the muscles only. Massage exerts a similar influence on the nervous system, and though the
immediate results may not be so striking in their character,
·the actual changes are none the less important. During the
process itself, and often for hours after, the patient experiences
a sense of refreshing ease and comfort. Lassitude and pain
disappear; the capacity for work returns, and mind and body
alike regain their vigor. Probably this results in no small
measure from the improvement in the circulation, as the effect
at first is quite local; but from the way in which general
strength and voluntary power are restored, in what are known
as neurasthenic cases, massage must exert a very considerable
influence upon the whole of the nervous system.

In Recent Injuries.—The best proof, however, of the power
it possesses over absorption and circulation is shown by the
ease with which the swelling and tension can be made to disappear from sprained joints. It is true that in recent cases
the greatest care is required, and that nothing is so likely to
increase the mischief as rough handling of the part; but when
it is carried out quietly and gently, by one who has had some
experience, it is very difficult to find anything that acts in so
perfect a manner. The whole limb, perhaps, is swollen; the
joint distended with blood; the skin shining and tense, much
too hot to the touch, and exquisitely tender; but all this vanishes almost like magic. The tension disappears as the fluid is
carried off; the pain is relieved, the temperature falls, the
natural outline begins to be apparent once more, extravasated
blood is broken up, the *débris* dispersed, and adhesions between the torn and bruised surfaces effectually prevented.
Sometimes even tendons, which have been turned almost out
of their grooves by the accumulation of fluid in their sheaths,
can in this way be restored to their position without further
assistance.

Such results as these cannot, of course, be obtained in every
case of recent sprain, and even when the treatment is successful in relieving the pain and getting rid of the swelling, it

must always be remembered that time is needed for the repair
of structures that have been torn. I am convinced, however,
that, especially when the stress of the injury has fallen on the
muscles, and when the laceration is not too great, this plan
may be adopted, not only with the greatest safety, but with
an infinitely better prospect of speedy recovery than under the
old established method of bandaging and rest. Graham, in
particular, lays stress on the fact that the sooner the treatment is commenced after the injury, the shorter its duration is
likely to be.

In Older Cases.—In older cases, where the effusion is denser
and firmer, and where, owing to the long-continued distention,
the tissues have lost their tone, and become sodden and œdematous, massage can be used with much greater freedom. The
solid part of the effusion is broken up and disintegrated by the
pressure, so that it is driven into the absorbents and carried
away by the increased force of the stream; the chronic congestion is dispersed, the blood circulates more freely, the tone of
the part returns, and the lifeless, helpless look disappears day
by day. The improvement is often surprising in its rapidity.
A joint that has remained for weeks cold and inactive, the
seat of a constant wearing pain, and quite incapable of per-
forming its proper movements, in a very few sittings begins to
recover its flexibility, loses the pain, and allows itself to be
handled, and passive movements to be carried out with ease
and readiness.

Active movement, in general, takes some time longer, for
the muscles grow so stiff and rigid from prolonged disuse that
they require as much education as the joint itself. The case
that furnishes the most striking cure is a sprained joint that
has been treated by bandaging in the conventional way, where
the œdema still persists, and where there are no adhesions
round other than those caused by the rigidity of the capsule
and the swelling of the soft tissues. Even if weeks have passed,
the effect may be seen after the second or third sitting. Only
where, owing to the great length of time, the effusion has become thoroughly organized, and where the structures round
are shrunken and matted together by dense, unyielding fibrous
tissue, it is of little avail until the joint is set free, and full
range of action restored by vigorous passive movement.

Method.—The method of application is not easy to de-

scribe, and it can only be learned through practice, even by
those who already possess a fair knowledge of anatomy. This
is indispensable; without it, massage must degenerate into
mere rubbing. Each group of muscles must be known, where
it ends and begins, how thick it is, and how the tendons lie,
where the intermuscular septa of connective tissue come, and
where the vessels and nerves that supply the part are situated.
All the natural movements and the different arrangement of
the structures in various positions of the limb must be perfectly familiar. The synovial cavity of the joints and the tendon sheaths must, as it were, be mapped out underneath the
skin. In short, there must be a thorough practical knowledge,
not only of the anatomy of the part at rest, but of the direction and mutual relations assumed by the different structures
when at work.

Supposing the case of a sprained ankle of moderate severity
in a healthy person, a few hours after the accident the ligaments are strained, perhaps even slightly torn; the synovial
cavity is distended with fluid, the tissues round are swollen out
with extravasated blood, the skin is hot and discolored, the
normal shape of the joint is lost, and all the hollows between
the bones are filled up. The patient must be seated comfort-
ably, so that the muscles are, as far as possible, relaxed; the
knee must be bent, and the foot and ankle given over altogether to the manipulator. The foot is to be held gently but
firmly, so that the patient may make no incautious start, and
the whole proceeding from first to last should be entirely devoid of pain. The operator should have plenty of room, so
that he is not cramped; perhaps as convenient a position as
any is kneeling on one leg, or sitting on a low seat in front of
the patient, with the heel of the injured limb resting on the
front of his knee. The movement at first must be exceedingly
light, and so directed as to diminish as much as possible the
sensitiveness of the skin, commencing with the part above
(nearer the trunk) the injured joint, and working gradually
downward. The thumb, or the tips of the fingers, or the palm
of the hand, should be used according to the shape of the surface, taking care always to employ as much as possible.

The direction of the movement must always be toward
the trunk, from the insertion to the origin of the muscles, in
the direction of the returning current of the circulation, com-

mencing over a part where the swelling has not yet shown itself, and gradually working on to the rest. The most tender spots must always be left till last. If, for example, the foot has been twisted outward, there is nearly always great sensitiveness over the tip of the internal malleolus, and a considerable amount of swelling along the course of the tendons behind, extending a variable distance up the leg, and into the hollow in front of the tendo-Achillis. This must be left until friction has been applied over the whole of the rest of the foot and leg; if this is carried out thoroughly not only does a great deal of the swelling disappear of itself from the injured part, but owing to the condition of the circulation through that which has been already manipulated, the remainder is absorbed much more readily than it otherwise would be.

Gradually, if the treatment is persevered in, the tendency to start on the part of the patient, and even the involuntary shrinking, disappear; the foot is given up to the operator with greater confidence, and the superficial general swelling begins to diminish. More attention may then be paid to the spaces in which the extravasated blood has collected to the cavity of the joint and the tendon sheaths. The tips of the fingers, or the thumb, may be made to trace out the irregular intervals between the bony prominences moving round and round in small circles on the skin. The two hands should be used close together, so that the paths the fingers traverse intersect each other, and the manipulated surfaces overlap. Gradually, as the effusion subsides, the circles increase in size, the pressure becomes firmer, and the deeper-lying structures are treated in their turn. The individual muscles and tendons are grasped and squeezed in the direction of their fibres, the fingers being always carried onward toward the trunk in the interspaces between them; and the soft tissues are firmly pressed, and, as it were, rolled along by one hand after the other, until all the excess of fluid has returned once more to the blood stream, and slight passive movements of such a nature as not to exert any traction on the injured ligaments are allowed without resistance.

This is to be taken as the sign of success in the treatment of recent cases. How long before it is reached differs naturally in each individual, and no rule can be laid down. Sometimes in slighter injuries a single short sitting suffices; at

others the process must be repeated for several days. The
time that has elapsed since the accident, the condition of the
joint, the degree of swelling, and the severity of the pain, all
possess some degree of influence. As a general rule, if the
injury is recent, there is more tenderness about the part, but
the swelling disappears sooner; in older cases firmer pressure
may be used from the first, as the skin is less sensitive; but
the time before the swelling is absorbed, and movement becomes free and painless, as a rule is much longer.

At the close of the sitting the joint and the limb must be
bandaged with pads of cotton wool, so arranged as to fill in
all the natural depressions of the part. If they are held in
place with a flannel, or better a Domett bandage, the joint
may be moved a little, though the pressure is sufficient to prevent the return of any great degree of swelling and œdema.
But, however carefully the bandage is applied, it nearly always
happens that the next day some of the fullness and tenderness
of the part returns, so that another sitting is desirable. If
the case is going to terminate favorably, each application is
shorter and less painful than the last, and each time the range
of passive movement is increased.

It must clearly be borne in mind that, though this method
of treatment causes the swelling to disappear more rapidly
than any other, and allows the return of slight degrees of
movement without pain almost from the first, a ligament that
has been torn across requires nearly as long for repair as when
it is left alone. Consequently, when it comes to the question
of dealing with sprains of great severity, such as often are
met with in the ankle, all that is done, and, indeed, all that
can be done, is to restore the parts to the condition best suited
for repair, and to guard, as far as possible, against the after
troubles of stiffness, chronic œdema, and pain.

In older sprains, the method of application is somewhat
different. Here much less stress is laid upon light friction, and
much more upon deep manipulation and rolling of the parts.
The object is not so much to cause the absorption of a fluid
exudation as to stimulate the muscles and nerves to greater
activity, and to increase the amount of blood and lymph circulating through the deeper strata. The grasp is firmer, and
the pressure greater; the whole hand is used, and both at the
same time; if, for example, the limb is not too large, one may

be placed opposite the other, so that two groups of muscles are manipulated together, the fingers of one hand partly reaching on to the territory of the other. One hand contracts as the other relaxes, each, in its turn, squeezing the tissues onward and away from the middle line, and stretching the parts that lie between them. Care, of course, must be taken not to stretch the tissues in opposite directions at the same time; and it is a wise precaution to go over the surface gently and superficially before attempting deep or thorough manipulation.

Where other joints are concerned, the treatment must be conducted on essentially the same principles, varying the details according to the circumstances of each case. The operator should always keep sufficiently far off so that his movements are not cramped or constrained, and he should always endeavor to make use of as much of the surface of his hand as possible. The fingers must be kept close together for the sake of mutual support; they should not be allowed to slip too much upon the skin, which should move with them as far as possible, or the operation may be a very uncomfortable one for the patient. For this reason ointments and other similar applications are very rarely used unless it is wished either to diminish friction or to produce some specific effect.

The patient must be placed in an easy and comfortable position, with the limb well supported, and, where possible, well raised, so as to assist the return circulation. If, for example, the wrist is the part in question, the point of the elbow should be resting on the table; if it is the elbow itself, or the shoulder, the patient should either rest his hand on the shoulder of the operator, or should even lay hold of something higher still.

The hands must always lie in the direction of the muscular fibres, and the rolling and squeezing always tend upward from the extremities toward the trunk. The rate of movement and the amount of force that is used must vary with each individual; but there should never afterward be any sign of bruising due to the manipulation. It is always present, of course, to a greater or less extent, in recent sprains, and it is nearly certain to be there if adhesions are broken down or a joint is forcibly manipulated under an anæsthetic; but it never occurs after massage unless the force used has been ex-

cessive and unjustifiable, and its presence generally means
that more harm than good has been done. Instead of assisting in the repair of the damage it has inflicted more.

It is most essential to commence as gradually and as gently
as possible, only working on the deeper tissues after the more
superficial ones have become thoroughly accustomed, and have
been unloaded of their surplus fluid. The skin, the soft subcutaneous tissue, the muscles, and the deeper layers, must all
be worked in turn. Nor should the manipulation be confined
to the injured part. In a sprain of any standing the whole of
the limb is affected more or less. It is usually better to de-
vote attention first to the parts nearer the trunk, than to deal
with those around the injured area, and only afterward, when
the circulation is thoroughly re-established, to manipulate the
joint itself.

The tendency is to make the sittings last too long. Deep
manipulation itself rarely requires more than five minutes;
but in dealing with a recent injury it may be advisable to
spend a longer time than this over the friction and other pre-
paratory measures, so that a quarter of an hour soon passes by.
When the tenderness is very great, and the amount of swelling
excessive, much longer than this may be necessary, but short,
frequently repeated sittings are of greater benefit than one
long one. A skilled operator, too, will often effect more in
a few minutes than an ordinary rubber will in as many sittings.

CHAPTER XI.

SPRAINS OF TENDONS.

SPRAINS of tendons are deserving of as much consideration as those of joints; they are almost as common; the changes in the tissues are nearly as serious, and the results, though they vary a good deal, are in many respects quite as important. Unless perfect freedom of movement is regained, there is an amount of suffering and inconvenience often altogether out of proportion to the extent of the mischief.

Structure.—In one respect the question is much easier; the structures concerned are not nearly so complicated. The shorter tendons are merely unyielding bands of various shape, directly connecting the muscle to one of the adjacent bones. They are formed of tough fibrous tissue, continuous, on the one hand, with the membrane investing the bone, and, on the other, spread out to receive the attachment of the muscular fibres. The longer ones are more or less rounded in shape, and are inclosed in a synovial sheath, practically identical with that which lines the interior of joints. The surface is as smooth as it can be, so that the tendon glides without friction in its groove, no matter how many bends or curves it makes, or how often the position and direction of these vary in different movements of the limb. The interior is lubricated by a fluid identical in character with that in joints, just sufficient in amount to fill up all the interstices, and enable the sheath to fit closely and evenly round the tendon. The outer wall is formed of a fibrous layer, which, though apparently distinct (just as the capsule of a joint appears distinct), is only a layer borrowed, as it were, from the delicate tissue round. Owing to the friction, this is condensed into a firm membrane, smooth and polished on its inner surface, but rough on the outside, where it still retains its connection with the fibrous tissue from which it was formed.

In some parts of the body each tendon has a separate

sheath surrounding it like a tube. At the ends this is continuous with the sides of the tendon, so that the cavity is completely closed. It is largest and best developed where there
are projecting points of bone, and where the direction of the
pull is consequently altered. In many parts the sheaths of
two tendons lying side by side communicate with each other;
and where, as ,in the wrist or ankle, the number of those running in the same direction is considerable, there is only one
large sac surrounding them all. Sheaths of this description
are much stronger and stouter, the walls are thicker, and
owing to the bundles of tendons lying side by side, each moving independently of the rest, are ribbed, as it were, on the
inner surface with longitudinal ridges, which sometimes project as actual folds, inclosing between their layers a mass of
soft and delicate tissue well supplied with minute vessels. In
the young the lining membrane itself is quite smooth, so far
as its inner surface is concerned; but as age advances, particularly in those whose work is laborious, or whose joints and
tendons are exposed to heavy or repeated strains, it undergoes
great alterations. The folds grow stouter and longer, their
free margin becomes irregular and broken up into fringes, and
the tissue of which they are composed becomes tougher and
firmer, until in some instances the surface is as irregular and
as shaggy with villous processes as the interior of a joint
affected with chronic synovitis.

Effects of Age.—This, however, is not the only alteration
found in tendon sheaths after adult life. There is a slight but
constant tendency for them to enlarge and encroach on surrounding structures. Where two lie side by side, or where
one is in contact with the capsule of a joint, the dividing wall
in course of time grows thinner and thinner until it gives way
altogether, so that the cavities communicate with each other.
In other instances, where the tissues round are soft and yielding, the sac expands unevenly, and becomes covered over with
irregular dilatations. If the wall is especially weak at any
one spot, or if from some accident the fibrous layer of the
sheath has been torn, the lining membrane is forced out little
by little into the interspace, until it assumes the shape of a
pouch, opening into the sheath by means of a long and sometimes very narrow neck. When one of these is once formed it
generally continues to increase in size. Fluid is driven into it

with very considerable pressure every time the tendon moves without there being any corresponding force to insure its return; the sac grows larger and larger until it projects beneath the skin, or even opens up a communication with some more distant cavity. It is in this way that tendon sheaths become connected with neighboring joints, the pouch developing originally sometimes from the one, sometimes from the other.

In the majority of instances it is difficult to say how far these changes are the result of time alone, and how far they are the product of repeated sprains, and of attacks of rheumatic gout. In joints there is no question that these causes are of material assistance, to say the least. Whenever large diverticula are present, or the interior of the synovial membrane is more than usually irregular, one or other of these has been at work. The same is probably true of tendon sheaths and of bursæ; the alterations are not serious except under these conditions. Slighter degrees, however, tending in the same direction, but not going further than a moderate amount of dilatation and thickening, are so common, and so consistent with what takes place under the same conditions in similar structures, that there is no doubt they are due, in part at least, to the natural degeneration of the tissues occurring everywhere as age advances.

Extent of Injury.—The tendons themselves rarely sustain much injury in the case of sprains. They are formed of little more than tough bundles of fibrous tissue closely woven together, so that if they escape being torn in two, or wrenched from the muscle to which they belong, they generally escape altogether. The sheaths, however, in which they lie make up for them in this respect. They are so delicate in structure that they are torn or bruised by the least unusual strain, and the relation they bear to the tendon they inclose is so accurate that the slightest alteration is sufficient to produce a very considerable effect.

Overwork.—Serious consequences are, of course, much more likely to be produced by violent injuries, but mere overwork is sufficient to affect the synovial lining and to cause inconvenience and actual pain. It need not be excessive; it is enough that it should be more than usual, and that it should be kept up for some time. Instances of this are of every-day occurrence when an unusual degree of exertion falls on a group of muscles that are not accustomed to it. The movements of the tendons are no longer easy and natural; a hot, burning sensation is felt each time the muscle contracts; there is a feeling of tenderness and fullness over it; the temperature (as taken by a surface thermometer) may even be slightly raised, probably from the larger amonut of blood that is flowing through the part; and, what is the most striking and characteristic symptom of all, as the tendon plays backward and forward in its sheath there is communicated to the finger a delicate sense of crepitation and rustling, as when two surfaces of silk are being rubbed together. Sometimes this is perceptible to the patient himself, at others it can only be elicited by carefully applied pressure over the tendon sheath. Whenever it occurs it may be accepted as clear proof that there is some alteration in the relation between the tendon and the membrane round it. Naturally it can be felt most plainly where a number lie close together beneath the skin, as on the front of the ankle joint or the back of the hand. In situations such as these, any unaccustomed degree of exertion, walking, for example, some distance unusually fast, or feathering in rowing at the commencement of the season, or even carrying a heavy weight in the hand, is sufficient to cause it.

Tenosynovitis.—It has been imagined by some that this peculiar sensation is the result of the sheath becoming dry. The synovial fluid is, as it were, used up, and the movement of the tendon over the dry and roughened surface causes friction. It is very difficult to understand how this can occur; such a condition of things would be almost unique; nowhere else does use, even when carried to the greatest excess, entail any similar result. The immediate effect of muscular contraction is to increase very largely the amount of blood flowing through the part, and to cause a much larger quantity of lymph to pour out through the walls of the vessels into the surrounding tissue spaces. It is difficult to understand how, under such conditions, the sac of the synovial membrane could become dry. The walls contain a greater amount of blood, they are softer and thicker, the lining layer of cells is not so perfect, their growth is more rapid, so that they have no time to assume their normal flattened shape, and the character of the fluid in the interior is modified by being mixed with the exuded lymph and with the cast-off cells; but the quantity is rather increased than diminished.

Lawn Tennis Arm.—The same symptoms (with the exception of the rustling) are produced by over-exertion when the tendon is attached directly to bone without the presence of any investing sheath of synovial membrane. A common instance of this is met with in a variety of what it is the present fashion to call lawn-tennis arm, though a similar thing was described long since in Australian diggers. There is a tender spot about the middle of the forearm, on the outer side of the bone, corresponding to the attachment of one of the muscles that is used especially in back-handed strokes; and sometimes the tenderness is so great that I have known it the source of great uneasiness. The skin appears slightly swollen and raised above the normal level; but it is quite white, even whiter than the surrounding part, and the swelling so soft that it can be appreciated much better by the eye than by the touch. In moderate cases it is limited to this point, and the muscle itself is not affected; only when it contracts there is a feeling of soreness and stiffness, not, perhaps, amounting to actual pain. In severe ones the swelling extends over the whole muscle.

The changes here are essentially the same; owing to the increased wear and tear more blood flows through the part; a larger amount of exudation is poured out into the tissues, through the walls of the vessels; the skin becomes more highly sensitive, so that it feels sore and tender when even light pressure falls on it; and the action of the muscles is difficult and painful. Only there is no crepitation or rustling, because there is no synovial sheath in which the fluid can collect.

Muscular Strains.—Under some circumstances the exertion required to produce such a result may be exceedingly trivial. It is not uncommon for patients who are recovering from an attack of severe illness, when they are allowed to sit up for the first time, to complain, after an hour or two, of soreness over certain bony prominences, and of a sensitiveness of skin that is sometimes mistaken for hysteria. There is a line, for example, at the back of the head, or a space between the shoulder blades, where the least pressure is painful, especially after they have been sitting up some time. In the morning, or after a long rest, nothing of the kind is felt; the muscles can act freely and naturally. It is only when they are tired out

that these symptoms begin to appear. The work that they
are called upon to perform is too much for them; they have
been weakened to such an extent by prolonged illness and
want of exercise that the exertion of sitting upright is as much
out of proportion to their strength as severe and prolonged
labor would be if they were in good training. There is, it is
true, no appreciable amount of swelling, but it is quite sufficient for the purpose that the tender points of bone correspond
with very fair accuracy to the attachments of the muscles
that receive the strain. Rest at once relieves it, and as the
nutrition improves and strength returns the symptoms rapidly disappear.

The same thing is frequently met with in connection with
the abdominal muscles after vigorous efforts of any kind, and
it is sometimes so marked that I have known it mistaken for
more serious disorders, especially as the muscles are often
thrown into a state of cramp, so that they do simulate, to
some extent, internal tumors. There is the same burning sensation when contraction takes place; the skin feels tender and
sore, and its sensitiveness is extreme (as it frequently is in
hysteria), the patient wincing at the slightest contact. Sometimes the feeling of soreness is worst over the points where the
muscles are attached to the bone; but more often the patient
refers it to the junction of the muscular and tendinous fibres;
and it is remarkable and very characteristic of this muscular
overwork, that nearly always, in indicating the seat of the
pain, the patient moves his hand, quite unconsciously, in the
direction of the fibres that have had the severest strain.

Injury to the Sheaths of Tendons.—In sprains, however,
the trouble is generally more serious, and the symptoms more
definite. When, for example, a man falls down with his hand
and forearm doubled up beneath him, so that the whole of the
stress falls on the tendons at the back of the wrist, and the
soft and delicate tissues lying underneath are crushed against
the bone, the amount of damage sustained is not to be mistaken. Within a very few minutes the wrist swells up, the
tissues are bruised, the vessels torn across, and blood poured
out into the tendon sheaths and the structures round, just as
it is when any other part of the body is injured. Only because
there is a sac in which the fluid can collect, the swelling is
unusually rapid in making its appearance, and is limited at

first in shape. Soon, however, it begins to spread; the back of the hand swells up, though here it always feels softer than it does elsewhere; then it extends along the forearm, and even makes its appearance on the front of the wrist, probably because the tissues in this situation were crushed and squeezed at the moment of the fall. The skin becomes hot and tender; movement at the wrist is completely lost; the joint is kept nearly straight, and can neither be bent nor extended; the former movement is too painful, because then the extensor tendons are pressed against the part of their sheath that has already sustained the severest hurt; the latter is almost impossible, as tendons cannot work when their sheath is distended with fluid. Even the fingers suffer in the same way; though a certain amount of flexion is permitted, they cannot be bent into the palm of the hand or completely straightened out.

After a few days the bruise begins to come out near the elbow (generally on the front surface of the joint) and, perhaps, in the hand; the coloring matter from the blood soaks by degrees into all the surrounding structures, and spreads along the looser planes of cellular tissue until it reaches the skin. The swelling slowly diminishes, remaining longest over the tendons; the tenderness becomes more definitely localized, being chiefly felt over that part of the back of the wrist which corresponds to the spot where the tendons were most bent and crushed against the edge of the bone; the movement becomes more free; the amount of grating and creaking grows less and less, and if no adhesions have formed, and there are no other troubles to hinder the progress of recovery, voluntary power slowly comes back, though even in a moderately successful case it is sometimes months before all the thickening has disappeared and the joint can be completely flexed.

Inflammation.—Sometimes it happens that instead of the extravasated blood being absorbed, and the movements returning in this way, inflammation sets in either as the result of some constitutional predisposition, such as gout, or from the excess of tension in the tissues. Ordinarily speaking, it is not present at all. The changes which have been described above are identical with those that accompany any severe bruise; the swelling has been already accounted for; the increased amount of blood flowing through the part, causing the skin to become hot and sometimes red, and making it at the

same time more sensitive to pressure, is only what is required
by the increase in the need for repair; the pain is due to the
tension caused by the extravasation and effusion; and the loss
of mobility is the result in the early stages of the distention of
the sheath (for unless the tendon is tightly grasped it loses all
its power) and of the pain when the torn and bruised tissues
are pressed on; in the later ones, of the imperfect absorption
of the lymph that has been thrown out and of the stiffness
caused by prolonged rest. These are the great causes of the
delayed convalescence and of the obstinate rigidity that so
often follow such injuries. In the majority of instances there
is no more inflammation after these than there is after a simple fracture or a severe bruise.

When it does break out the severity of the symptoms is
not easily mistaken. The pain is intense; it is no longer a
question of a hot or burning sensation felt when an attempt is
made to move the tendon; the whole extremity throbs from
one end to the other. The temperature rises rapidly; the skin
grows red, and, if suppuration is going to follow, becomes
thick and swollen, so that it pits on pressure and can no
longer be raised up from the structures that lie beneath. At
the same time there is high fever, with headache and constitutional symptoms of great severity.

Inflammation of this description rarely remains limited to
the space in which it begins. Sheaths of tendons and bursæ
are, so far as their development is concerned, merely great interspaces in the cellular tissue, and they never lose their connection with the others around them. If they become inflamed, and their contents suppurate, the way lies open for the
pus to spread through all the cellular tissue of the limb. It
may even extend into the neighboring joints without there
being of necessity any direct or open communication between
them. I have many times seen complete destruction of an
articulation, even of such a one as the knee, occur as a result
of deep-seated suppuration that had found its starting-point
in the inflammation of a neighboring bursa or tendon sheath.

Imperfect Recovery.—Imperfect recovery, stiffness, and
loss of power are much more common. For a week or two
everything goes on well; the symptoms gradually diminish in
severity; the pain becomes less and less; the swelling disappears, except immediately over the tendons (there it always

lasts the longest), and a certain amount of voluntary movement is regained. But then the improvement stops. Every
attempt at further progress is checked at once by pain, and is
followed by an increase in the swelling. The muscles begin to
waste; the neighboring joints and tendons become stiff from
prolonged disuse; and sometimes the improvement already
won is lost again, and free movement of the tendons never returns completely.

There is no doubt that this is much more likely to happen
if the tendon sheath has been inflamed, and that then the results are, generally speaking, much more serious. Even when
it subsides fairly soon, inflammation, if it once involves a tendon sheath, always leaves behind it extensive, and sometimes
permanent, changes. But it is also certain that loss of movement, and other troubles, are met with after injuries of tendons in which inflammation never occurs at all. Complete
and permanent wasting of the muscles, and an absolute degree
of rigidity, may be uncommon; but, independently of these,
sprains are liable to be followed by a number of other consequences, which have nothing to do with inflammation, and
which are quite sufficient to give rise to the gravest inconvenience, and even to prolonged suffering.

Stiffness, for example, is rarely absent altogether. Some
time always passes before the tendons move, as they ought to
do, so easily that there is no consciousness of their existence.
Pain is equally common, and, indeed, is in general severe in proportion to the stiffness. It differs immensely in different cases.
In some there is a constant sense of aching, and of soreness
over the whole part, even when it is at rest. In others it is
only felt on movement, and then with great severity over certain spots. Swelling nearly always persists for a time. The
sheath is distended with fluid, or cysts develop in connection
with it; or there is some effusion into the cellular tissue round,
sometimes soft and yielding, at others hard and irregular. It
may continue without material change for an almost indefinite
time; more often it increases slightly in amount as often as
the tendon is much used. The skin may remain exceedingly
tender, especially over those spots where the swelling is
greatest, or where pain is felt when the tendon is moved.
Creaking and grating are almost universal. It is not merely
the delicate rustling, already mentioned, due to the alteration

in the lining cells, or to blood or lymph being mixed with the
synovia, but a much rougher, coarser sound, caused by the
presence of fringes, projecting up from the folds of the lining
membrane, like those in joints; or else by myriads of loose
bodies floating about in the fluid, in which the tendon lies and
moves.   Louder noises even may be audible in the later stages,
caused, in all likelihood, by the sudden separation of two surfaces that accurately fit each other.

Very often there is a peculiar feeling of weakness—not so
much actual loss of power in most cases as a sense of insecurity.   It occurs even with an ordinary ganglion on the back
of the wrist, and is almost invariable when one of these is
large enough to project distinctly under the skin.   The patient
complains of inability to use the hand, the flexor muscles being
as much interfered with as the extensor, owing, no doubt, to
the way in which they are always trained to act together.
When the dilatation involves the sheath itself, the sensation is
never wanting.   I have seen an instance in which a patient
was quite unable to bend his middle finger, merely because the
sheath of the flexor tendons along the under surface was distended with fluid.   There was no other obstacle; it could be
bent by the other hand, as far as mechanical considerations
would allow; and as soon as the fluid was removed by subcutaneous puncture, full power was regained.

Even this does not exhaust the list.   There are other consequences following sprains of tendons, similar to those already
described in the case of joints, involving parts that have not
sustained any direct injury.   Wasting, rigidity, and loss of
power in neighboring muscles; stiffening of the capsules and
sheaths of other joints and tendons; filling up of the cavities
of bursæ and other periarticular spaces; and many others
which are probably the result of prolonged rest and confinement in one position, rather than of anything else.   Inflammation, when it does break out, makes them all tenfold worse;
but it is not by any means necessary for their occurrence.
The injury sustained when a tendon sheath is badly bruised,
and then kept perfectly quiet for an indefinite length of time,
is quite sufficient to account for them in most cases without
calling in the aid of anything else.

Treatment.—So far as general principles are concerned, the
treatment of tendons, after they have been sprained, is very

similar to that already described in the case of joints. The great object is to restore the power of voluntary movement as soon as possible; everything else must be subordinate to this. Until this is perfect, recovery cannot be said to be complete.

The first obstacle is the extravasation of blood into the tissues, and the amount of lymph poured out afterward to effect the repair of the injury. The soft and vascular tissues, some of the most delicate in the body, are crushed and torn; blood flows out in all directions, until, if it is not checked in some way, the sheath and the cellular spaces round can contain no more. Then all the vessels dilate; everything swells up and becomes soft; the interstices in all directions are distended with lymph, which gradually takes the place of the blood as this is absorbed; and if no steps are taken to prevent such a result, the tendon, its sheath, the delicate tissues round, and even the neighboring muscles and fasciæ, so far as the injury has extended, become glued together. Of course, the extent to which this change takes place in the different tissues varies within very wide degrees. The tough, unyielding, and almost non-vascular substance of which a tendon is composed scarcely shows the change at all, while the soft and delicate tissue round and between the folds of the synovial sheath is so altered that it can hardly be recognized; but the principle is the same. The change is an essential one, the natural consequence of the injury, and has nothing to do with inflammation. Under certain conditions it may be carried to excess, and then it becomes a source of danger, and may even, by the help of other agencies, become the starting-point of this complication, the cause rather than the consequence. But this ought never to happen, and if the effusion can be restrained within proper limits, and the predisposing causes are not too strong, never does happen. No doubt inflammation follows if a patient, who is on the verge of an attack of gout, by some fall, strains or otherwise injures one of his tendons. It is only natural that it should, and it may come on within an hour after the accident, but it is not fair to put this down entirely to the credit of the injury.

There is another reason for trying to check the effusion as soon as possible. After tendons have been sprained there is always a certain degree of stiffness. This is dependent on

many things, and cannot be helped at first. But the perma-
nence of this stiffness, and its degree, are regulated almost entirely by the extent of the effusion, and by the changes that it
undergoes. If it is slight and quickly reabsorbed, leaving only
so much as is needed for the repair of the tissues, perfect movement is recovered spontaneously; but when it is excessive, and
all the surrounding structures are softened and infiltrated,
this can only happen under the most favorable conditions. As
a rule, much of it becomes organized; and then all the tissues
are made stiff and rigid, and are matted together by adhesions. The minute interstices between them, for the purpose
of allowing free and even play of movement, are filled up.
Probably during life they contain a semifluid material, so that
the structures on either side can easily accommodate each
other in their various movements; this quite disappears. In
worse cases, the opposite surfaces grow together, and the tendon becomes adherent to its sheath, either in places, here and
there, so that fibrous bands pass across from one to the other
and limit the range of action, or even all over, so that recovery,
so far as movement is concerned, is quite hopeless.

Pressure.—Heat or cold may be tried at first, as already
directed in speaking of joints, but by far the most efficacious
method is to apply well-graduated pressure from the very
commencement. The details, of course, must vary in each
case, but when this can be done systematically, not as bandaging ordinarily is, with the whole of the pressure on the
bones, nothing succeeds so well. Only there must be a
thorough knowledge, not only of the structure and arrangement of the parts, but also of the exact nature of the injury
sustained in each case.

Massage.—Massage or kneading is even more useful in the
treatment of sprained tendons and muscles than it is in the
case of joints. The second day, when the pads and bandages
are removed, the limb appears misshapen from the pressure to
which the soft tissues have been subjected, and stiff from their
confinement. Kneading and working the part thoroughly
every day causes this to disappear more rapidly and more
effectually than anything else. It must, of course, be done
with a definite idea of the purpose in view, and with a knowledge of the structure of the part itself. Further, as the accident is so recent, the ordinary rules must be observed with

even more than usual care. The rubbing at the commencement must be very light, affecting only the skin at first, and
then later the deepest structures. Tender spots must be ap-
proached very carefully; they need even more attention than
the rest, but, unless it is very cautious, manipulation makes
them more painful still. Every movement must be commenced
at the end of the limb, working gradually toward the trunk.
Properly managed, and used at the same time as passive
motion, the relief this gives is immense; the pain is exceedingly slight; the swelling disappears more rapidly than it does
under any other method, and the chances of after stiffness are
materially lessened.

Passive Movement.—There are the same rules with regard
to passive motion. It must be employed regularly and systematically every day without fail. The loose tissues round
the tendon sheath are softened and thickened; the surface of
the synovial sac is rough from the rapidity with which the
new cells are formed to line it in place of the old ones; and it
is irregular from the swelling of its folds and fringes. Unless
movement is kept up from the first this must end in some degree of stiffness. It need not be repeated often at each sitting;
once is quite enough, but it must be thorough. Every joint
and every tendon near the part that has been injured must be
worked at least once a day through its whole range of action.
Slight and faint-hearted attempts, apparent movements really
taking place at another joint, are useless, and throw discredit
on the treatment. They do not prevent the formation of adhesions, or break down those that are already established;
they merely pull and strain on the stiffened structures round,
and make them painful and tender without setting them free.
The adhesions, before they are too firm, are easily separated
by definite and well-regulated manipulation without any fear of
exciting inflammation. Even after they have become organized it is safer, as has already been shown in speaking of joints,
to break them down thoroughly and effectually with one single
effort than to keep perpetually straining and worrying them.
Weak and ineffectual attempts, carried on hap-hazard, without
any definite object in view, do more harm than good. They
increase the pain that is left, cause more lymph to be poured
out, prevent the absorption of that which is already there, and
allow it to accumulate until, as the adhesions grow thicker

and stronger, the prospect of recovery becomes more remote
than ever.

In the later stages, when the signs of bruising have nearly
disappeared, if the movement of the tendons remains painful
and constrained, and particularly if the patient can point out
certain spots which are especially tender after use, more energetic treatment is required, just as in cases of imperfect recovery after sprains of other parts.   Baths, douching, and
shampooing may be tried with success in many instances.
Tendons, even when very stiff, nearly always move more freely
after long soaking in hot water, and though they may not retain the whole, there is nearly always a certain amount of permanent improvement.   Galvanism, too, in these circumstances
is sometimes of great assistance in encouraging the circulation
and restoring muscular vigor.   Stimulating liniments, especially those containing the aromatic oils, are also most useful as
adjuncts.   They increase the flow of blood through the superficial parts, soothe the pain, and loosen and improve the nutrition of the skin.   In this way they are of assistance to other
measures which they cannot replace.   If there are large and
tender muscular masses, which remain stiff and painful, acupuncture often acts with good effect, as described in speaking
of sprains of the back; and counter-irritants and small light
blisters, often repeated, are of excellent service in many of
these cases.   If, however, the tender spots are very definitely
marked, and if they become more painful and tender regularly
after certain movements, these methods are rarely sufficient
to secure more than mere temporary relief.   Something further
is required.

More Permanent Changes, Adhesions, etc.—It may be
that there is the residue of an old organized blood clot, outside
the sheath altogether, forming a little hard, irregular mass,
that is pressed on in certain positions when the tendon is
stretched.   I have known this it the neighborhood of the knee,
in the fibrous expansion given off by the extensor muscle.   It
was merely a little blood clot, following a blow, lying underneath the fibres; but probably there was a nerve filament
near it, for the least contraction of the muscle gave rise to an
amount of pain seemingly out of all proportion.   I have little
doubt that the same thing sometimes occurs in connection
with deeper tendons.

In other cases there is an adhesion, or some thickening on the tendon sheath, or there are fringes or loose bodies in the interior continually shifting their position, and keeping up a certain amount of effusion, by the way the sheath is bruised when the tendon moves over it. It is extraordinary what a degree of pain and tenderness may be caused by a body of this kind, whether in a tendon sheath or bursa. Quite recently a patient, a woman of middle age, with rather stout and shapeless limbs, was sent to me, complaining that she had received a blow on the knee about a month before, and that ever since she had suffered such an amount of inconvenience that she could scarcely get about. Walking had become very painful; going upstairs was bad, but coming down she had such a sense of insecurity that she was obliged to cling to the banisters, a statement which I have often heard when there was anything interfering with the action of the extensor of the knee. On examining the joint, it appeared slightly enlarged, but most of the swelling was below the knee-cap on each side of the ligamentum patellæ, caused apparently by the enlargement of the bursa, which exists naturally in this situation, and which is always larger and more prominent in women than it is in men. It was over this that she had received the blow, and here on firm pressure could be felt a large loose body, which, when the muscle was relaxed, slipped easily under the ligament from one side of the joint to the other, causing each time a very peculiar and sickening sensation.

In the same way I have on several occasions been able to trace the development of foreign bodies in the bursa lying in front of the knee-cap. In this situation they give rise to little inconvenience, as a rule, until in kneeling down and reaching forward the weight of the body is brought to bear upon the patella; then there is a sudden stab of acute pain, and within a few hours the bursa becomes filled with fluid. Sometimes there is only one, irregular in size and shape, but often, owing probably to the repetition of the injury before advice is sought, the number is very considerable; or if the first is due to injury, the others may result from the persistent degree of irritation, and even of inflammation, maintained by its presence.

When the pain can be traced definitely to a cause of this kind, there is no alternative. The patient must be placed under an anæsthetic to avoid suffering, and to secure complete muscular relaxation; the part must be thoroughly examined, and the adhesion, if one is present, broken down, or the foreign body removed.   Whatever the cause of the continued tenderness may be, it very rarely happens that it is of a nature to be cured by prolonged rest.   In the great majority of instances it is due to this having been too much prolonged already. Most of the crippled joints and tendons that are met with after sprains are due* to the fact that passive movement has not been employed sufficiently early or sufficiently thoroughly; and they are only to be cured by the adoption of measures that must be energetic in proportion to the delay.

Ganglions.—Some of these after-consequences, ganglions, for example, require a certain amount of notice, as they either do not occur in connection with sprains of joints, or, when they do, must be treated in a special way.   There are two varieties of these; one is a small cyst, originally in connection with the sheath, and probably due in the first place to a protrusion of the sac through a weakened or ruptured part of the wall; the other is a dilatation of the sheath itself.   There is no essential difference between these, so far as their origin is concerned; they both frequently originate in strains, though it is possible some may arise from inflammation or in other ways; they contain the same kind of fluid, a clear gelatinous substance, much thicker than natural, and devoid of all lubricating power; and it is often possible to find transition forms between them, sheaths, that is to say, irregularly distended, so that they appear to be sacculated; but the symptoms to which they give rise, and the method of treatment to be adopted, are very different.   The former are by far the most common, and occur with especial frequency on the back of the wrist, where they give rise to much annoyance by their unsightly appearance, and by the sensation of weakness that accompanies them. They are met with, however, as well on the foot, on the outside of the knee, just by the head of the fibula, and in other places; indeed, there is hardly a tendon sheath in the body from which they do not sometimes project.   As a rule, the inconvenience they cause is not serious, but it is not uncommon to meet with instances in which neuralgic pain of a severe character is a prominent symptom, probably because some small cutaneous nerve happens to be pressed upon by the cyst in certain positions of the limb.

Simple Ganglion.—The ordinary method of treating these is to crush them by direct pressure, and then gradually squeeze the contents into the surrounding tissues, so that they may be absorbed, assisting the process from time to time by friction and kneading, or by the pressure of a leaden plate. Or they may be punctured, and the fluid let out, and if they fill again, injected with iodine, or a small seton passed through them. Or a small tenotomy knife may be introduced on one side of the cyst, and the whole mass divided in two by a horizontal cut; this answers better than the others, as it is impossible for the sac, when it has once been treated in this way, to fill again; but none of these methods are quite satisfactory. They often succeed, it is true; but, even when the cyst does not return, it is very common for a hard irregular mass to be left behind, interfering with the action of the tendons, and causing an unsightly tumor. I have known a swelling of this kind persist unaltered for twenty years in spite of continued attempts by kneading and other measures to get rid of it.

When it is desired to remove them thoroughly and finally, it answers much better to dissect them out. There is no difficulty unless they have been ruptured and squeezed several times before; they separate readily from everything round except the tendon sheath. Generally they are firmly attached to this, and often when the uniting band is severed the tendon may be caught sight of, lying in its groove, and showing that the cyst was in communication with its sheath. If the operation is done carefully, and the hand kept on a splint for a day or two after, the cure is effectual, and the scar can scarcely be seen at the end of a week. If, however, the cyst has been much handled first, particularly if several unsuccessful attempts at squeezing it have been made, it must be left for some time before attempting any such proceding.

Compound Ganglion.—It is more serious when the dilatation involves the sheath itself, especially if it is a large compound one, including many tendons, such as that in the palm of the hand, or if it is in the immediate neighborhood of a joint. Even where there is only a single tendon, and the size of the sheath is not very great, the inconvenience is often considerable; but in these cases the character of the wall rarely undergoes much change, and if they are not cured by blistering or tapping they are certain to yield to subcutaneous incision,

followed by pressure and passive motion. In the larger ones
the lining membrane and the contents have, generally speaking, undergone such modifications that it is often impossible to
promise more than relief.

Like the others, their origin may sometimes be traced to
a single strain, though it is more usual for them to develop as
a result of repeated injury. In proportion to their number,
communications with joints are certainly more frequent; but
this, of course, is mainly regulated by anatomical considerations, and by the condition of the joints themselves. If these
are affected by rheumatic gout, or if cysts develop from them
for other reasons, it is all the more likely to occur. Sometimes
the connection is due, as I have seen myself, to the enormous
size of the ganglion; it grows larger and larger until the
structures in between are so thinned by absorption that they
give way, but more often, as Morrant Baker has shown, the
reverse of this happens, diverticula form along tendon sheaths,
or through weak parts in the capsule of joints, and appear
perhaps some distance off as cysts which closely resemble
ganglions.

The fluid in the interior may be identical with that found
in the smaller forms, or it may be more liquid and less gelatinous. It develops in a very short space of time; I have
found it present and of typical consistence within three weeks
of a strain. The wall is usually much altered in character; in
one instance it was in a condition almost identical with that
met with in joints as a result of strumous inflammation, greatly
thickened, that is to say, much too vascular, semi-translucent
in appearance, and covered over on its inner surface with
numerous little granulations. In other cases it is much tougher
and firmer, and projects into the interior in great folds and
fringes, which lie between the tendons, and seriously interfere
with their action. Occasionally, the sheath is divided into
chambers, and very often it contains numbers of minute bodies
of the same shape and size as melon seeds. What these are
formed of is not absolutely certain in all cases; it seems most
probable that, in the majority, they are developed either from
the fibrin of extravasated blood, or from lymph that has collected in the sheath, and has been worked continually backward and forward by the movements of the tendons. When
they are present in any number the wall is, as a rule, coated

over and roughened with material of the same character, so that probably the latter explanation is correct. They contain no cells or fibres; on the addition of acetic acid they swell up so as to become translucent. All that can be made out is an indistinct concentric marking, as if they were formed of layer after layer of some fibrinous material.

Ganglions such as these must be treated on totally different principles to the smaller ones. Palliative measures are of little use; free subcutaneous division of the wall has been practiced with success in some of the simpler ones, where there are no melon-seed bodies; and in the case of the great palmar one, section of the ligament that divides it in two has been recommended, but I have had no experience of it. Generally speaking, the sac must be laid open freely, the whole of the fluid removed, together with the melon-seed bodies present, any partitions that exist, dividing the interior into chambers, thoroughly broken down, and even in some instances it is necessary to scrape the wall, so as to clear it from the adherent lymph. Then it must be drained so that it does not refill. Naturally this operation is a very serious one. There is great danger of inflammation setting in, and even if it does not, some permanent degree of rigidity, in spite of the early use of passive motion, is always left behind. If it does, the consequences may be disastrous to the very last degree.

Cysts that develop in connection with joints, whether as a result of injury or of rheumatic gout, or of both together, must either be left alone or treated in the same way. In this one would be guided mainly by the age and constitution of the patient, the condition of the joint as regards security and movement, and the size and rapidity of formation of the cyst. I have seen them in connection with the shoulder, ankle, and knees; and no doubt they may occur in other joints as well. Sometimes they caused but little inconvenience; at others they spread so rapidly, and attained such a size, that it was absolutely necessary to drain them. In nearly all there was a great deal of stiffness afterward, but this was due in part to the original disease; one of them suppurated.

CHAPTER XII.

SPRAINS OF THE BACK AND NECK.

SPRAINS of the back and neck are sufficiently common and important to deserve a certain amount of separate consideration. The structures concerned are exceedingly complicated; there is an immense number of separate joints of various shape and size, and in addition there is the spinal cord running in a canal down nearly the whole of its length, and giving off the nerves which pass out on either side between the bones. Nor do the injuries themselves vary less in character and severity. In some they are exceedingly slight; in others the consequences are as serious as any that occur in surgery. Some, too, have gained a most unenviable notoriety from their connection with railway accidents; for whatever may be the truth as regards many of these cases, whether they are deceptions or not, there can be no question that sometimes very considerable injuries are produced by the way in which the backbone, and the structures in connection with it, are strained and wrenched when the body is thrown violently backward and forward as it is in collisions.

One of the most singular features in connection with these sprains is the way in which the backbone itself, and the muscular and ligamentous structures around it, are overlooked and ignored. Even in the ordinary accidents of every-day life there is a great tendency to lay everything that is serious or lasting to the credit of the spinal cord. In railway cases there is no hesitation at all; if any serious result ensues it must be the consequence of damage this structure has sustained, or of inflammation following it; little or no attention is paid to anything else. Yet it is difficult to see why the other structures should enjoy immunity. The vertebral column may be strained, especially in the cervical and lumbar regions; the ligaments torn or stretched; the nerves bruised or crushed; the smaller

joints between the segments twisted and wrenched; the muscles detached from their bed and torn across, or thrown into
such a state of cramp that they become rigid and unable to
act with freedom; or the fibrous sheath which contains them
and helps to secure the bones laid open and filled with blood.
Results, in short, of the most serious description are not uncommon, and often leave lasting evidence of their existence behind, when the spinal cord itself escapes completely.

Injuries of the Spinal Cord.—When it is hurt the symptoms cannot easily be mistaken. There may be insensibility
for a time even when the head is not injured. A certain degree of shock is always present, and when this has passed off
there is paralysis or loss of power, corresponding in extent
and degree to the amount of injury sustained. This may
make itself apparent at once, or some time, even hours, may
elapse before there is any definite evidence of its presence.
Sometimes it is so slight that it can only be detected by the
most careful investigation; at others it is so severe as to give
rise to the suspicion of fracture or dislocation. Generally
speaking, when it is due to bruising, or to what is still more
common, effusion of blood into the tissues round the cord so as
to compress it, the symptoms begin to diminish at the end of
a few days. Recovery may then progress without interruption
until it is complete, or it may be arrested at any point, leaving behind it greater or less impairment of power. Sensibility
is frequently affected, too, but it rarely suffers in anything like
the same degree. If it is lost completely the prognosis must
be regarded as exceedingly grave, for it nearly always indi-
cates that at some one point the cord has been crushed and
disorganized. Sometimes a certain amount of hyperæsthesia
or increased sensitiveness of skin may be detected over a small
area immediately above the seat of injury, but the general
tenderness all down the spine, which is such a common symptom in sprains of the back, whether they occur in railroad accidents or elsewhere, and the strange sensations, such as
crawling, creeping, or tingling, experienced in the limbs, are
probably due entirely to other causes. They are certainly
met with in cases in which there is no reasonable ground for
suspicion that the cord itself has been hurt in any way.

Into this part of the question, however, it is not my intention to enter at present. Injuries of the spinal cord, and the

consequences that may result from them, are matters much
too serious to be regarded merely as complications of sprains
of the back, and the subject has been already exhaustively
treated by Page in his work on "Injuries of the Spine and
Spinal Cord." My contention merely is that a very large
number of the symptoms which are usually considered as
definite proof that the spinal cord has been hurt may be, and
in a large proportion of instances probably are, due altogether
to the injuries that the other structures in the back must sustain in such accidents.

Injury to the Muscles and Ligaments; Sprains.—S. C.,
thirty-two years of age, a strong, healthy man of exceptionally
good physique, in getting out of a barge slipped and pitched
head-foremost into the hold among some bales of goods. The
shock was in a measure checked by his hands, or he would
almost inevitably have broken his neck. As it was, he lay for
some moments unable to extricate himself, with his head
doubled under him and his chin driven down upon his chest.
He did not lose consciousness; there was no concussion or
other injury to his brain; there was no fracture or dislocation
anywhere about his spine, though, owing to the severity of the
shock he had sustained, he was unable to stand upright, and it
was almost certain that his spinal cord had not suffered any
very serious hurt, for after he had recovered from the shock he
was able to move his arms and legs about freely in all directions.
Sensation was not in the least impaired; there was no tingling
or feeling of pins and needles; nor was there that peculiar
sense of constriction round the body as if a string were tied
round it, of which so many patients complain. The stress had
fallen almost entirely on the muscles and ligaments at the
back of the neck; these, no doubt, were severely strained, and
it seems probable from what followed that the nerves running
from the spinal cord had suffered in the same way.

The next day the shock had completely passed off. He
had slept but little during the night, and he still felt giddy,
everything seeming to go round when he attempted to sit upright; but he had recovered his natural color and expression,
and the pulse and temperature were perfectly normal. He
had completely lost, however, the power of moving his head
or neck; the least attempt, especially nodding, brought on
severe attacks of pain, shooting up over his head and behind

his ears on each side, so that he sat either with his chin resting on his hand, or with his thumbs behind his ears and his fingers grasping his face. Indeed, without support of some kind he seemed unable to hold his head upright. He complained of his back and neck feeling weak, as if he were going to be paralyzed, mistaking, as Hood has pointed out, the fear of movement due to the pain it causes for actual loss of power. The skin was exceedingly tender to the touch, as it is over every sprained joint, and there was a certain degree of swelling, very ill-defined in outline, over the part that had been most severely strained. What caused him most apprehension, however, was the difficulty that he felt in opening his mouth. He could shut it easily enough, but slight as is the muscular effort required to move it in the opposite direction, it was almost too much for him. The muscles which act from the upper part of the chest, and help to form a fixed point from which the lower jaw can work, were unable to do their fair share. They had not been injured themselves, but the nerves supplying them had been strained in the neck at the moment of the fall, and were unable to carry the necessary stimuli. For the same reason his breathing was very shallow and his speech slow and deliberate.

In a few days this began to pass away; the sense of strength returned, and movement became much more easy; but for a long time a peculiar sensation could be detected in the neck when the head was turned from side to side, as if two roughened surfaces were being rubbed against each other, or some dense fluid, such as extravasated blood, were being squeezed to and fro in the meshes of the cellular tissue. Gradually this, too, disappeared, but in spite of repeated blistering, the stiffness still persisted in the back of his neck. Improvement went on fairly rapidly up to a certain point, but then came to a standstill. Forcible manipulation, however, assisted by thorough kneading, soon effected a cure.

In this case the mischief was well defined, the ultimate recovery, though it was delayed for some time, was complete, and there was no inflammation or other complication. The cord itself was not injured, though just at first there was reasonable ground for suspicion; the whole of the symptoms were due to the damage the muscles and ligaments had sustained, and to the way in which the nerves were stretched.

In all probability, as Page has pointed out, many of the cases of what is sometimes called railway spine may be accounted for in this way. The symptoms, because they are serious and persistent, are referred to the spinal cord, instead of to the structures which surrounded and are especially intended to protect it.

Paralysis is one of these. Where this really exists there can be no question that the spinal cord, or the nerves at their exit from it, have sustained some exceedingly grave hurt. It may be that curious, almost indefinable, effect known, for want of a better term, as shock to the nervous system; or it may be actual bruising and laceration; something of the kind there must be, and in such a case it is necessary to exercise the most extreme precaution in the question of prognosis. But it often happens that, without the least intention of deceiving, patients describe themselves as paralyzed, or unable to perform some particular action, when, as a matter of fact, the attempt is merely prevented by pain, or, what is still more singular, by the belief that they cannot. Hood has pointed out how patients often describe a joint as feeling weak, speaking of it as if it were in need of some mechanical support, when the real cause is the dread of calling into action muscles that are stiffened from disuse or rheumatism. So it is with the spine; after a severe strain there is a certain amount of difficulty about calling the muscles into play, just as there is when they are affected by lumbago, and the patient is naturally very apt to think that he has lost power over them, and is going to be paralyzed. This was the case in the instance that I have quoted above, and similar examples affecting different parts of the body, according to the seat of injury, are of exceedingly common occurrence.

Hyperæsthesia, again, or increased sensitiveness of the skin, is always regarded with great apprehension. In some particular cases, as I have mentioned already, it is true that it is a symptom of injury to the spinal cord; but in the great majority, especially in those in which it extends down the whole of the spinal column, it occurs for exactly the same reason that it does over any sprained ligament, or muscle, and means nothing more.

The crawling sensations, too, that are complained of in various parts of the body, the tingling, and pins and needles, are still more ambiguous. Often they are due to causes of an entirely different nature, pressure or traction, for example, on some of the nerves, or some alteration in the amount of blood flowing through the part; they cannot, at least in the absence of other evidence, be regarded as proof that the spinal cord has suffered to the exclusion of everything else. Occasionally even more remarkable symptoms are met with. In one case under my own observation, where the patient sustained a very severe strain with some contusion in the lower part of the dorsal region, there were typical attacks of what are known as lightning pains, shooting round the body with great intensity, and then ceasing abruptly; yet there was no evidence at any time that the injury had involved the spinal cord itself.

In short, these symptoms, which are usually regarded as definite proof that the cord has been injured, so far as they prove anything, are rather suggestive of injury to the structures that lie round it and protect it. These must sustain the brunt of the violence in any accident; the cord itself is placed in the position of the greatest possible security, protected as far as it can be from any external hurt, so that in the vast majority of instances it (very fortunately) escapes. From its great importance, and from the disastrous results when it is injured, it has caused everything else to be overlooked and forgotten.

Injury to the Bones.—Of the frequency with which the bones are affected there can be little doubt. Injuries of the back, in the shape of blows or strains, have to account for a very large proportion of cases of disease of the spine; and, probably, if the history of the rest could be obtained, it would be found to be true of most of these. It is difficult, of course, to bring forward direct proof of this; but a certain amount of confirmation may be obtained from the locality in which this affection is most common. A blow may affect any part; but strains, in such a structure as the vertebral column, are always felt most severely where a rigid and a flexible segment are joined together—where, for example, the neck or the lumbar region joins the thorax, which, from the attachment of the ribs and for other reasons, is peculiarly stiff. At any rate, whether this is the explanation or not, it is a fact that disease of the spine is particularly common at these two spots.

Injury to the Smaller Joints.—Sometimes the strain falls

on the smaller joints between the vertebræ, though it must be
admitted that it is rarely possible to find any direct evidence
of their being hurt. There are so many of them; they lie so
close to each other; and the amount of movement possessed
by each is so slight that unless the injury is extremely localized its effect is spread too widely to strain any single one.
It is not improbable, however, that they suffer more often than
is generally suspected; only the injury, owing to the depth at
which they lie, and the way in which they are covered in by
muscles, is not correctly diagnosed. At least, evidence of
past mischief is sometimes found post-mortem, long after all
history is forgotten; and suppuration even has been known to
occur, and to spread until it made its way into the spinal canal,
and involved the cord itself.

Ligaments.—The structures, however, which bear the
brunt of strains, are the bands of fibrous tissue, and the muscles on the back and on either side of the vertebral column.
With regard to these, the part played by the former is entirely
mechanical. Close under the surface there is a broad sheet of
extraordinary strength, extending outward over the muscles,
binding them down, and protecting them so far as it can from
being overstretched. A little deeper it is much more delicate
and vascular, forming sheaths for all the separate slips, and
uniting them closely to each other. Deeper still it becomes
strong again; but here the fibres are short and irregular in
direction, running between the prominences with which the
bones are covered, and acting the part of ligaments. This
fibrous tissue cannot stretch. When the violence is so great
that the muscles are overcome, or so sudden that they are
caught unawares, it resists as long as it can; then it gives
way, rarely at any one single spot; more often here and there,
where it is attached to the bones, or becomes continuous with
the muscles.

Muscles.—These, on the other hand, are the most active
ligaments the back possesses. Not only do they move one
bone upon another, but, within certain limits, they are the
main agents by which the extent of the movement is regulated.
When those limits are passed, and, as a rule, not till then, the
purely passive fibrous bands are called into play.

The result of this is that, as a rule, in accidents of this kind,
the muscles suffer to a very serious extent. Sometimes they

are overstretched, and lose their power of contracting again;
or they are seized with cramp; or they are crushed together
and bruised. Sometimes there is a great effusion of blood into
their substance, so that they become swollen and painful; or
the sheath of fascia which surrounds them is split open to such
a degree that they are displaced entirely from their surroundings, and dislocated; or they are even torn in two or wrenched
from their attachments.

Dislocation of Muscles.—Many of these injuries occur
commonly in sprains of other joints, but one of them, dislocation, is, if not confined to the back, at least very rarely met
with elsewhere. It is most common in the neck, for here the
movements are very rapid and extensive, while the muscles
are especially long and slender. The head is suddenly twisted
round to look in some awkward direction; there is a sudden
sharp stab of pain, often causing the patient to cry out; something appears to be caught, and the head is held fixed. In a
minute or two, when the acute pain has subsided, it can generally be brought nearly straight again; but it requires considerable effort, and it cannot be turned so as to face in the
opposite direction, or even kept straight for long. As soon as
it is allowed to assume the position of least discomfort, it bends
over once more to the affected side. Careful examination in
these cases sometimes shows a tender spot on the contracted
side, slightly too prominent. If this corresponds in position
and direction to some muscular slips, and if, when the part is
manipulated, the swelling disappears, and full and painless
mobility is instantaneously restored, it can hardly be doubted
that the symptoms were due to the dislocation of one of these,
which has slipped back into its place again. In some cases an
audible snap can be heard by the patient at the moment of
reduction; and, in one under my own care, an incautious movement on the part of the patient, before repair was complete,
reproduced the displacement.

I have known several instances in which, from the practically instantaneous character of the relief, it is almost certain
that this had happened; but I must admit it is much more
common for the swelling to disappear gradually and for voluntary power to return by slow degrees. Probably, in these
instances, there is no real dislocation; the muscular fibres are
either in a state of painful and spasmodic contraction, such as is

common in the leg after unusual exertion, or some of them have been torn and strained, so that movement is painful until the injury is repaired, and the extravasated blood absorbed again.

I have never met with any similar unmistakable dislocation in the loins, though, no doubt, from the description given by Callender, its occurrence is quite possible. The patient, he narrates, was carrying a heavy weight on his shoulders, when he suddenly slipped, and, in spite of all he could do, was swung round by the momentum. The pain for the moment was intense, and though it did not continue his back remained stiff, so that he could not move about with proper freedom. On examining the part there was one very tender spot in the muscles by the side of the spine, where a decided irregularity could be detected; this was diagnosed as a dislocation. The patient was instructed to repeat, so far as he could, the movements he went through as he fell; and while doing this firm pressure was made on the painful spot. The swelling disappeared at once; full power of movement was regained; and the sensation of stiffness completely vanished. The case was completed, and the diagnosis verified by a subsequent repetition of the accident.

Method of Reduction.—In any injury of this description, even if the presence of a dislocation is not certain, it is always worth while to carry out some simple manipulation such as that described above. Whatever may be the reason, whether it relaxes spasm, or whatever it does, it is a fact that almost immediate relief is sometimes gained by this, though the symptoms are not in the least characteristic. In one case under my own care there was no history of an accident at all. The patient was a young man, healthy enough himself, but of rheumatic and gouty parentage. He had been sitting incautiously in a draught when overheated, and got an attack of muscular rheumatism. Curiously enough, however, the pain was limited to one side, and almost to one spot; had he met with an accident, I should at once have suspected the existence of a strain. In spite of the history, however, I determined to try the effect of sudden vigorous contraction, and accordingly made him sit down on a low seat, with his feet firmly pressed against the wall in front, so that the pelvis should be securely fixed. The tender spot was carefully marked, and then it was explained to him that he must stoop forward as low as possible, and at the word of command suddenly straighten himself up. One arm was placed under his chest to assist him in this, and the thumb of the other hand firmly pressed upon the tender spot. The patient carried his part out loyally, in spite of the pain, and was completely and thoroughly cured at the second attempt. Some pain and stiffness returned in the course of the next day, but determined extension and contraction of the muscles involved, relieved him without further assistance.

It is very important in accidents of this kind to get a perfectly accurate account of the way in which it happened, and the smallest details often prove of great importance. The chief difficulty is to determine whether the seat of injury is one of the smaller joints, or a muscular slip by the side of it. Sometimes a soft and rather indefinite swelling can be made out beneath the skin; more often there is merely a certain amount of local tenderness, with a sensation of stiffness, or of inability to execute some particular movement, amounting in some cases, as has been already mentioned, even to a suspicion of paralysis in the patient's mind. Bruising is rarely seen, owing to the depth at which the injured part lies.

If the situation corresponds fairly well with the position and direction of some slender slip of muscle, the assistance of the patient must be called in, and what is required of him thoroughly explained. There are two chief ways in which the reduction may be effected; sometimes one succeeds, sometimes the other. In the first the patient is placed in an attitude that relaxes the injured part as much as possible, and then, while the hand or finger is firmly pressed upon it, is made to bring it suddenly and vigorously into action. In the second, which is rather the better—for it is very difficult at once, and when suffering pain, to move the back or neck quickly in any given direction at a moment's notice—the body is placed so that the dislocated slip is put upon the stretch, and held in that position by the operator, while the patient endeavors to straighten himself up against the resistance. The muscle suddenly contracts, alters its shape and consistence, and, from the relief that is experienced afterward, must, apparently, slip back again into its bed. Sometimes there is a sharp feeling of pain at the moment, and the preliminary stretching is always disagreeable, but the use of an anæsthetic is, of course, impossible.

Muscular Pain.—The most common trouble, however, after

sprains is something different to this, and is probably closely
allied to muscular rheumatism. It may be the result of unusually severe, or of unusually prolonged effort; nothing is
felt at the time, or for a few hours; then, generally speaking,
at night a peculiar aching sensation begins to make itself felt.
The skin is often tender to the touch, especially over the points
that correspond to the exit through the fascia of the cutaneous
nerves; but there is no heat or redness. The tissues show no
sign of bruising; steady pressure, though it is unpleasant at
first, gives relief rather than causes pain; and, except as a result of disturbed rest and sleep, there is no fever or constitutional disturbance. There is merely a constant wearing pain,
with a sensation of stiffness and want of power, that renders
rest for any length of time impossible, and entirely prevents
the patient holding himself upright or moving about with
freedom.

What may be the actual nature of the change in the tissues
is uncertain in many of these cases. In some, no doubt, there
is rupture, or straining of the muscular fibres, or there are
minute hæmorrhages; but from the practical identity of the
symptoms with those of myalgia, due to cold or gout, it seems
probable that the cause is to be sought in the 'changed condition of the circulation, or of the nutrition of the part. During
contraction of the muscles a much larger amount of blood
flows through them than when they are at rest, and the blood-
vessels are very much dilated. It is possible that when this is
carried to excess by prolonged overwork it is succeeded by a
condition of passive congestion, the vessels being overloaded,
and the blood unable to circulate as freely or as rapidly as it
should. Then the waste products accumulate and act as
sources of irritation, and fresh material to replace that which
is exhausted by fatigue is not supplied in sufficient quantity.
Probably in those who are young and healthy this is not of
material consequence; it merely causes a certain amount of
muscular stiffness, which soon subsides when the part is rested
and the natural equilibrium once more restored; but if any
constitutional taint, such as gout or rheumatism, is present
too, it seems to stamp the complaint with its own peculiar
character, and makes it tenfold more severe.

The most common situation for this to occur is in the loins,
owing to the large masses of muscle situated there, and to the

way in which they are called upon for unusual or sudden exertion in lifting heavy weights; but it may occur anywhere,
even in the extremities. Wherever it is, care must be taken
not to confound it with other disorders. It is not uncommon
for affections, even of such distant parts as the viscera, to be
attended by pain in various regions of the spine. To say nothing of examples which must occur to every one, I have known
the back-pain of incipient small-pox treated as lumbago, and
massage has before now been vigorously applied to a case of
stone in the kidney.

General Treatment.—In the milder cases merely local
treatment may suffice, but it is so common for an outbreak of
some complaint (the existence of which may hitherto not have
been suspected) to follow strains, that practically in all general
treatment adapted to the particular constitution of each
patient is essential. Just as an injury to the foot is often the
apparent cause of the first attack of gout, so many of the
muscular strains of the back owe at any rate their persistent
character to the presence of some similar complication. It is
for this reason that careful attention to diet is so necessary;
and that such drugs as colchicum, iodide of potash, chloride
of ammonia, the carbonates of the alkalies, and others prove
so useful. Only it rarely happens that any indication as to
which of these internal remedies is likely to prove most beneficial can be derived from the condition of the back itself.
This is only to be ascertained by carefully inquiring into the
previous history of the patient, and thoroughly investigating
the other symptoms that are present. In other words, local
measures should be employed to relieve the pain and stiffness,
and to restore the condition of the muscles as soon as possible;
but it must not be forgotten that the general state of the patient in most instances needs quite as much attention.

Local Measures. Warmth.—Warmth, either applied to
the part itself, or generally over the whole surface of the body,
is of excellent service in relieving the consequences of strains.
The simplest plan is to wring a piece of flannel out of water as
hot as can be borne, or to roast it in front of a fire, and press
it firmly upon the affected area, renewing it from time to time
as it cools. The skin becomes red; more blood circulates
through it, and probably a considerable amount is diverted
from the deeper parts; the congestion is relieved for the time

being; the waste products are carried away; more nutritive
material is supplied, and the stiffness certainly diminishes. Or
bags of hot sand, or salt, may be used; they retain the heat
considerably longer, and from the way in which they can be
fitted into any irregularity of surface, are particularly suited
to certain parts of the body. If this is not convenient, the
electric brush may be tried, passing it regularly all over the
surface of the skin after it has been thoroughly dried first to
increase the resistance. It is probable that the benefit derived
from this is due almost entirely to the influence it possesses
on the blood-vessels, and not in any way to the chemical effects
of the current.

Baths.—Hot-water or vapor baths are almost too well
known to require mention. Turkish ones also enjoy a great
reputation, especially for recent cases, and among those who
are accustomed to them. For others, they must be recommended with a certain amount of caution, and the subsequent
treatment in any case requires much more attention than it
usually receives. At Aix, when the full effect is desired, the
patient, after his bath, is quickly dried, wrapped in blankets,
and carried in a sedan chair to his hotel. As soon as he reaches
his apartment he is lifted into bed, still swathed like a mummy,
covered up with additional blankets and a quilt, and left to
perspire for a longer or shorter period. After twenty minutes
or half an hour he is carefully rubbed down by an attendant
who had accompanied him from the bath. Where this is im-
practicable, the patient should at least be very careful not to
hurry away, but to remain two or three hours if necessary, and
above all, to make sure that he is properly covered up.

When the complaint has already lasted some time, douche
baths may be employed, conjointly with vapor baths. The
patient should be seated on a wooden stool, with the feet immersed in warm water so as to avoid chill, and then jets may
be directed against his back in any required direction. The
size of the jet must be regulated by the amount of pressure,
and by the temperature of the water; but it is rarely advisable
for it to be more than a quarter of an inch in diameter, and it
is always best to begin with warm water, and gradually replace it by cold. The effect is greatly enhanced by massage
afterward.

Those who have never tried these baths, or who suffer

either from giddiness and a feeling of fullness in the head, or from a sensation of faintness after their use, may be recommended to take local ones with perfect safety. If the patient is in bed, a cradle may be placed over the body so as to leave a space round him, beneath the bedclothes, and the steam of a kettle introduced by means of properly-arranged tubing, until the desired effect is produced, taking care not to scald the patient's legs. Where he can sit on a chair, it is more convenient to arrange a mackintosh, or, if this is not available, a blanket, round his neck, so as to reach the floor on all sides, and then to place under the seat of a chair a spirit lamp with some boiling water. Both these methods insure copious perspiration within a very few minutes, and possess the great advantage of not affecting the patient's head or interfering with his respiration. Further, there is less risk of catching cold afterward, and aggravating or reproducing the original trouble; if the bath is taken of an evening, the patient can be placed in bed at once, and nearly always can make sure of some hours' refreshing sleep.

At Aix-les-Bains, according to Dr. Stewart, the method is still more highly elaborated. When the patient is sent to have a steam bath (the Berthollet, as it is termed), he is directed to an apartment which contains a curious wooden box, with a round hole in the movable lid. After undressing, he steps into the box, and finds that he is shut in all but the head, the round hole being occupied by his neck. Immediately a valve on the level of the floor is opened, the hot vapor rises about him, and he soon begins to perspire freely. The perspiration running down his brow trickles from his face. Presently he feels the streams flow down his sides and legs, and very speedily a feeling of oppression and debility comes on. After ten or twenty minutes the bath is opened up, the patient carefully dried, and removed to his hotel.

Hot-water baths act in the same way. The beneficial effect they exercise is almost entirely due to their temperature, and proportionate, within limits, to the length of application. The salts that they contain, whether neutral, alkaline, or sulphuretted, are of very little consequence. If they exist in certain degrees of concentration, they stimulate the cutaneous circulation, but that is all. For this reason peat or mud baths are, as a rule, more efficacious. The one feature common to

all bathing establishments which enjoy a high repute is the
temperature of the water, and probably the benefit derived
from .the use of the baths (as distinguished from a sojourn at
the place) is due entirely to this.

Friction.—Friction, either with the hand or with a flesh
brush, is very grateful in these cases. The direction should be
upward, toward the head, and the strokes light and rapid.
The effect is, to a certain extent, the same as that of heat;
there is a temporary contraction of the vessels near the surface, followed by a more lasting dilatation and more rapid circulation of the blood. It possesses, however, in addition, considerable influence on the nerves of sensation, and it is not
improbable that it is felt even more widely than this would
imply. At least, it is difficult to explain on other grounds the
undoubted power which steady friction along the back seems
to possess in allaying some forms of nervous excitement and
inducing sleep.

Liniments.—Stimulating liniments, containing camphor,
ammonia, or turpentine, may be usefully employed in conjunction with either friction or heat. Sprinkling a few drops of
turpentine on the heated flannel before applying it is generally sufficient, or some of the liniment may be rubbed in with
the hand. This acts as a mild form of counter-irritant, probably temporarily withdrawing the blood from the deeper parts
toward the surface, and where the stiffness and pain have
lasted some time this is more effectual than either heat or friction by itself. If the tenderness is limited to one or two spots,
and especially if these correspond to the places where the
nerves perforate the fascia, blistering fluid, painted on once or
twice, according to the thickness of the skin, answers better
still.

In rare and exceptional cases more powerful applications,
even the actual cautery, may be used. How these act is not
clear; they may merely withdraw blood from the deeper parts
or they may act in some way through the nervous system;
for there is little doubt that certain organs are always in
definite nervous relation with certain parts of the surface of
the body, and are affected when these are in any way stimulated. However this may be, there is no question that sometimes this agent may be employed in relieving deep-seated
pain, especially about the bones, with conspicuous success.

When the skin feels sore and tender after a sprain, the essential or aromatic oils often give very great relief. Many of the quack remedies employed to soothe pain, even the deep-seated pain of acute gout, owe what merit they possess almost entirely to these. A very favorite application in Germany, known as Hoffmann's balsam of life, consists of an alcoholic solution of balsam of Peru and seven of these aromatic oils mingled together. They may be either painted on the skin, and left exposed, or dissolved in spirit in various proportions, and covered over with oiled silk to prevent too rapid evaporation. Menthol is one of the most convenient, and acts especially well when mixed with camphor or croton-chloral, so as to form a thick oily liquid. Probably in this instance, too, the relief is in no small measure due to the effect produced upon the cutaneous nerves.

In certain cases minute quantities of morphia, belladonna, or veratria may be combined with these. It must, however, be remembered that if chloroform is used as a solvent, a considerable amount is absorbed through the skin, particularly if friction is used at the same time, and that in spite of the comparative thickness of the cutaneous covering of the back and the paucity of sebaceous glands. Belladonna plasters, which are strongly recommended by some, not only share with all other plasters the objection of being intolerably dirty, but have the additional disadvantage of sometimes causing an acute attack of eczema. Quite as great benefit may be derived by wearing a belt of flannel or, if this is too irritating, one of silk next the skin.

The hypodermic injection of anodynes, such as morphia, may occasionally be necessary, but it is always as well to postpone this until all other remedies have been exhausted. The very ease with which it gets rid of the pain is its greatest danger. It rarely cures the complaint, though it gives a temporary sensation of comfort, and is only too likely to be required again before many hours are past.

Ironing.—Besides these there are other remedies which are especially suited to deep-seated and large muscular masses, such as exist on either side of the spine in the loins. Ironing has already been alluded to. The patient should lie in bed, rather on his face, with the body supported by pillows in as comfortable a position as possible, and should turn from side to side as occasion requires. A well-warmed piece of flannel (great stress is laid by some on its being unwashed) is then stretched over the affected part, and the muscles on either side of the backbone thoroughly ironed in all directions with an iron as hot as can conveniently be borne, using considerable pressure at the same time. The best for this purpose are those of rather small size, with the edges and angles well rounded off, so that they may be pressed into all the depressions between the bones without causing pain.

Acupuncture.—Acupuncture, again, though it is rarely employed nowadays, and seems, like bleeding, to have gone out of fashion, is at times very efficient in removing chronic muscular pain. How it acts is not thoroughly explained. Ordinary long darning needles answer very well. They are simply thrust through the skin, deep into the muscles, and withdrawn again after a few minutes. If the plan is successful they leave behind a bright red areola, which varies considerably in size and duration in different cases, and probably is dependent on the condition of the nerves that are stimulated. The pain is exceedingly slight, especially if the thrusts are made firmly and rapidly, and the punctures scarcely bleed.

Galvanism.—Galvanism, too, is very successful in treating muscular stiffness. The skin should be well sponged over first with warm salt and water, so as to avoid irritation as much as possible, and either the labile or the stabile plan adopted. The latter is the best to commence with, and then, after the current has been passing some time, the direction may be reversed once or twice. The electrode applied over the muscle should be of large size (a zinc plate covered over with leather, well moistened, answers as well as anything, as it may be cut or bent to any shape), and the current used of proportionate strength. Then, before leaving off, a smaller electrode may be substituted, and passed over the whole of the surface with a weaker current (if possible in an ascending direction) so as to secure its refreshing action and remove any sensation of fatigue. The sittings should not last longer than five or ten minutes, and it will generally be found that every other day is sufficient, especially if kneading or ironing is used on the alternate ones.

Massage.—Massage, if it is thoroughly carried out, is more successful still. Its action is most refreshing and invigorating.

Under its influence the aching and stiffness disappear, the blood circulates more freely through the muscles, the waste products are carried away, nutrition improves, and strength and voluntary power begin to return at once. It seems to possess the same restorative influence over the deeper structures that friction has upon the skin.

Percussion and kneading are both recommended. The former is the easier, and does not require so much skill or experience; but it only affects superficial parts, and is altogether of more limited application. The ulnar side of the hand may be used, or an instrument which bears a general resemblance to a hammer, with a stem of whalebone to secure elasticity, and a head faced with India-rubber. With this, held rather lightly, the whole of the stiff and painful part of the back is thoroughly percussed, the number of strokes rising to as many as three or four hundred in the minute, until the skin begins to glow.

Kneading is of much greater service, but requires practice before the full benefit can be obtained. The object is to compress and relax alternately the deeper-lying muscles, and to squeeze their contents onward, so as to insure a more rapid flow of blood and plasma through their substance. Consequently the movement must be regular, definite in direction, and well ordered.

A muscle at rest receives an exceedingly small quantity of blood, compared to what flows through it when it is contracting. So long as it is doing no work, the plasma which pours through the walls of the vessels into the interspaces round remains almost stagnant; the fibres are very slow in getting rid of their waste and in receiving a fresh supply. As soon as the muscle begins to act, the vessels dilate, the current of blood is quickened, the plasma is driven on at a much faster rate, and the nutrition improves beyond all measure. This is helped to no slight extent by the alteration in the shape of the muscles. These are all incased in a comparatively unyielding fibrous sheath, differing in strength and density in different places. The plasma collects underneath this, filling up all the clefts and spaces left between the fibres. Each time the muscle contracts it compresses some of these, and causes others to dilate, so that it alternately sucks and drives the fluid plasma on. And, as a matter of fact, it is well known that the flow of plasma, as well as that of blood, through the substance of a muscle, increases immensely as soon as it begins to work.

Massage aims at imitating this. Its object is, by the rolling and kneading of the muscles, to increase the flow of blood and plasma through them, get rid of the accumulated waste, and stimulate nutrition by supplying fresh material in larger quantity. If carried out thoroughly it is almost certain to give relief, but it is not a thing to be undertaken rashly, without previous training, and without some knowledge of anatomy. Massage and rubbing are not synonymous terms.

Supposing the lumbar region to be affected, the patient must be placed upon a couch of convenient height—as already described in speaking of ironing—and well supported from underneath by cushions, so that the muscles of the loin may stand out beneath the skin without being contracted. The operator should stand over him, at a suitable distance, so that his movements are not cramped; and then, with both hands, moving one after the other, knead and squeeze the muscles, first on one side and then on the other, rolling them, as it were, away from the middle line, and pressing them onward and upward toward the head. The whole hand must be used, the fingers, as it were, being insinuated, as far as possible, under and between the groups of muscle, the skin being allowed to glide, to a certain extent, over the structures beneath. Then, if there is any very painful spot left, the muscles may be grasped with the hands and firmly kneaded with the thumbs, moving them round and round in small circles intersecting each other over it so as to knead and squeeze the structures round it from all sides.

The pressure should be gentle at first, and then gradually become firmer and firmer. No liniment or oily substance can be used, as it weakens the grasp of the hands and tends to defeat the object of the manipulation. If it is desired it may be rubbed in afterward. The rate of movement must vary with the thickness and depth of the tissues to be manipulated, and with the amount of pressure used. Within reasonable limits, the slower the better. There is a great tendency on the part of many, who are supposed to practice massage, to use much too much force, and to make all the movements too rapid. Five minutes, as a rule, is sufficient for a sitting, though it is often beneficial to apply an ascending constant current to the muscles for a minute or two more afterward. It answers better to repeat the manipulation later on in the day than to continue too long at one time. The golden rule is never to fatigue the patient, or to produce the least degree of tenderness or bruising. Those who have not had much experience or a thorough training are very apt to overdo it.

CHAPTER XIII.

INTERNAL DERANGEMENT OF THE KNEE.

THE knee joint is occasionally the seat of a peculiar kind of accident, which, for want of a better name, was called internal derangement by Hey, who first described it. It is extremely painful; it occurs during perfect health from most trivial causes; if it happens once it is always liable to occur again; and after a time the joint is very likely to become seriously crippled. Yet, mainly owing to the fact that opportunities of examining the interior of the joint are seldom met with, its pathology is almost as much a matter of discussion as ever it was.

It is undoubtedly connected with two flattened structures in the joint known as the semilunar cartilages. Roughly speaking, they form two circles, lying side by side between the bones. The margin of each is the thickest part; from this they slope off gradually toward the centre, where there is a perforation. The circumference, especially that of the internal one, is attached to the bone more or less firmly all round; but the part corresponding to the centre of the joint, where the two cartilages touch each other, is much the most secure. At this point each of them is interrupted for a short distance, and the four ends so formed are firmly united to the bone beneath. The outer cartilage forms nearly a complete circle, so that its ends lie close together; the inner, on the other hand, barely forms two-thirds of one. This peculiarity of shape, and the presence of several accessory bands, tend to make the inner of the two the more secure. It scarcely moves at all in ordinary actions of the joint, merely, when the weight falls on it, expanding a little in all directions from its centre. The outer one, on the other hand, glides backward and forward freely.

It is generally supposed that in a typical case of internal derangement one or the other of these cartilages slips from its position and is caught between the bones. As a consequence the movement of the joint is abruptly checked; complete extension becomes impossible; the two bones are forcibly wedged apart from each other, and the ligaments that hold them together are stretched and strained. The internal, in spite of its greater security, suffers more often; the external, perhaps from the very way in which it can accommodate itself, nearly always escapes.

Rupture of the Semilunar Cartilages.—Sometimes they are torn completely away from their attachments. Godlee mentions one instance in which the external was found rolled up toward the centre of the joint, having been separated from the bone all around the margin. Annandale has described the anterior end of the internal one, stretched or wrenched away from the bone; and probably they may be injured in other ways as well, torn across, for example, or twisted round in various fashions, or, if the violence is sufficiently severe, forced out from the joint altogether until they project beneath the skin. Then there is, generally speaking, laceration of the lateral or of the internal ligaments of the joint as well, so that the bones are dislocated from each other.

If the joint is the seat of chronic synovitis, or is subject to attacks of rheumatic gout, or if, in younger people, there is that peculiar loosened condition of the ligaments which I have already described, the displacement may be much more complicated. It is not unusual to find in these circumstances that the cartilages may be made to slip backward and forward between the bones by the mere pressure of the finger. It is not fair, however, to regard these as genuine examples of internal derangement. In this, the joint is, to all appearance, perfectly sound and healthy; the violence is exceedingly slight; and the relief is instantaneous. There may be a transient effusion into the cavity of the joint after the displacement has taken place, but clearly there can be no tearing or even severe bruising of any of the internal structures. The greatest injury must fall short of this, or the time required for repair would naturally be much longer.

Displacement Without Rupture.—The best description is given by Knott, of Dublin, who has suffered from it himself on repeated occasions. It first occurred to him when he was a boy, as he was walking quietly along. All of a sudden, without having sustained any wrench or twist of which he was

conscious, he was seized with such agonizing pain on the inner
side of the knee joint that he half fell, half sat down, on the
ground, sick and faint, with a sensation of utter helplessness.
The knee was slightly flexed; he could not move it one way or
the other, and voluntary power over it was entirely lost. Instinctively he applied his hands one on either side of the joint,
and made as powerful a pressure as he could in the hope of
relieving the suffering. This caused the flexion to diminish;
when suddenly the pain again became almost intolerable, a
clicking sensation was conveyed to his hand and his ear at the
same time, and perfect relief came at once. He managed to
walk away, and no after trouble of any kind followed.

After that the accident happened to him on many occasions; he noticed that it never occurred during active movement, but only when the muscles were off their guard; and
that if the knee-joint was slightly bent, the least force applied
so as to turn the toes outward was sufficient to cause it. So
long as he walked with the toes turned in the joint felt secure;
the reverse of this is the case when the displacement concerns
the external of the two cartilages.

From this he is convinced that, at least in his own case, the
displacement consists in the posterior part of the internal
cartilage gliding forward from its position until it is caught
between the bones. This forces them apart, like a wedge, and
completely stops the movement of the joint. The muscles
round contract at once, and become perfectly rigid, so that
voluntary action is out of the question for the time. Afterward, when they are tired out, and the joint fills with fluid,
the power of movement returns again; but complete extension is not possible so long as the displacement lasts.

Hey's account is closely similar. He describes the knee as
being not unfrequently affected with an internal derangement
of its component parts, as a consequence of trifling accidents,
and states that the trouble is now and then removed as suddenly as it is produced, by the natural movement of the joint,
without surgical assistance of any kind; but that it may remain for weeks or months, and then become a serious misfortune, as it causes a considerable degree of lameness.

"The disorder may happen with or without contusion. In
the former the symptoms are equivocal, until the effects of
the contusion are removed. When no contusion has happened,

or when the effects of it are removed, the joint, with respect to its shape, appears uninjured. If there is any difference from its usual appearance, it is that the ligament of the patella appears more relaxed than in the sound limb. The leg is readily bent and extended by the hands of the surgeon, and without pain to the patient. At most, the degee of uneasiness caused by this flexion or extension is trifling, but the patient himself cannot freely bend or extend the limb in walking; he is compelled to walk with an invariable and small degree of flexion; yet in sitting down the affected joint will move like the other."

Bonnet, from experiments on the dead subject, confirms Knott's views of what takes place in these cases, and shows clearly that it is produced by twisting the leg outward when the limb is slightly flexed. Certainly there is no laceration or extensive displacement of any internal structure. Sir Astley Cooper wrote of it in much the same terms, stating that it may be produced by striking the inner side of the great toe against any slight projection, when the knee is bent as in walking. I have seen the same thing myself on several occasions, but the most interesting example with which I am acquainted was told me by a medical man of himself. During his student days, while playing at football, he suddenly made a violent kick, missed his aim, and fell down, feeling very sick, with intense pain on the inner side of his knee. He was entirely unable to move the joint, but after a friend had slowly flexed the limb as much as he could, and then rapidly extended it, the pain disappeared all of a sudden, and he could walk as before; only for some days there was a considerable amount of swelling, and a sense of insecurity about the joint. The same thing happened to him on several occasions afterward.

These symptoms agree so closely with those described by Hey, Knott, and Bonnet, that there can be no doubt the actual derangement is the same, though the way in which it is produced is apparently altogether different. I say apparently, because, if the action of the knee joint under these conditions is considered for a moment, the difference completely disappears. When the leg is extended, just as it comes to lie in the same straight line with the thigh, a slight amount of rotation outward takes place at the knee joint, so that the ligaments become tense, and the joint sufficiently secure to bear the

weight of the body in walking. In this particular instance
extension was extremely rapid and vigorous; there was no
weight resting on the limb to keep the bones in apposition,
and, consequently, there was nothing to check the rotation
outward. This allowed the posterior margin of the internal
cartilage to be carried forward until it was caught and fixed
by the spasmodic contraction of the muscles. Voluntary
movement at once became out of the question. I have since
been told that accidents of a similar character, only not sufficiently severe to cause any actual displacement, are not uncommon at football; there is merely a sickening pain on the
inner side of the joint for a few minutes, and in some instances
a slight amount of effusion afterward; but the displacement
is not carried far enough for the cartilage to be caught and
fixed.

Reduction.—The method of reduction has been already
mentioned; nothing is easier when once it is understood, especially if the patient is under an anæsthetic. Hey recommended making him sit on a high chair, facing the surgeon,
who should grasp the limb firmly, extend it until it was as
straight as the circumstances would allow, and then rapidly
flex it again. Later surgeons have reversed this proceeding
with some advantages, as preliminary extension is much more
painful than flexion, and in the second step rapid flexion is
somewhat difficult to carry out. Whichever way is adopted,
while it is being done firm pressure must be made with the
thumb of the disengaged hand over the position of the displaced
cartilage. As soon as free movement is restored the limb is
carefully padded with cotton wool, and thoroughly bandaged to
prevent any accidental redisplacement, and to limit the effusion that is almost certain to follow

After Treatment.—This apparently trivial precaution
should never be omitted. The chief danger of this singular
accident is its extraordinary liability to occur again and again.
If the effusion is not checked at once the capsule and the ligaments yield until the natural tension of the joint is lost, and
the displacement becomes easier than ever. When once a
commencement has been made these two things act and react
continually on each other; each displacement causes a fresh
amount of effusion; each time the effusion occurs it makes
the displacement more easy. At length it often happens that

the distention becomes chronic and that the joint is seriously disabled, though it must be admitted that when this has happened the displacement does not cause so much pain as it did.

After the effusion has been absorbed it is always advisable to wear a retentive apparatus for some months, especially when indulging in any exertion which, like lawn-tennis, has a particular tendency to produce this derangement. If it has only happened once, an elastic knee-cap, strengthened and padded opposite the internal cartilage, may suffice; but care must be taken with an appliance of this description that more harm than good does not result. It must never be worn at night; and when it is taken off the knee should be thoroughly rubbed and kneaded to restore the circulation through it, or else the tissues waste away and the elastic becomes so comfortable that it is regarded by the patient as indispensable.

If one of the attachments of the cartilage has been torn, so that there is a definite displacement recognized by the projection it forms beneath the skin, on the outer or the inner side of the joint, this is not sufficient. Either a mechanical contrivance must be worn for the purpose of checking irregular movements of the leg when the lateral ligaments are slightly relaxed, or else, as Annandale has done on several occasions, with conspicuous success, the joint must be opened, and the offending cartilage stitched into position.

A very good arrangement for cases of this kind consists of two well-padded metal plates accurately fitted round the knee-cap, one on either side and held together above and below by short straps. These plates are connected together by a steel spring passing horizontally across behind the joint, so that when the splint is in position they press firmly on the unprotected portion of the capsule, where the displacement is most likely to occur. If this does not answer, or if it is thought, from an examination of the case, that the derangement in the case of the internal cartilage is really due rather to outward rotation of the leg while the ligaments are relaxed, the best kind of apparatus is formed on the principle of two lateral bars jointed opposite the knee, and connected together above and below by a circle round the limb, formed partly of metal and partly of leather. An additional strap across the joint above and below the patella is sometimes of service. This is heavier and more cumbersome, but much more efficient than the former in checking irregular movements of rotation in either direction. Flexion and extension are not in the least impeded, and after the patient has once grown accustomed to it even lawn-tennis is possible in it.

CHAPTER XIV.

CONTRACTION OF THE FINGERS.

IT sometimes happens that sprains, instead of running an ordinary course, are liable to be followed by unusual results, due either to some peculiarities of structure in the part itself, or to the presence of an overpowering constitutional taint, or to the influence of both together. One of these, which occurs in the hand, tying down the fingers, and giving rise to serious inconvenience from the way in which it interferes with their movements, is known as Dupuytren's contraction.

Structure.—The whole of the palm of the hand is invested by a sheet of dense fibrous tissue, which forms a sheath round all the muscles, and is closely united to the skin on one surface and the bones on the other. In the centre it is exceedingly strong, stretching over the tendons and retaining them securely in all the movements which the hand executes. It is to this, in great measure, that the palm owes its firm resisting feel. At the sides, where it is continued over the muscles of the thumb and little finger, the thickness is not so great; but where these portions join the central part there are two strong partitions passing deeply toward the back of the hand, and sending off side branches in a direction parallel to the surface between the deeper structures. At the clefts of the fingers the central part breaks up into four divisions, each of which again divides, so as to form bands running down the sides until they become attached to the bones and the sheaths of the tendons. Where the division takes place, and the several portions commence to diverge, another layer, lying deeper than the tendons, comes to reinforce it from below, and just here it is very closely attached to the skin. Sometimes, as a result of strains, this fibrous tissue slowly but almost irresistibly contracts, until the ring and little fingers, and sometimes even the middle one, are rigidly flexed into the palm of the hand so that no reasonable amount of force can straighten them again.

The first thing to attract attention is the presence of a small hard nodule in the palm of the hand, at a point corresponding to the lowest of the transverse creases into which the skin is thrown, and to the interval between the ring and little fingers. It is not painful unless pressed upon or roughly handled, and does not at first give rise to any inconvenience; there is merely a hardened inelastic spot, where the tissues are bound together so that they do not yield and give way to each other in every movement as they ought. Soon, however, the skin begins to waste and lose its flexibility; the fat disappears, and it becomes tied down to the fascia beneath so firmly that it is practically incorporated with it. Then prolongations may be noticed running from this point upward toward the wrist, and downward to the fingers. The latter are much the stronger, and if the process continues, the ring and little fingers become more and more flexed by the contraction of these bands until they are held down immovably in the palm. One of these two fingers is generally the first; but often both of them suffer, and sometimes the middle and even the index are affected as well. When the bending is complete, the finger catches in everything like a hook, so that it is liable to be pulled back and hurt at any moment, and becomes the source of extreme annoyance from the way in which it interferes with every action, even such apparently trivial matters as shaking hands.

Cause.—Dupuytren was the first to point out the cause of this deformity, and it has ever since been known by his name. He showed that the flexion and subsequent rigidity were due entirely to the contraction of the fascia by the side of the fingers, and that the tendons themselves took no share of any kind in its production. They are and remain perfectly free. It is not, however, quite so simple a process as it appears to be from this; the shortening does not take place merely in one direction. If the part is carefully examined, the first thing that is noticed is a depression of the skin where it is tied down to the tissues beneath. The shrinking is general; the fibrous tissue contracts in all directions, and the change is made more conspicuous still by the absorption of the fat, and the wasting of the soft parts as the blood-vessels become more and more constricted.

It is this which renders the difficulty of effective treatment so great. If the contraction merely took place in one direction, simple division of the shortened band would be sufficient. Unhappily this is rarely the case. The whole of the fibrous tissue of the palm at the affected spot becomes so dense and rigid that such a proceeding scarcely produces any effect. The contraction is as great in depth as it is in length. The fat is absorbed; the muscle wasted; the skin loses it suppleness and flexibility, and the texture is so changed that in advanced cases the whole of the tissue between it and the bones beneath appears to be converted into a dense fibrous mass, which creaks and grates under the knife when an attempt is made to divide it.

Much of the interest that is always expressed about this deformity arises from its supposed connection with gout. It is believed by many that this alone, without injury of any kind, is sufficient to produce it. It is certainly true that it is much more common among men than women, and that many more cases are met with in private practice where gout is frequent than among hospital patients; but it hardly seems probable that this can be the only cause.

If this is the case, it is not a little singular that a Frenchman should have been the first to give a true account of its pathology; and even if the presence of this complaint is admitted as one of the reasons for the obstinate persistence of this contraction, it hardly seems probable that it can be the sole cause of its commencement. In a certain proportion of cases it is impossible to obtain any history of gout, either in the patients themselves, or even in their families; and though it is more commonly met with, it is true, after middle life, it certainly does occur long before. I have seen it as early as one-and-twenty, and one of the worst cases that has ever come under my notice (it was so bad that one of the fingers was amputated) was in a man only four years older.

Urate of soda, too, is rarely found in connection with this, unless there is a general deposit in other parts of the body; and, so far as I know, this form of contraction has never been described in connection with the feet, though it is notorious gout has a special predilection for this region, and there is a layer of fascia in them almost identical in structure and arrangement with that of the palm of the hand. The immediate cause is either a single, sudden strain, bending the fingers back, or long-continued irritation, such as that produced by the constant pressure of a round-headed stick in the palm of the hand, especially during convalescence from illness. Gout very probably is one of the conditions that predispose to its occurrence, but it is almost certain that it is not the only one.

It is more common among the upper and middle classes (or, perhaps, it would be more correct to say that they more commonly apply for relief) than among laborers, because in these the hands are thoroughly hardened and trained to work of all kinds, and a strain that would cause serious injury in the one is hardly felt by the other. It does, however, occur among out-patients, especially among those who are employed in engineers' shops; I have seen many such cases, and have been assured by the men that quite half of their number are affected more or less, only they do not consider it worth while applying for relief. With regard to this it is significant that, among the class of people who furnish the majority of the out-patients in a general hospital, it is almost as common among women as it is among men.

The comparative weakness of the fingers on the inner side of the hand is sufficient to account for the fact that they are affected almost exclusively. The muscles attached to them are so much weaker that they are unable to stand a strain that is at all sudden or severe, and give way before a force the others can bear with ease.

It is the obstinate and progressive character of this contraction that renders it so serious. When once it has commenced, though it may remain quiescent for long periods, it has on the whole a decided tendency to grow worse and worse. In the earlier stages it may be relieved, or even cured, without great difficulty; in the later ones this is impossible without operation, and sometimes this condition becomes so bad that the patient prefers the permanent and distressing deformity of losing his finger.

Treatment.—Before contraction has made its appearance, when there is only a small hard nodule to be felt beneath the skin, the very simple device of repeatedly working the part with the thumb of the other hand, while the fingers support the back, is often sufficient to arrest its progress, only it must be carried out regularly and systematically. Rotatory motion, with the affected finger well stretched out, so as to make the contraction tense, is the most useful, changing the direction now and then, and keeping up firm pressure all the while. ` If this is carefully carried out every day, or better still two or three times a day, and if at the same time further flexion is checked by constantly straightening out the fingers and the palm, pressing them spread out upon a table or other firm object, the tendency can certainly be kept in check for years. Too often, however, this precaution is so simple that it is neglected, and when advice is sought the contraction is already well marked and the skin firmly adherent.

Even then much may be accomplished by the same means, supplemented by the use at night of an appliance devised to exercise a certain amount of continuous traction. In the later stages, and after operations, some contrivance of this description is essential. When the deformity is only slight, I have found an ordinary wooden splint, firmly padded opposite the knuckles, very useful. It must be well fastened by means of straps and buckles to the wrist and the two first fingers; and little caps made of some soft metal, such as thin sheet lead, fitted on to the under surface between the affected joints. Steady continuous traction can then be made on these at night by means of elastic bands; and, if the angle is still more than a right angle, a great amount of improvement can generally be effected in a comparatively short space of time.

Where the flexion is more advanced, or where an operation has been performed, so simple a contrivance is rarely sufficient. It is generally necessary to have an appliance constructed by an instrument-maker. The principle on which they work is essentially the same. There is a broad, well-padded metal plate fitted to the back of the hand, so as to be quite firm, and provided with extension racks lying over the fingers, and bent at an angle to suit the deformity. This is buckled on of an evening, and screwed up until the desired position is obtained.

The difficulty is to graduate the tension with sufficient nicety. On the one hand the continued use of the instrument becomes exceedingly irksome, unless a certain amount of improvement is visible; on the other, there is the pain due to the tension on the fibrous structures of the palm, and the fear of injury to the skin from pressure. It is a rough but fair rule, when no operation has been performed, to straighten out the fingers each time as far as the patient will allow them; and then to relax again slightly. Progress must be slow, and, if the degree of pain is at all severe, the patient, as a rule, refuses to continue, and remains satisfied with a slight and temporary degree of improvement. Care must be taken as often as the splint is removed, and again before it is applied, to knead the tissues of the palm thoroughly, and to soak the hand in water as hot as can be borne; otherwise a great deal of the benefit that may be derived from the extension is almost certain to be lost.

An immense amount of improvement in the method of operating has been effected in recent years by the ingenuity of various orthopædic surgeons, and especially William Adams. Dupuytren himself merely made a transverse incision through the skin and fascia, at the most resisting point, so that when the finger was straightened out there was a lozenge-shaped wound, the sides of which might in successful cases grow together. This, however, rarely happened; the wound nearly always had to heal by granulating, and the resulting cicatrix possessed, as it always does under these conditions, so great a power of contraction that the deformity was reproduced often in a worse degree. I have seen a finger irretrievably tied down within a month by the cicatrization of a comparatively superficial wound along its under surface, not deep enough to involve either the tendon or its sheath.

This was improved upon first by Goyrand, who, before dividing the contracting band, made a longitudinal incision through the skin so as to improve the chance of primary union. In some cases (those, for example, in which the contraction is deep rather than broad, and does not involve more than one finger) this answers fairly well, especially as the means for securing early union are much better understood at the present day. The skin must be detached first on either side with the greatest care, and the band, besides being completely divided, must be separated as far as possible from its deep connections by incisions parallel to the surface. When so much as this is done, however, it is more satisfactory to isolate the whole of the contracted tissue from its surroundings, and remove it bodily. I have known this done on several occasions with the most excellent results. The most serious objection is that, when the adhesions are spread over any extent of surface, a great deal of manipulation is required to detach the skin, and, consequently, there is some danger of impairing its power of recovery. If it does perish, the wound that is left is large, though superficial, and there is a great tendency to contraction, so that in cases where the lateral extent is considerable it is, as a rule, advisable to select another method.

For this reason, as soon as the merits of subcutaneous tenotomy became known, other methods were almost entirely superseded. At first the band was divided in one single spot, without much benefit resulting. Then a totally different plan was adopted, minute punctures, as many as may be required, being made wherever the contraction stood out prominently beneath the skin, recollecting that the shrinking is a general one, taking place equally in all directions. The number is not regarded as of any moment. The object is to divide the contraction thoroughly, wherever it resists, and to separate it from the parts beneath.

The palm of the hand is dealt with first, selecting those points where the skin is movable over the subjacent tissue; then each side of the affected fingers by itself. The skin wounds are scarcely visible; there is little or no bleeding, and if they are covered up at once, and firm pressure made with little pads of lint, they ought to be perfectly sound within three days. No attempt at extension must be made until they are.

Where the position of the fingers is such as to allow it, massage is of great assistance, both as a preliminary measure and in the after treatment of the case. It loosens the attachment of the skin, gets rid of the thickened epidermis, so that the wounds close more accurately, and does away, to a great extent, with the necessity of detaching it from its deep connection. But three clear days at least must be allowed to pass before the operation. There is always a certain amount of hyperæmia attendant on kneading and manipulation, and under these conditions this is not advisable.

After the punctures have healed, massage is of even greater service. There is no fear of their being reopened if sufficiently firm pressure is employed. The surface is fixed in this way, so that no tension can fall on them; while the lymph that fills up the interstices of the deep incisions is dispersed, and driven into the absorbents, so that the amount of fresh-formed cicatricial tissue, and the danger of recontraction, are both of them re-

duced to a minimum. It is not uncommon, where the operation
has been thoroughly carried out, to find the hard nodules, left
behind at first, becoming smaller and smaller, until they
either disappear altogether or cease to give rise to any trouble.

Extension, by means of instruments, should be steadily
employed, at first all day long, and then, according to the
progress made, at night only. The same general rules must be
observed as when no operation has been performed, not going
too fast, for fear of reopening the punctures and injuring the
skin, or too slow, for then the contracting bands will reform
and reproduce the deformity.   As a rule, it is advisable to
make as much progress as possible during the early days, for
then the tissues that unite the severed portions are still soft
and yielding. If it is to be successful, the whole must be accomplished within three weeks, though the appliance must be worn
for some time longer on account of the danger of recontraction.

CHAPTER XV.

MUSCULAR CONTRACTION.

In speaking of the results of sudden twists and sprains, it was mentioned that the muscles and tendons rarely escape altogether, and it was pointed out that sometimes, even when the joints are not concerned, they sustain very serious injuries from being crushed or bruised, and, perhaps, torn in two, in the effort they make to save the joint. This, however, is not all. Though there may be no visible effect at the time, it is not uncommon for changes in the nutrition or the activity of the muscles to make their appearance at a later period, and to become worse and worse as time goes on, until they interfere seriously with the use of the limb, and lead, perhaps, to very grave results.

These may be distinguished from those already described as secondary or remote. There is no fixed time for their occurrence. They may appear within the first few days, or three or four weeks, or even more may pass without any change being noticed, and their variety is almost unlimited. Some are probably the result of inflammation, as when groups of extensor muscles, to the complete exclusion of the rest, waste or atrophy shortly after the injury. Others appear to be dependent on some morbid condition of the nervous system. Many are the direct consequence of the accident, without which they would never have occurred; many more, like those complaints known as hysterical, are merely the local manifestation of a general condition, determined to one particular part by the occurrence of the accident. Some few are still only capable of a conjectural explanation.

Cramp.—In some instances the muscular contraction is of a very simple character, when, for example, after some sudden strain, a particular group, or set, becomes hard and tense, and passes almost at once into a state of spasmodic rigidity. It may last for the instant only, subsiding of itself, and merely

leaving the part stiff and tender for the next day; or if the
tension is not relieved it may be kept up until exhaustion com-
pels the fibres to relax. When this occurs, as, for example, in
internal derangement of the knee, the joint is said to be locked.
So far as the patient himself is concerned it is fixed entirely
beyond control. Except by making use of his hands to move
it, or by placing it in such a position that the weight of the
limb can bear upon it, he has not the least power over it. The
spasm does not yield until the cause has been removed by
manipulation, or by other suitable measures. It is the direct
result of the strain; the muscles and nerves are stretched, and
their ends dragged asunder, either by the accident itself or by
the displacement of some internal structure. This acts as a
stimulus. The contraction is the result, and, until some relief
is afforded, voluntary movement is out of the question.

The pain in sudden twists of the loin or neck, when, for instance, the head is quickly turned round for the purpose of
looking at something above and behind, is in many cases due
to this. The attack is always sudden; the pain very severe,
often sufficient to make the patient cry out, and for the moment he feels as if it were impossible to move. Then the head
is slowly and cautiously brought round again to the natural
position with a perceptible sense of effort. In a few of these
there is dislocation or rupture of some of the slender muscular
slips that lie by the side of the vertebral column, or bruising
of the delicate tissue round and between the smaller joints.
Accidents of this kind are well known to occur occasionally,
and some instances have been already mentioned. At first
the symptoms are very much alike, but there is rarely any
difficulty in distinguishing them afterward. The cramp due
to a sudden strain disappears much sooner than the others;
relief is rapid and often spontaneous; a feeling of soreness may
persist, it is true, for days, but the part can be used at once
with a fair degree of freedom. In the other cases, owing to
the tearing and laceration at the time of the injury, the effects
are much more serious. They last a longer time, and it is
often necessary for the patient to submit to a long and careful
course of treatment before the part is recovered sufficiently to
be used again with comfort.

The muscular cramp, which is so common after unusual exertions, among those especially who have a tendency toward

gout, bears a close resemblance to this. It is true that the immediate cause is very trivial, as a rule, and that the contraction rarely involves the whole of the muscle, but the difference almost disappears if due allowance is made for the condition of the tissues at the time. Instead of being fresh and active, they are tired out from overwork; waste products, probably of an acid nature, accumulate in their substance, and there is need of a long period of repose before the blood circulating through them can restore their strength and vigor. In these circumstances a very insignificant stimulus is sufficient to excite contraction. Merely holding the limb in an awkward position will cause it. Some fibres are unduly stretched. Suddenly they swell up, become hard, nodular, and painful; and then, as they tire themselves out, slowly relax and become soft again, leaving the part sore and tender. The muscles, which preserve the most perfect sequence of action so long as they are fresh, become more and more irritable as they are exhausted, so that their fibres are thrown into a state of irregular and spasmodic contraction by stimuli, which, under ordinary conditions, would not have the least influence on them.

The remedy is to straighten out the muscle quietly, but firmly, with as little delay as possible. The patient is generally unable to do it for himself, and then it must be done for him. The head, for example, must be steadily and firmly brought round until it faces the opposite direction. If this is done before complete rigidity sets in the pain and tenderness are much less severe. At the same time great relief may be obtained by kneading and rubbing any hard or contracted mass that can be felt under the skin, the pressure following the course of the fibres until they relax and become soft again. Where the resistance is very obstinate spongiopiline, or flannel wrung out of water as hot as can be borne, may be applied with benefit, and if the tenderness is extreme the rubbing may be continued with an anodyne liniment. As a rule, it is fairly easy to make the contraction subside, but it is as well to caution the patient to be careful afterward about the position in which the part is held. If the muscle is slightly strained again, or kept in a state of tension before recovery is perfect, the cramp is very likely to return at the same spot, and be much more painful.

It does not seem improbable, from what is known of the

use of massage in restoring the energy of overworked muscles
and relieving the pain of sudden strains, that great benefit
might be derived from it in those cases in which the limbs or
particular groups of muscles are liable to be seized with cramp
at frequent intervals, without there being any definite cause to
account for it, other than the presence of some impurity in the
blood. It has a most wonderful influence on the circulation
and nutrition; it relieves the exhaustion of fatigue more
thoroughly and rapidly than anything else; and it is only reasonable to think that if it were systematically applied the
same effects would follow in cases such as these.

Tonic Contraction.—Muscular rigidity after sprains is
not, however, always instantaneous or spasmodic; sometimes
it comes on quietly and slowly, and persists without any apparent relaxation for an almost indefinite time. It is not painful so long as it is left alone; the joint is merely held rigidly
fixed in one position until the tissues become wasted and
spoiled for want of use.

In Children.—One variety is often met with in children,
and, as Paget has shown, may be regarded as in some degree
the result of fear, though it can hardly be due to this alone.
The main features in the history are nearly always the same.
Some joint has been slightly strained; perhaps it is the elbow,
owing to the way in which children are swung round by the
hands. A few days after, it is noticed that the arm is held
continuously in one position, and then it is found that the
muscles on one side of the limb are in a state of rigid contraction, which is maintained so long as the child is awake. Any
attempt at straightening it out meets with steady resistance
and a peculiar elastic recoil. If the attention is diverted, or,
in a still greater degree, if the child is placed under the influence of an anæsthetic, the joint can be moved freely and
easily, so that it is clear there are no adhesions or fibrous contractions round. Nothing is out of place; there is no sign of
inflammation; the stiffness is purely muscular. It cannot be
called voluntary; children cannot, by any effort of will, keep a
limb straight and rigid for hours; nor is it due to reflex disturbance starting from the joint, for not only does it involve
muscles (*e.g.*, the extensors of the knee) which would never be
involved in this way, but the contraction shifts at times rapidly
from one set to another, and even from one joint to another.

It is not even necessary that a joint should be involved at all. One of the most obstinate cases I have ever seen was in a boy who had a small ganglion on the back of his wrist; this had been ruptured subcutaneously twice before, but each time it filled again, as they often will. If it was even touched, all the muscles on the back of the forearm quite involuntarily became rigid, so that any attempt at bending the fingers caused severe pain. When the ganglion was removed all the contraction disappeared at once, and did not return.

Now, in some instances, no doubt, this is the unconscious result of fear. The joint has been hurt once, and the child instinctively keeps it stiff to prevent its being hurt again. But this is not all. The child really has not the power of straightening out the muscles, and the longer the case lasts the more marked the inability becomes. Voluntary control is not yet throughly developed. The emotional side of the mind is stronger than the will, and muscular contraction such as this takes place because there is not the power to help it.

The diagnosis seldom presents much difficulty. Self-consciousness in children is not perfect enough to be constantly on its guard; sooner or later something occurs to distract their attention from themselves, the crippled limb is forgotten, and the rigidity vanishes, to return again instantly if the part is touched. In sleep, too, it rarely persists, and it is seldom necessary, even in the most doubtful cases, to resort to the use of anæsthetics. It is quite exceptional in them for the contraction to last long enough to excite any organic change in the muscular substance or the structure of the joint; and the mimicry of inflammation is rarely perfect. Either the position is exceptional, as when the knee is kept straight instead of flexed, or the temperature of the skin is never raised, or something so unusual or incongruous is present, that the suggestion of serious joint disease is put out of court at once.

Treatment.—In many of these cases, where, for instance, a limb has been kept obstinately fixed in one position for some length of time, it is almost impossible to dispense entirely with the use of splints, but it is as well to employ them as little as possible. The object is to strengthen the limb, and to accustom the muscles to act in obedience to the will, not to confine them or to restrict their action. Much more may be effected by quietly making the position of the limb uncomfortable, varying the method according to the particular circumstances of each case. A mild counter-irritant, for example, may be applied in the angle where one surface presses on another: this is generally sufficient to induce the patient to alter the position of the limb, without anything further, but care must be taken not to blister the skin, which is certain to be soft and tender at this spot.

In other cases it answers better to leave the contraction entirely alone, and to divert the attention successively to different parts of the body. I have seen several instances in which this method of treatment has been followed by conspicuous success; and though the cure may not have been permanent, yet time was gained for the adoption of other measures, and the danger of degenerative changes avoided. Quite recently, two children were brought to me separately on the same day for exactly the same affection. In each a knee had been sprained some time before, and the limb had become stiff and rigid in a position of extreme extension. The least attempt at bending it caused severe pain. There was no heat or redness, or any sign of inflammation, and certainly there was no displacement. Acting on a suggestion of one of the friends, a small blister was placed in each case on the knee of the opposite leg, with the best result; free movement returned within twenty-four hours.

It must not be forgotten, however, that this method of treatment does not aim at permanent success; it merely relieves the symptoms of the moment, and prevents the occurrence of serious after-consequences. It has no influence of any kind on the real cause, which is nearly always some disordered condition of the general health. Until this is set right by measures, which, of course, must vary in each individual case, it is almost hopeless to look forward to any lasting benefit from other plans.

In Adults.—Muscular rigidity of this description is not confined to children. It is nearly as common in young adult life in one sex as well as the other, and is liable to be followed by consequences of a much more serious character. Sometimes it come on suddenly, so that the patient on waking up of a morning is unable to straighten out a limb; sometimes it is so slow and gradual that no one can quite call to mind when it first appeared; there has only been a stiffness, increasing gradually from day to day, until some accidental circumstance calls attention to it.

Many of these cases resemble, in their chief features, those already described. They are in reality the result of defective voluntary control. Mental power has either never been developed thoroughly or else it is not exercised. It may be that it has remained in the state so characteristic of childhood, or that it has become entirely subordinate to an excessive longing for sympathy. Whatever it is, the cause is not any mischief in the joint; there is no disease or inflammation in the part, though there may be a close resemblance to it. However serious the final result, and it may end in complete loss of use, at any rate at the beginning, the contraction can only be regarded as the local expression of a constitutional weakness, which may show itself in a variety of ways.

Simulation of Joint Disease.—The most striking feature about it is the way in which it can imitate real disease. The resemblance is sometimes extraordinary. In the one case the joint is inflamed and the muscles are tightly contracted, because the least movement of the bones causes intense pain; in the other, the rigidity is merely the act of an emotional or an excited frame of mind, of little importance in itself, and serious only in proportion to the likelihood of its continuance and the secondary changes that follow. Yet the difficulty is sometimes extreme, and it is not lessened by the fact that it is advisable to come to a definite conclusion, and adopt suitable measures as soon as may be. Whatever the cause, if left to itself it is a condition only likely to become steadily worse.

Fortunately, the evidence, if it is properly interpreted, is clear and distinct in the great majority of cases. In some, the first glance is enough. There is a certain order and regularity present in the symptoms when a joint is inflamed; they vary, it is true, according to the joint, but, for each individual one they are fairly constant, and if there is any glaring inconsistency, such as is met with sometimes, the idea of inflammation may be set aside without hesitation. In others, however, the question is not so easily answered, and it is only after repeated examination and the most careful weighing of evidence that such a conclusion can be formed.

The previous history is of very little use. Very often, without the least intention of deceiving, it is entirely mislead-

ing. If at any time, no matter how remote, there was an accident, the symptoms are always dated from it, and if nothing
deserving of such a name can be remembered, repeated ques-
tioning is sure to suggest it at length. It is only in accordance
with human nature that, as a result of continued trying, vague
recollection should become a definite picture, the details growing more and more circumstantial each time until the whole
thing is clear, and the friends at least are thoroughly convinced. As a matter of fact, it is not unusual for them to be
much more certain on such a point as this than the patient
himself.

Nor is any great degree of help to be derived from the
position of the limb. In cases of emotional contraction in children it is often unusual or inconsistent with the presence of inflammation, as when the knee is kept rigidly extended, but in
adults it is commonly identical with that assumed in real disease. So with the locality in which pain is felt. This may
correspond exactly, even in such strange features as pain on
the inner side of the knee when the hip joint is inflamed.

Sometimes the difficulty is increased by the addition of
symptoms that are ordinarily regarded as characteristic of
inflammation. The part, for example, may be swollen, and the
temperature of the skin raised; there may even be a distinct
blush upon the surface; but close examination, even in cases
such as these, nearly always reveals their true character. The
increase in size, for example, is never very distinct; often it
appears to be more considerable than it is, from the wasting
of some of the tissues and the passive collection of fluid in
others; the rise of temperature (which should always be esti-
mated by a surface thermometer; the hand may easily be deceived) is never above that which is normal in the more protected parts of the body, and the blush, if it were really due
to inflammation, would indicate a degree of severity that is
certainly not present.

In many instances information may be gained from the
length of time that has elapsed since the accident, or at least
since the commencement of the symptoms. Muscular rigidity
is one of the earliest signs of inflammation, but it never remains the only one. At a very early period others are sure
to make their appearance, and as they become more numerous
and more marked the diagnosis becomes more easy. Emo-

tional contraction, on the other hand, may last for an indefinite period with no further change than that which has been already described as the result of prolonged inaction.

Unhappily the methods that are so successful in children do not give nearly such certain evidence in the case of adults. In the former it is, comparatively speaking, easy to divert attention from a suspected joint, so that if it is not inflamed the tonic contraction of the muscles quietly disappears and the angle changes. In the latter it is much more difficult. Chance moments of forgetfulness seldom present themselves in them, and the case may be watched for a very considerable time without any change being detected.

Sometimes after all the evidence has been carefully weighed it seems impossible to arrive at a definite conclusion. There is then only one alternative; the patient must be placed under an anæsthetic. This rarely fails. The joint may then be examined without the least pain; the muscles are completely relaxed; the movements are not interfered with; and it becomes possible to ascertain definitely how much of the rigidity is due to spasmodic contraction, and how much to other causes. It often happens that a limb, apparently as rigid as a bar of iron, becomes perfectly flexible as soon as sensibility is lost.

There is, too, as Paget has pointed out, another advantage to be gained by doing this. Valuable information may often be obtained by carefully watching the condition of the muscles while the patient is coming round again. If the rigidity is due to the pain of an inflamed joint they begin to contract and steady the bones long before consciousness has returned; and they do it so gradually and imperceptibly that it is almost impossible to say when the change commences. The rigidity is an instinctive act, independent altogether of the mind or of the higher cerebral centres, and it returns of itself long before these have reassumed their influence. When, on the other hand, no such cause is present, the relaxation continues until some notice is taken of it; then it disappears almost instantaneously, and the muscles become even more rigid than they were before.

At first sight it appears improbable, but it is, nevertheless, true, that the danger of overlooking the presence of inflammation is not nearly so great as that of imagining that it exists when the real cause is the lack of voluntary control and prolonged disuse. It is, comparatively speaking, rare for disease, even of such an obscure and deep-seated joint as the hip, to be mistaken for hysteria; the opposite is much more common.

Not Merely Hysteria.—This, however, is not the only reason why these cases of emotional contraction deserve special attention. There is another danger to which they are exposed, scarcely less serious and infinitely more frequent. It is one of the commonest mistakes to regard a case in which it is clear there is no inflammation, merely as hysterical, and to dismiss it summarily as the product of some transient phase of mental emotion. The joint is hysterical, and that is enough; local treatment is not required; indeed, it is considered by many to be actually injurious, as it tends still further to attract the attention of the patient to the part; general measures only are recommended, and the contraction is left entirely to itself.

The result might be anticipated. As I have described already, a part that is kept at rest and never used cannot remain healthy; certain changes inevitably make their appearance; they need not be gross ones, or produce conspicuous alterations; the nutrition of the part suffers, and that is quite enough; the tissues are impoverished and lose the power of working with that complete unconsciousness and absence of effort which is so characteristic and striking a feature of health.

A good example of this may frequently be met with in the case of the arm, because, from the ease with which the shoulder-blade moves upon the chest the shoulder-joint itself can be kept almost at rest for an indefinite period without attracting much attention. The patient is almost always a young girl; there may be a history of injury; more often this cannot be relied on; or there may have been some mental trouble. At any rate, there is sure to have been something that either receives, or wants, the constantly and loudly expressed sympathy of others. The symptoms at first do not seem in any way imperative; there is always a certain amount of pain, which is borne with much resignation; and the movement of the part is constrained and awkward, especially when any attempt is made to raise the hand above the level of the shoulder; but there is nothing apparently serious until the part is examined and compared with the opposite side. Then it is found that all the time the shoulder-joint itself has been kept perfectly quiet, and

that the clumsiness is due to the attempt that has been made
by one joint to supply the place of two. The muscles are
wasted; the bony prominences stand out unduly; the rounded
contour is lost; the arm cannot be lifted from the side; rotating the limb is almost impossible; the soft tissues round the
joint have become firm and unyielding, and the patient is un·
able to raise the hand to the back of the head. The joint is
almost rigid; the whole of the movement, or nearly the whole,
is apparent only, and is really due to the freedom and ease
with which the shoulder-blade glides upon the chest.

A joint in this condition cannot be called hysterical. It is
of no consequence whether it originated in hysteria or not.
The starting point of the contraction may have been an injury,
or it may not; that has nothing to do with it. The joint has
been kept at rest and never used; its tissues are starved and
wasted; and they are unable to do their work. It is no longer
a question of want of voluntary power; the muscles are rigid
and the soft tissues round are stiff and unyielding; and until
their natural condition is restored by local measures the part
cannot work, whether the patient has the power to will it or
not. The fault may have been that of the patient originally,
but now it has passed entirely out of her control.

This is even more serious than it appears at first sight. A
joint that is stiff and painful is always liable to become the
seat of hysteria, even when this is not the cause. The patient's
health suffers; every attempt at movement causes pain; the
existence of the joint is continually being forced upon the mind,
it is impossible to forget its condition, and at length it may
happen that from this alone, even in those who are, comparatively speaking, strong of will, a condition closely resembling
hysteria, if not identical with it, becomes developed. It is for
this reason that active, vigorous local treatment, such as I
have described already in speaking of the effects of prolonged
disuse, is so essential in the treatment of what are called hysterical joints. Until the nutrition is thoroughly restored, and
the tissues have recovered their natural power, it is hopeless
attempting to effect any improvement by general methods.
The two lines of treatment must be carried on together; one
without the other is almost useless. It savors of the ridiculous
to assure the friends of a patient that if the condition of the
joint could only be forgotten recovery would follow at once,

when all the time the tissues are too wasted to do their work, and the least attempt at movement causes pain.

Muscular Contraction from other Causes.—Now and then instances are met with which cannot be explained by any of these causes. Some accident, apparently quite trivial in character, is followed by persistent muscular contraction, without the least trace either of hysteria or inflammation to account for it. One of these that came under my notice recently was in many ways most striking. The patient was a young man, tall, and of good muscular development. While at sea, about a twelvemonth before I saw him, he had strained his knee in getting out of the hatch. His account of the accident was perfectly clear. He had to take a step of great height to obtain a purchase for his foot, and to raise himself up at the same time with his hands; while doing this, pulling on his knee joint with all the strength of which he was capable, from a position of extreme flexion, he felt something snap; there was a moment of intense pain, and he fell back almost helpless. When his knee was examined it was full of fluid, but there was no displacement, and it was not locked. It was thought at the time that it was merely a sprain, and that if it was kept bandaged for a week it would get quite well. In spite of this, however, it was nearly a month before he could rest any weight on it; and even before this he noticed that the muscles which bend the joint were slowly contracting, and that he was gradually losing the power of straightening it out. This grew worse and worse, until at length he was so disabled that he was forced to lay up and consult a surgeon, who placed him under an anæsthetic and straightened the limb by main force. He could walk better after this, but he was still compelled to wear a leather splint to keep the joint extended. As soon as he left it off the knee began to bend itself in a manner entirely beyond control, and, of a morning particularly, it was only after great effort, and with much pain, that he was able to stand upright. To complete his misfortune, he had slipped off the curb-stone and sprained his knee again only a few days before. Since this the loss of control had been worse than ever; it was only with the greatest effort that he could get the limb straight at all; the morning that I saw him he had fainted twice in the attempt; his health was failing, and he was reduced by pain, and by the loss of his appointment, almost to a state of despair.

On removing the splint it was at once apparent that the whole limb was wasted to a certain extent from pressure, but mainly from disuse. There was no discoloration, swelling, or pain; and the only tender spot was the one on the inner side of the knee cap, of which almost all patients complain. The muscles on the front of the thigh had suffered most severely; the flexor ones at the back felt unusually firm and hard, though their bulk, as compared with those of the opposite side, had diminished too. The strangest thing was, that while looking at him, the knee gradually began to bend, until in about three minutes it had reached a right angle without the patient having the least power of preventing it. The movement was perfectly smooth and quiet. There was no cramp; the hamstrings felt somewhat firmer, and that was all. It required the exercise of very considerable strength to bring the limb again into a straight position.

I recommended at first that the limb should be thoroughly encased in a plaster of Paris splint, thinking that the muscles would soon become tired out by the unyielding resistance, assisted by the pressure, but it was of no use; and after being on for a few hours it had to be removed on account of the pain. It did not seem advisable to try the action of local sedatives; the case had lasted too long for them to be of any permanent service, and the patient would not submit again to an anæsthestic, so that it was not possible to manipulate the joint freely. Under these conditions I determined to try the effect of faradization, applied to the weaker muscles on the front of the limb, and met with the most surprising success. During the first application he was able to extend the limb with much greater ease, and after the third he could do it himself, when the current was not being applied. In short, he was completely cured, and returned to his occupation, though the limb, when I saw him again some months later, had not yet regained its normal proportions.

There can be no reasonable doubt that in this case the muscular contraction was the result of the sprain, though unhappily it was impossible to ascertain what was the precise nature of the injury that had befallen him; and no one who saw him, and who witnessed his anxiety to return to duty, would have entertained for a moment the suspicion of hysteria. What may have been the explanation of the unbalanced con-

traction is very doubtful.   It seemed as if the nerves supplying
the weaker muscles were unable to convey a sufficiently powerful stimulus; that, to use the phrase adopted by Vivian
Poore in his Bradshawe lecture, they were blocked, so that
the tonic contraction of the other muscles gradually overcame
them.   The muscular substance itself seemed equally affected
on both sides of the limb, so that it could scarcely have been
due primarily to this; and there was no reason to believe that
the mental determination of the patient was in any way defective.   It is possible, it is true, that a condition of irritation
may have been induced in one of the nerve twigs supplying .
the interior of the joint by the changes following the sprain,
and that it had travelled, after the fashion of the neuritis de-
cribed by Erb, to the muscular branches supplying the flexors,
stimulating them to increased and disproportionate vigor;
but, if this were the case, it is difficult to understand how it
was so easily cured.   Whichever explanation is correct, it remains an example of muscular contraction, persisting for over
a twelvemonth after a sprain, not due to inflammation or
hysteria.

CHAPTER XVI.

MUSCULAR WASTING.

WASTING of the muscles is another common consequence of sprains. They lose their tone; the firm elastic sensation when they are pressed on with the finger disappears; they feel soft and pulpy; their strength diminishes and their size decreases until, in extreme cases, they may seem to have disappeared altogether, so plainly and distinctly does the outline of the bones show itself through the skin. ·

Degeneration from Disuse.—There may be many different reasons for it. Want of exercise, for example, may induce it. A limb kept perfectly at rest and never used, of course, must waste. The structure of the tissues degenerates; they either become infiltrated with fat or replaced by it to such an extent sometimes that the real amount of wasting is concealed. The muscles in some cases appear to retain their normal shape and size; the outline of the limb is nearly perfect, but the vigor and strength are gone, and everything feels soft and inelastic to the touch. In others, when, for instance, the patient is suffering from some disease that drains all his strength away, the wasting is so extreme and the amount of fat deposited so slight that they seem to have vanished altogether, and to leave the bone covered in by nothing but skin.

This change is a general one; it affects all the muscles— indeed, all the tissues of the limb alike; no set or group suffers perceptibly more than the rest; and unless the constitutional affection from which the patient is suffering is such as to preclude it, the prospect of recovery, so far as the muscles are concerned, is exceedingly good, even in extreme cases. There is little or no destruction of the living active portion of the muscle. No matter how diminished in size or strength the residue may be, as soon as it is exercised and the circulation through the limb increased by general treatment (especially a liberal

supply of food), assisted by local measures, such as massage
and galvanism, the size and strength return, and in the majority of instances the whole of the former vigor is regained.
I have seen this happen on more than one occasion when there
literally did not seem a particle of muscle left.

Wasting from Compression.—Wasting of a description in
some respects similar to this occurs with great rapidity under
the use of constant compression. The worst form is caused
by the constriction of an elastic bandage. Sometimes after
sprains it is thought advisable to wear one of these. If there
has been a great deal of effusion into the cavity of the joint,
especially if it has been allowed to remain unabsorbed for any
length of time, the capsule becomes softened and stretches
until it fails to exert any pressure on its contents. It becomes
loose and flaccid, and there is a continual sensation of insecurity
and want of strength. The joint itself is actually firm enough,
but the patient does not feel that it can be trusted as it was
before. What is the reason of this is not certain; it is probably dependent on the nerves that supply the joint, for the
same complaint is made of muscles when the sheath of their
tendons is distended; and it certainly supplies a very strong
argument in favor of removing the surplus fluid from a joint
after an injury, by some means or other, with as little delay
as possible. However this may be, when the capsule has been
left in this condition a patient often feels the greatest comfort
from the use of an elastic support, such as an anklet or knee-
cap; and, wearing it at first only when he is taking exercise,
gradually continues it until it is scarcely left off, even at night.
The result may be imagined. In a short time a wasted band
is seen all round the limb corresponding accurately to the size
of the elastic; the superficial structures are more affected than
the deeper ones, owing to the way in which the blood is kept
constantly squeezed out of them; and where a muscle lies next
the skin, with a broad flat surface of bone beneath, it is wasted
to such an extent that its presence can scarcely be recognized,
and years may elapse before it recovers. Such appliances
may be used when any very unusual degree of exertion is undertaken, for just the same reason that laborers strap a piece
of leather tightly round the wrist, but nothing can be worse
than wearing them habitually.

These kinds of wasting are not limited to sprains, and their influence is not confined to the muscles; they are due to general causes, and affect all the tissues of the limb, though, owing to their vascularity and softness of texture, there are differences in degree. Others are the direct consequence of these injuries, and are different in many points. They have no relation to disuse; are not the result of compression; do not involve equally all the muscles of the limb; are not due to fatty degeneration; and what is more serious and more important than all the rest together, unless active measures are taken, sometimes show little or no tendency to recover.

Wasting of Extensor Muscles Only.—One of these affects the extensor muscles almost exclusively, and is remarkable both for the very early period at which it shows itself and the rapidity of its progress. I have been able to detect a distinct change in the tone of a muscle three days after a sprain, and it is common for the diminution in size to be visible at the end of a week. Simple rest, no matter how complete, does not produce the same result in anything like the time. The wasting, too, is often extreme; a few weeks after the receipt of a strain or blow the bony prominences may stand out with great hollows between, so as, for the moment, to give rise to the idea that something is out of joint.

Only the extensor muscles are affected, and the broad ones of coarser texture, such as those covering over the hip or shoulder, suffer most, even when full allowance is made for the peculiarity of their shape. In these two situations in particular the effect is so considerable that it rarely escapes notice, and often is sufficient to attract the attention of the patient even before anything is said about it.

At first the wasting is limited entirely to this particular group; the deltoid, for example, which gives the shoulder its smooth and rounded outline, is the earliest to show the change; then it spreads to those that cover in the shoulder-blade behind. Only after it has lasted some considerable time does it involve the rest, and, as the whole of the limb is affected more or less, then probably as the result of confinement and disuse rather than anything else. The atrophy, too, in these cases is simple, and bears no relation to fatty degeneration. This may set in later, and involve all the muscles of the limb, especially if it is allowed to remain unused for any length of time; but as Valtat, in particular, has shown, both by experiments and clinical observation, the two processes are essentially different.

Many suggestions have been offered in explanation of this, but the most reasonable is that which refers it to influences exerted through the nerves supplying the joint. Some have supposed, as it is common in the shoulder, that it is the result of injury to a nerve which winds round the bone in such a position that it might easily be bruised in falls or strains. But even if this were to happen, it does not follow that the muscles would become wasted in this way. They certainly do not when the ulnar nerve is bruised, and, as a matter of fact, the wasting is not limited to the muscles supplied by this particular branch, but involves all those which straighten out the joint, and which are not in any way connected with it; nor would this explanation be of any service in the case of other joints, such as the hip or knee.

Wasting from Inflammation.—Wasting of this description may be taken as a sure sign that the joint is inflamed, or, more correctly, that it has been, for it continues after the other symptoms have subsided. Its degree and rapidity de-pend mainly on the cause and severity of the attack. When this is but slight, affecting the vascular tissues of the joint only, or due to such transient local causes as the tension set up by the accumulation of fluid in the interior, it is least marked. If, on the other hand, the deeper textures of the joint, particularly the cartilages, are involved, or if the cause of the inflammation is some condition of acute blood poison-ing, it is rapid and extreme. In children it is not common, unless at the commencement of strumous disease. Atrophy of the extensors never fails to appear early in this, though, owing to the slowly progressive nature of the disorder, it is often some time before any well-marked degree is perceptible. In adults it is most often seen in those who, later in life, are subject to attacks of rheumatic gout; and its importance de-pends in great measure on the warning it gives of this. In itself, it is merely a sign that the joint has been inflamed; it means nothing more, and it gives no indication of the cause. But subcutaneous injuries, such as sprains, are so rarely fol-lowed, in young and healthy adults, at any rate, by this com-plication that when it does occur the existence of some addi-tional reason is always to be suspected. Occasionally it is the outcome of indiscretion, or of some mistaken method of treatment; sometimes it is due merely to tension, but most frequently when inflammation and wasting follow a simple strain there is a history of gout or rheumatism, or both together. The injury assists the constitutional predisposition by selecting the part to be attacked, and, as it were, antedates the outbreak; in after years, as age advances, it is generally found that assistance of this kind is no longer required, and similar attacks, producing even more severe degrees of wasting, occur independently, without any blow or strain to excite them.

I have known this happen on many occasions. The patient generally gives a history of a sprain or of some unusual or sudden effort a few days before. Very likely nothing is felt at the time; but at a few hours later there is a sense of uneasiness and stiffness about the joint. It is not sufficiently severe to occasion serious anxiety; often there is no complaint about it until the question is asked; but yet it does not get well. Then quite suddenly, ten days or a fortnight after the accident, the condition of the muscles is noticed for the first time. The signs of inflammation may still be visible, or they may have already passed away, leaving the wasting and a certain degree of stiffness; there may be a sense of insecurity and even pain, most severe at night and when the joint is moved, or some distention of the joint cavity; and even in a few instances a perceptible rise of temperature, or there may be other signs of what has been quietly going on; but, as a rule, they are so slight that the discovery is almost accidental, and the diminution in size is thought to have been even more rapid than it really is. In the case of a young officer, who had strained his shoulder while wrestling about a fortnight before, I was solemnly assured that the wasting had come on in the course of a night.

If left to themselves these cases sometimes, but not often, recover without further trouble; the effusion is absorbed; the muscles regain their tone; the stiffness passes off, and full movement returns. If, on the other hand, whatever may have been the original cause, the inflammation does not very soon subside, the changes progress and become exceedingly serious. At first merely the extensor muscles and the lining membrane of the joint are involved; but in a little while the cartilage that covers the ends of the bones and the bones themselves are

affected. Absorption takes place; the length and axis of the
limb are altered; symmetry disappears; the movements lose
their smoothness and freedom; the range is limited, and the
muscles, not only round the affected joint, but also those of the
whole limb, become atrophied. Changes of this nature are
most often met with after middle life in persons with a strong
tendency to rheumatic gout, but they are not confined to this
period. They occur as well in young adults, and are sometimes even more acute in them, so that I have known the
lower limb lose an inch of its length, and the patient become
completely crippled by the pain and wasting round the hip
within a twelvemonth of its having been sprained.

Wasting from Overwork.—Atrophy of muscle occasionally makes its appearance after prolonged overwork, and even
after a single sudden strain. In the former case there is a
great tendency for the wasting to spread from those that are
first involved to others; and when this occurs definite and
well-known changes are generally found to exist at the same
time in the cells of certain regions of the central nervous system. It is certain that there is a connection of some description
between overwork and these pathological changes, but it is
not easy to say how close this may be. One may be the actual
efficient cause of the other, or not improbably some grave constitutional disorder may be the real agent, and the overstrain
merely determine the particular group of muscles in which the
changes first show themselves. However this may be, there
is no question that the exceedingly serious disorder known as
progressive muscular atrophy not unfrequently makes its first
appearance in muscles that have been subjected to a long and
continuous overwork, such as those of the back in "hedgers
and ditchers."

Wasting from a Single Strain.—Atrophy due to one single, sudden effort is not so common. I have seen one well-
marked case in which the muscles of the upper extremities
were involved. The patient, who was a man of good muscular
development, had slipped suddenly down some steps while carrying a heavy weight in each hand. In trying to save himself
from falling, he made a sudden and vigorous effort with his arms,
jerking spasmodically upward the weight that he was carrying. The shoulders and arms were stiff and painful for some
time, but nothing remarkable was noticed for about three

weeks or a month, when he became aware of loss of power and
of wasting, which, when I saw him, was so extreme as to convey the impression that the whole substance of some of the
muscles had disappeared. The affection was nearly symmetrical, that is to say, approximately the same portions of both
arms were attacked, and they were those which it is reasonable
to imagine would have felt the strain most severely in such
an accident. It is possible, it is true, that the wasting was
secondary to the severe compression sustained by the nerves,
as they run down into the arm over the first rib, between this
and the collar-bone, at the moment of the fall. Loss of power
and permanent wasting of the muscles are sometimes occasioned in this way, as Dr. Vivian Poore has shown, though as
a general rule such momentary compression is not enough.
It must be continued for some time to cause so serious a result.
But the muscles that were affected in this particular case were
too distinct and isolated to admit of such an explanation.
They were not torn in any way; there was no evidence of the
nerves being injured. There was no loss of sensibility; the pain
was not severe; there had simply been one single, sharp contraction; and as a result of this (or at any rate after this) the
muscles rapidly wasted and lost their power. Unfortunately,
I was unable to watch the case further, and so cannot say
what effect galvanism and other treatment would have had,
or how it terminated at last. I should think it not improbable that it ultimately ended in the progressive form.

Local Wasting.—Lücke has described the same thing as
occurring in the great extensor muscle on the front of the thigh,
from the effect of blows or sprains. The wasting may involve
the whole of the muscle or only a part, one of the great divisions, for example, of which it is composed, or a smaller portion
still. In a case that was recently under my care, a gap could
be distinctly felt on the front of the limb, about halfway between the hip joint and the knee. It gave the impression that
the muscle had been torn across, and never reunited, though,
according to the patient's statement, which was quite clear
and definite, it was impossible for it to have been produced in
this way. The gap made its appearance slowly and gradually
after a strain, nothing being noticed for some days, and it
kept steadily increasing in width week by week. Moreover,
the electric reaction of the whole muscle was depressed, and

there was a general loss of tone and firmness. Lücke, who
has thoroughly gone into the question, has come to the conclusion that there is an actual loss of the contractile substance
in these cases similar to that found by Valtat in the atrophy
following inflammation of a joint.   There is no neuritis or
other affection of the nerves, and no extravasation of blood;
the wasting may follow either a blow or a strain; and its
rapidity is in no way measured by the severity of the injury.
There is often a certain amount of pain of a rheumatic character, and not unfrequently a slight amount of effusion into
the knee joint; but this is probably passive rather than active,
allowed to take place by the relaxation of the capsule of the
joint that always follows loss of tone in the extensor muscles.
According to the same authority, atrophy of the capsule of
the joint with stiffness, and, at a later period, wasting of the
other muscles of the leg, are not unlikely to happen, especially
in old people.

Muscular Impotence after Strain.—Another peculiar consequence of muscular sprains has been described by Duchenne
under the name of functional impotence.   It cannot be called
atrophy, for, in the earlier stages at least, no gross lesion of
any sort can be detected either in the nutrition or in the structure of the muscles.   They merely become tired out, and give
way with the slightest exertion, so that the joints are no longer
properly supported, or the bones sufficiently braced together.
Sometimes this is the effect of a single, sudden strain; more
often it results from continuing to over-work muscles when
they are weak and badly nourished; but it may be produced
by blows, and even, it is said, by exposure to cold.   At first
there is only an indefinite sense of pain and weakness, but
after this has lasted for some time the symptoms become more
conspicuous.   If there is the least exertion the affected muscle
is thrown into a state of rigid spasmodic contraction.   It does
not relax as it ought to in its proper turn, and allow the joint
to move smoothly and evenly, but remains tense, contracted,
and often in a state of painful cramp.   This lasts longer and
longer each time until the change becomes permanent; the
tendon stands out under the skin like a rigid cord; the sub-
tance of the muscles wastes, and is replaced by a kind of fibrous tissue which grows shorter and shorter until the joint is
fixed in one position, and a condition is produced almost identical with that which results from prolonged inflammation.

In the Spine. Lateral Curvature.—Functional impotence
of this description occasionally occurs in lateral curvature of
the spine; and probably is, in some cases, in no slight degree
the actual cause, especially when the deformity sets in with
great rapidity after a strain. In one instance under my observation, the patient, a boy of fifteen, was swinging by his
hands from a horizontal bar, when he was seized with sudden
pain running round the abdomen so that he felt sick and faint.
After lying down a short time this passed off, and nothing
further was noticed until, in a course of a few weeks, his back
gave way to such a degree that he was scarcely able to hold
himself upright. At no time was there any sign of inflammation or of disease of the bones; there was no bruising or tenderness of any description, so that nothing could have been
torn; the joints were uninjured and the movements perfect;
only the muscles, from the moment they had been strained,
had altogether lost their strength. By a vigorous effort after
a prolonged rest, they were able to get the back nearly straight
again, but they were quite unable to maintain it; almost at
once they began to relax and give way. There was no serious
alteration in their structure, for under proper treatment recovery was rapid and complete; they had merely lost their
power as the result of one single, but severe strain. Had the
case been left to itself, there is little doubt the deformity would
have continued to increase, and ultimately would have become
permanent.

In the Leg. Flat Foot.—Functional impotence is still more
common when the strain, instead of being momentary like
this, is kept up for a considerable length of time day after day.
The muscles then never have the opportunity of thorough rest
and relaxation; they are continuously overtaxed; and degeneration, often permanent in character, is very likely to be the
result. This is frequently seen in the common form of flat
foot occurring at puberty. Duchenne has shown that of the
arches of the foot the long one is maintained almost entirely
by the action of certain muscles on the outer side of the leg,
the peronæi. The posterior pillar of the arch formed by the
heel is almost vertical; the anterior, made up of the bones
which form the great toe, is long and slanting. When the
weight of the body falls on the crown of the arch, the posterior
pillar is fixed by the pressure; the other would slip forward,

and allow the arch of the foot to sink down, if it were not for the muscles that hold it back. After long-continued standing, kept up for many days together, for many hours each day, these muscles, especially in a growing lad, gradually become tired out and yield. Then the tension falls on the ligaments, which, like all such structures when exposed to a continuous strain they were never intended to bear, stretch, and become the seat of acute pain, spreading up either side of the leg. Finally, they give way; the arch of the foot sinks, and the internal border becomes proportionately elongated. If, when this stage is reached, the peronæi muscles are examined, the tendons in which they end are found to stand out like rigid cords. Under the influence of the unceasing strain to which they are unequal, they have passed into a condition of permanent degeneration, probably identical with the contracture that follows inflammation, and now by their shortening form one of the great obstacles in the way of recovery.

I must not be understood to say that all cases of flat foot originate in functional impotence of the peronæi muscles caused by overstrain; but I am quite sure this is the chief element in a very large proportion, and I am able to confirm this by a case of my own, in which the cause of the loss of power was entirely different, but the effect the same. The patient, who was a strong, athletic young man, about a month before I saw him had received a severe blow on the outside of the leg, immediately over the middle of these muscles. No especial attention was paid to it at the time; there was a bruise, and that was all. But in two or three days he noticed that walking, and to a still greater degree standing upright, caused him considerable inconvenience. This grew worse and worse, until, owing to the nature of the trouble from which he was suffering not being properly understood, he was reduced to such a condition that he could scarcely walk six steps at a time. The pain was so intense that he was compelled to stop and lift his foot off the ground. This gave instantaneous relief, but the moment he rested his weight on it again all the old suffering returned. The description he gave was exceedingly clear. At first there was merely a general and ill-defined sense of aching, with a feeling of pins and needles running down the outer side of the leg; then his foot felt tired out, especially in the sole; the aching became more definite, and transformed itself into a dull, numb pain, most severe behind the outer ankle, but spreading up the limb as high as the knee. The longer he stood the more intense this became and the wider the area it involved, until he was literally compelled to give in, and raise his limb from the ground. Throwing his weight on the outer side of his foot enabled him to walk a few steps further, and he always affirmed that a high-heeled boot enabled him to get about much better than a low one.

Careful examination made it plain that the cause of all his suffering was the injury sustained by this particular muscle. So long as it retained its natural strength, the weight of the body rested on those points of bone which are adapted to receive it, and which are held together by structures proportioned to the strain. The arch of the foot was as perfect as that of the opposite one. But when in a little while the muscle, unequal to its work, commenced to yield, the arch lost its main tie, and the anterior pillar began to slip forward until the whole of the strain fell on the ligaments, stretching them, and causing the peculiar sickening pain that always occurs under these conditions. Fortunately, in this particular case, the nutrition of the muscle was restored before either its structure had undergone a considerable degree of degeneration, or the ligaments had been seriously stretched, so that there was no serious sinking down of the instep. The pain was naturally less with a high-heeled boot, because the weight was then thrown more perpendicularly on the anterior pillar, and the strain on the ligaments was lessened.

Treatment.—The treatment of this complication of sprains requires the greatest care and consideration. It may be dependent on so many causes, and may be indicative of so many different pathological conditions, that of two cases, to all appearance identical, the one may recover easily and readily, the other may be merely a sign of the commencement of some serious disease. The first thing to determine in all cases is whether it is secondary to inflammation or not; if this is present nothing, of course, can be done directly to improve the condition of the muscles, as the majority of the remedies employed for restoring their strength and activity would only tend to aggravate the disorder of the joint. As soon as this has passed away, there is nothing peculiar about the atrophy it leaves, except the ease with which it can be cured in the earlier stages, and the extreme difficulty it presents in the later after degeneration has set in.

Question of Inflammation.—The best evidence that inflammation has subsided is afforded by the temperature of the skin, as compared with that of the corresponding point on the opposite side of the body. This can only be done satisfactorily by means of a surface thermometer, carefully packed; the hand may be deceived, but this scarcely can. The points chosen must exactly correspond, they must be under the same conditions of exposure, and the rise must be a distinct one. It is not well to attach too much importance to slight alterations if other signs are not present. It seems as if certain people, by directing their attention constantly to one part of the body, possess the power of raising the temperature to a slight extent, probably through dilatation of the blood-vessels, so that from this alone it becomes slightly warmer than its corresponding area. At least, I have on several occasions witnessed phenomena of this kind, for which I could find no other explanation; and the suggestion is quite consistent with what is known of the influence of the mind on other parts, as, for example, the lungs in cases of phthisis. As a rule, if the difference is inconsiderable and variable, it may be taken for granted that inflammation is not present; and that the sooner passive movement and more energetic treatment are adopted, even to the extent of forcibly breaking down adhesions, the better the prospect of recovery.

As I have shown already, in speaking of joints, the danger is that, disregarding the positive evidence of the thermometer, and relying on the fact that movement is painful, it may be imagined that inflammation still continues, and that further rest, with its inevitable consequences, further atrophy, is advisable on that account. The mistake is the more serious, as under such conditions the rigidity is constantly increasing, so that the prospect of recovery, when at length an attempt is made, is even more remote than it was before.

Local.—The local treatment of muscular atrophy is for the most part identical with that which has been described already in speaking of the condition of disused and stiffened joints. Everything is of service that helps to exercise them and to improve the circulation through them. Passive mo-

tion, working each of them alternately, first in one direction
and then in the other, sometimes with, sometimes without resistance; stretching them out; massage, in all its forms,
especially those which influence most the deeper-lying strata;
ironing; bathing and douching with hot and cold water;
shampooing; friction with stimulating liniments; and even,
where large masses of muscles are concerned, as in the back,
acupuncture.

Galvanism.—One other remedy that has scarcely been
mentioned yet may be used with the best possible result in
many of these cases, and that is galvanism. It is true it is
impossible for any one who is not a specialist in the subject
to undertake to form an elaborate diagnosis, or to give a definite opinion as to the extent to which degeneration has spread
in particular directions. But without attempting this, and
even leaving special and unusual cases aside, there is no inconsiderable number of others in which it may be employed
with immense benefit under the guidance of simple and ordinary rules. The object is entirely different. It may be impossible, without special education, to give an accurate opinion
from the electric phenomena alone as to the condition of the
muscles, and the probable course of the degeneration; but
this is not what is wanted. The diagnosis has been made
already. It is known from other symptoms that the atrophy
is the consequence of certain definite causes, such as inflammation, which may or may not have ceased to exert their
influence. This is sufficient in all ordinary cases. Galvanism
is employed, like massage and other remedies, solely as a
means for improving the nutrition of the tissue and restoring
the energy to the muscles. For this it is one of the most
valuable applications known, and if only there is a fair general knowledge of its use, and the method of its employment,
it may be applied in a very large number of cases with the
greatest benefit.

In Diagnosis.—It has been thought by some that elec-
tricity would be of service in diagnosing the presence of hysteria; that by its means it would be possible in any case to
ascertain whether the loss of power is due merely to loss of
will or to some actual lesion. If this were so, it would be of
the greatest use; the difficulty is a common one and often
very considerable. But, unhappily, it is of little or no use for

this particular purpose. It does not enable us to discriminate in any definite way between the slighter forms of traumatic or pressure paralysis, and that which is met with in hysterical subjects. When the atrophy is more advanced, and the degeneration plainly marked, the signs it gives are, it is true, much less equivocal; but the difficulty then has in great measure disappeared, and the diagnosis may be allowed to rest with safety on the other symptoms.

The Induced Current.—Faradization by itself is required only in exceptional cases. Its action, even when applied to the muscles, is mainly on the nerves and their motor ends, and this is rarely needed. I have mentioned one remarkable case in which it proved of value, restoring to full use, after a third or fourth application, a limb that had been almost crippled for over a twelvemonth. There was apparently some obstacle to the transmission of stimuli down the nerve into the muscle; the influence of the will was not sufficiently powerful to make its way along it. One set of muscles was, in consequence, seriously weakened, and the opposing ones, with their vigor unimpaired, kept the limb constantly contracted. Here faradization apparently opened up the path for the passage of other stimuli, so that full power of movement was regained. Such instances, however, in the absence of hysteria, are not common. When this is the exciting cause, faradization often proves a most effectual remedy, but it is not easy to say in such circumstances how far this is due to moral influences. Apparent paralysis of other muscles, at least where there has been no injury, is not unfrequently cured in this way.

In functional impotence, and in the early stages of the contracture that follows it, mild direct faradization sometimes restores the power more quickly than anything else; but, as a rule, the energetic and protracted action of a strong galvanic current answers better. Or, if a more powerful stimulus is desired, the positive pole may be applied over the muscle, and the current interrupted occasionally, and even reversed. I have had no experience of the simultaneous action of the galvanic and faradic currents, but from what is known of the refreshing influence of the former, and of the power it possesses of increasing the electric excitability of the parts to which it is applied, it seems reasonable to suppose that it would be of material assistance, especially in cases such as these; and by enabling a weaker current to be used would avoid the fatigue and exhaustion which might otherwise result. The alternate action of the two is certainly very sucessful.

The Constant Current.—For atrophy itself galvanism is more effectual than the interrupted current. It is a mistake to think that the beneficial effect of electrization is to be attributed in any way to the production of muscular contrac- · tion. If the nerve centres of the spinal cord are involved, it is impossible to prevent degeneration or wasting. The influence of the continuous current on their nutrition is to be attributed, rather, to its chemical action, to its influence on the circulation, and to the way in which it promotes the absorption of waste products and the regeneration of broken-down elements. As I have already pointed out, it must always be remembered that the nutrition of the tissues is ultimately dependent on the circulation of the plasma outside the walls of the vessels. The blood circulates in these, its fluid constituents passing out through the walls and permeating the tissues in all directions. The muscular fibres lie embedded, as it were, in a fluid plasma, which requires to be constantly replaced, and its renewal is dependent much more on the activity of the tissue elements themselves than on the mere circulation through the vessels. This, without the other, is of little service. If the tissues are leading an active and energetic life, the circulation of the plasma is carried on at its best; if they remain sluggish and passive, it stagnates round them, the part is badly nourished, and the tissues become sodden and œdematous. In this condition of things regular and systematic employment of galvanism is especially indicated. Whether its influence depends on chemical process or not, it causes the swelling to disappear, quickens the circulation, brings back the color to the skin, and restores the activity of nutrition in a manner equalled by nothing else. Faradization may be used in certain cases and, as already pointed out, is of great assistance sometimes in conjunction with the constant current; but so far as muscles are concerned in everything beyond the mere production of contraction, the latter is far the most useful.

Generally speaking, it is sufficient that the limb should be

galvanized every other day, alternating it with massage for
five or ten minutes each time. In certain cases it may be
used more frequently, but there is often a tendency, especially
on the part of the patients, to over-galvanize the limb. Dis-
appointment must not be felt if it is some time before any decided improvement makes its appearance. The regeneration
of the tissues must be a slow process; absorption and nutrition may be assisted, but they cannot be hurried.

The strength of the current should always be moderate,
though it is difficult to lay down any definite rules. It is not
possible to be accurate without the aid of delicate and complicated instruments. Specifying the number of cells gives little
or no idea; allowance, for example, must be made for difference in the resistance of the skin in different parts of the body.
Where it is thin, or where there is a large number of sweat
glands, the current passes much more easily than it does elsewhere; and the resistance diminishes with moisture, with
pressure, and with the length of time the current is applied, this
being due in all probability to the fact that after it has been
passing some time the blood circulates more freely through
the superficial parts. It should never cause the least suspicion of pain; if actual contraction is desired, each muscle must
be stimulated in turn by applying the electrode to its motor
point or points, as the case may be; or if the nerve that supplies the muscle is more easily accessible contraction may be
produced in this way, but the weakest current that will effect
this must always be used. In the case of galvanism the size
of the electrodes is a most important consideration. The
strength of current passing through the body from a certain
number of cells is, other things being equal, dependent on the
extent of their surface. Consequently, where there are large
masses of muscle, as in the back, and where, accordingly,
large plate-like electrodes are employed, a current of proportionate strength should be used. If they are large enough,
and kept well moistened, there need be no fear of injuring the
skin.

When galvanism is used, for its refreshing action, after
faradization or to relieve the sensation of fatigue, the positive
pole should be applied to a point more distant from the trunk
than the negative in order to obtain as far as possible an
ascending current. In other circumstances the cathode is

placed directly over the structure it is intended to galvanize, and either held there or slowly moved over in the direction of the fibres. The latter method is much more stimulating; the current is always varying in intensity, being most vigorous immediately under the electrode, and the energy with which it acts upon the muscles beneath is constantly changing as it moves over their surface; so that in addition to the chemical influence it possesses it calls out moderate contration of all the fibres in turn. The rapidity of the movement is as important in determining the amount of muscular contraction as the strength of the current, owing to the suddenness in the variation, when the position of the electrodes is changed.

Even when there is no atrophy galvanism has a very beneficial influence on sprains in their later stages. The action of the muscles, perhaps, is embarrassed; every movement is attended by a sense of stiffness and fatigue; the tissues are rather swollen; the skin feels cold, and the muscles do not respond readily. The injury has been repaired, it is true, and there is no definite alteration in the structure of the part, but it does not perform its function properly, and recovery is not perfect. The circulation requires a stimulus; the conducting power of the nerves is enfeebled; the muscles need educating again, as it were; their contraction is not orderly, as it should be; they do not assist each other, and the movement is not passed on from one to the other as smoothly and evenly as it is in health; the result is a sensation of pain, which prevents freedom of action, and by encouragng the patient to keep the part at rest delays convalescence more and more. Under these conditions the thorough electrization of the whole, using the interrupted and constant currents alternately, often effects a cure in a very short space of time, especially if it is assisted by massage. Nothing restores power and freedom of movement more easily or more quickly. If it fails, and there is no serious disease or inflammation to account for the persistence of the symptoms, the presence of some adhesion, too strong to give way before such mild measures, is to be suspected, and it becomes advisable to examine the joint under an anæsthetic.

INDEX.

ABSORPTION, 66–67
  of effusion in sprains, 66
Accidental bone-setting, 112
Acupuncture in treatment of
  sprains, 168
Adhesions, 108 .
  in joints, 74
  treated by division, 109
  treated by manipulation, 110
Adults, tonic contraction in, 192
Age, effect of, on joints, 27
  effect of, on tendons, 134
Anæsthetics, advantages of, 31
Anatomy of joints, 9
Arnica in sprains, 87

BACK, dislocation of muscles in
  the, 56
  dislocation of tendons in the, 56
  injury to the bones of, 157
  injury to the smaller joints of,
    157
  sprains of, 152
Baths in treatment of strains, 164
Biceps, displacement of, 58
Bones, 11
  injury to, 59
  of the back, injury to, 157
Bursa, Rider's, 50
Bursæ, 44

CAPSULE, 11
Cause and prevention of sprains, 18
Children, tonic contraction in, 190
Chronic sprains, 23
Cold as a temporary application, 85
  continuous application of, 86
  in treatment of sprains, 83
  method of application of, 85
Compound ganglion, 149
Compression as muscle degenera-
  tor, 202
Contraction, muscular, 187
  of the fingers, 179
Cramp, 187
Creaking in joints, 74

DIAGNOSIS, 30
  galvanism in, 214
Difference between male and
  female skeletons, 22

Discoloration, 34
Dislocation of muscles of the back,
  159
  of tendons and muscles, 55
Dislocations, 36
Distention of tendon sheaths, etc.,
  61
Division, adhesions treated by, 109
Dry synovitis, 79
Dupuytren's contraction, 179

EFFECT of age on joints, 27
  of muscular development, 21
Effusion and distention, 61
  in sprains, 61
Elbow, dislocation of, in children,
  34
Exercise, manipulation as an, 117
Extensor muscles, wasting of, 203

FARADIZATION in muscle atrophy,
  214
Feebleness of muscular system, 25
Fibrous tissue, 12
Finger contraction, cause of, 180
Fingers, contraction of the, 179
  injuries of the, 47
Flat-foot, 209
  treatment of, 211
Forcible manipulation in treat-
  ment of sprains, 108
Fractures, 38
Friction, 122
  in treatment of sprains, 122, 166

GALVANISM in diagnosis, 214
  in treatment of muscle atro-
    phy, 214
  in treatment of sprains, 168
Ganglion, compound, 149
Ganglions, 148

HAND, displacement of tendons on
  the, 58
Heat in treatment of sprains, 88,
  163
Hemorrhage, 42, 43
Hyperæmia and softening, 61
Hyperæsthesia in sprains of the
  back, 156

IMPAIRMENT of mobility, 73
Imperfect recovery, 71
Impotence, muscular, after sprain, 208
   muscular, in the leg, 209
   muscular, in the spine, 209
Inflammation, 60
   in muscles a cause of wasting, 104
   in sprains of tendons, 139
   question of, 212
Injuries of the fingers, 47
   of the spinal cord, 153
   to bones, 59
   to the muscles of the back, 154
   to the sheaths of tendons, 138
Injury of the knee, 47
   of the ligaments, 45
   of the muscles, 48
Ironing in treatment of sprains, 167

JOINT disease, simulation of, 193
   interior of the, 78
Joints, anatomy of, 9
   changes in the tissues of, 77
   effects of age on, 27
   effects of prolonged rest on, 98
   movable, 10
   neuralgia of the, 80
   stiffness in, 63
   yielding, 9

KNEE, injury of the, 47
   internal derangement of, 172

LATERAL curvature of the spine, 209
Lawn-tennis arm, 137
   leg, 51
Leg, muscular impotence in the, 209
Ligaments, 13
   of the back, 158
   of the back and neck, injury to, 154
   injury of, 45
Liniments in treatment of sprains, 166
Local measures for relief of sprains, 163

MANIPULATION, adhesions treated by, 111
   as an exercise, 117
   forcible, in treatment of sprains, 98, 108
   rapid, method of, 116
   rapid, preparation for, 115
Massage, 120, 124
   in injuries not recent, 127
   in recent injuries, 126

Massage in treatment of muscular pains, 168
   in treatment of sprains, 120, 144, 168
   in treatment of tendon sprains, 144
   method of application of, 127
Mobility, impairment of, 73
Movable joints, 10
Movement and inflammation, 102
   in treatment of sprains, 102, 146
   passive, 103
   time for, 104
Muscles, condition of the, 18
   degeneration of, from compression, 202
   degeneration of, from disuse, 201
   dislocation of, 55
   injuries of the, 48
   of the back, 158
   of the back and neck, injury to, 154
   of back, dislocation of, 159
   wasting of, from inflammation, 204
   wasting of, from overwork, 206
Muscular contraction, 187, 198
   impotence after strain, 208
   impotence in the leg, 209
   impotence in the spine, 209
   pain, 161
   pain, general treatment of, 163
   rigidity, 73
   strains, 137
   wasting, 201

NATURE of the injury, 40
Neck, sprains of, 152
Neuralgia after sprain, 80
   of the joints, 80

ORGANIZATION between muscles, 64
   not due to inflammation, 65
   of tissue, 62
   of tissue in bursæ, 64
   of tissue in joints, 63
Overwork, a cause of muscle atrophy, 206
   effects of, on tendons, 135

PAIN, 34.
   muscular, 161
Paralysis in sprains of the back, 156
Passive movement in treatment of tendon sprains, 145
Percussion, 123
   in treatment of strains, 169

Permanent changes following tendon sprains, 146
changes in substance, 68
Peronæi tendons, displacement of, 57
Pressure, effects of, 68
in treatment of sprains, 91
in treatment of tendon sprains, 144
Prevention of sprains, 18

Railway spine, 156
Rapid manipulation, preparation for, 115
Recovery, imperfect, of tendon sprains, 140
Rest, 97
in treatment of sprains, 97
prolonged, changes in tissues due to, 99
prolonged, effects of, on healthy joints, 98
Rider's bone, 120
bursa, 50
sprain, 49
Rigidity, muscular, 73
Ruptured veins, 59

Sartorius, dislocation of the, 56
Semilunar cartilages, displacement of, 173
cartilages, ruptures of, 173
Skin in sympathy with parts beneath, 20
Softening of vessels, 61
Soreness, 34
Spinal cord, injuries of, 153
injuries of, by sprains, 153
Spine, lateral curvature of the, 209
muscular impotence in the, 209
railway, 156
Spongiopiline in treatment of cramp, 189
Sprains and dislocations, 36
and fractures, 38
cause and prevention of, 18
chronic, 23
diagnosis, 30
effusion in, 61
forcible manipulation in treatment of, 108
general considerations, 5
imperfect recovery in, 71, 140
inflammation and the process of repair, 60
massage in treatment of, 120, 144, 168
nature of the injury, 40
neuralgia after, 80
of tendons, 133
of the back, 152

Sprains of the neck, 152
of the back and neck, 152
prevention of, 18
treatment, 82, 142, 163
Strains, 161
muscular, 137
treatment of, 163–171
Structure of the fingers, 179
of tendons, 133
Swelling, 32
Sympathy of parts, 15
Synovial membrane, 14
Synovitis, dry, 79

Tenderness, 34
Tendon sprains, treatment of, 142
Tendons, dislocation of, 55
effect of overwork on, 135
effects of age on, 134
extent of injury to, 135
injury to the sheaths of, 138
sprains of, 133
structure of, 133
Tenosynovitis, 136
Thumb, sprain fracture of, 38
Time for repair, 69
Tissue starvation, 80
Tonic contraction, 190
contraction in adults, 192
contraction in children, 190
Treatment, 97
general, of muscular pain, 163
of finger contraction, 182
of sprains, 82
of sprains by application of cold, 83
of sprains by application of heat, 88
of sprains by application of pressure, 91
of tendon sprains, 142
of tendon sprains by massage, 144
of tendon sprains by passive movement, 145
of tendon sprains by pressure, 144

Warmth for relief of muscular pain, 163
Wasting, muscular, 201
of extensor muscles, 203
of muscles from compression, 202
of muscles from inflammation, 204
of muscles from overwork, 206
Whole limb should be carefully examined, 31

Yielding joints, 9

www.ingramcontent.com/pod-product-compliance
Lightning Source LLC
Chambersburg PA
CBHW030324270326
41926CB00010B/1488

* 9 7 8 3 7 4 4 6 9 2 8 9 2 *